ANXIETY
Second Edition

Anxiety

Second Edition

S. Rachman
University of British Columbia, Canada

Psychology Press
Taylor & Francis Group

HOVE AND NEW YORK

First edition published 1998 by Psychology Press Ltd
Reprinted, 1998, 2001 and 2002

Second edition published 2004 by Psychology Press Ltd
27 Church Road, Hove, East Sussex, BN3 2FA

www.psypress.co.uk

Simultaneously published in the USA and Canada
by Taylor & Francis Inc.,
270 Madison Avenue, New York, NY 10016

Psychology Press is part of T&F Informa plc

Copyright © 2004 Psychology Press Ltd

Cover design by Jim Wilkie
Typeset in Palatino by Garfield Morgan, Rhayader, Powys
Printed and bound in Great Britain by TJ International Ltd, Padstow, Cornwall

British Library Cataloguing in Publication Data
A catalogue record for this book is available from the British Library

Library of Congress Cataloging-in-Publication Data
Rachman, Stanley.
  Anxiety / S. Rachman.– 2nd ed.
      p. cm. – (Clinical psychology, a modular course, ISSN
1368-454X)
  Includes bibliographical references and index.
    ISBN 1-84169-515-7 (hardback : alk. paper) – ISBN 1-84169-516-5 (pbk.
: alk. paper)
1. Anxiety. I. Title. II. Series.

  RC531.R334 2004
  616.85'22–dc22

                                                        2004001276

  ISBN 1-84169-515-7 (hbk)
  ISBN 1-84169-516-5 (pbk)
  ISSN 1368-454X (Clinical Psychology: A Modular Course)

Contents

Series preface

Clinical Psychology: A Modular Course was designed to overcome the problems faced by the traditional textbook in conveying what psychological disorders are really like. All the books in the series, written by leading scholars and practitioners in the field, can be read as stand-alone text, but they will also integrate with the other modules to form a comprehensive resource in clinical psychology. Students of psychology, medicine, nursing, and social work, as well as busy practitioners in many professions, often need an accessible but thorough introduction to how people experience anxiety, depression, addiction, or other disorders, how common they are, and who is most likely to suffer from them, as well as up-to-date research evidence on the causes and available treatments. The series will appeal to those who want to go deeper into the subject than the traditional textbook will allow, and base their examination answers, research projects, assignments, or practical decisions on a clearer and more rounded appreciation of the clinical and research evidence.

Chris R. Brewin

Other titles in this series:

Depression
Constance Hammen

Stress and Trauma
Patricia A. Resick

Childhood Disorders
Philip C Kendall

Schizophrenia
Max Birchwood and Chris Jackson

Addictions
Maree Teesson, Louise Degenhardt and Wayne Hall

Preface

Surging advances in the understanding and treatment of anxiety disorders have made it necessary to revise and expand this book. Signs of impending change were evident in the research described in the first edition but the progress made in the past 6 years has exceeded expectations. At least 12 new theories of psychopathology have been published in this period, and 7 of them deal with the anxiety disorders. Some of them are causal theories—unusual in clinical psychology—and all of them incorporate cognitive concepts. The theories are becoming increasingly specific and most provide platforms for the derivation of equally specific methods of treatment. The evaluation of theories and treatments is an unavoidably lengthy and demanding process and definitive conclusions about particular theories, and the general pattern of these developments, is some way off.

The basic science deals with the psychology of anxiety but the current emphasis on applied science, on the nature and treatment of disorders of anxiety, overshadows the basic research. The preoccupation with anxiety disorders, and the pressures to master these distressing problems, are understandable but they have tilted the balance from basic to applied research. However, the interplay between basic and applied research is a two-way process that benefits both. Advances in understanding the phenomena and mechanisms of anxiety disorders help to illuminate fundamental psychological processes. The expansion of understanding of the emotion of fear was largely the result of clinical research. An excellent example of the interplay is now taking place in current analyses of the intriguing disturbances of memory that are so conspicuous in PTSD. Intensive studies of the clinical phenomena have already begun to expand our conceptions of basic memory processes.

S. Rachman,
Vancouver, 2003

The nature of anxiety 1

In this chapter, the nature of anxiety is defined and its significance discussed. Anxiety is distinguished from fear, the main types of fear are described, and the concept of anxiety disorders is elucidated. 解释.

Research on anxiety has accelerated since the 1980s. Specialized clinics for dealing with anxiety disorders have been introduced and self-help groups established in many parts of the world. This growth is justified because anxiety is one of the most prominent and pervasive emotions, and large numbers of people are distressed by inappropriate or excessive anxiety. In part, the steep increase in interest was prompted by the decision of the American Psychiatric Association committee responsible for preparing a new diagnostic system for "mental disorders" to create a separate category for anxiety disorders and to introduce clear definitions and criteria for diagnosing these disorders (Barlow, 2002; Norton, Cox, Asmundson, & Maser, 1995). The introduction of this classification system—*The Diagnostic and Statistical Manual of Mental Disorders* (DSM)—was a major advance on the chaos that prevailed before 1980 but the system has serious shortcomings. It is a categorical classification where a dimensional system would be preferable, and it encourages the unfortunate idea that all anxiety problems are pathological: are indeed mental disorders.

The present book is a description and psychological analysis of the phenomena of anxiety. The therapeutic implications of current knowledge and theorizing are dealt with because anxiety is a central feature of many psychological problems, including those that were formerly called "neuroses". Anxiety disorders are distressing, often disabling, and costly. Large-scale surveys carried out in the US have led to the conclusion that "anxiety disorders represent the single largest mental health problem in the country" (Barlow, 2002, p. 22). If they are left untreated, anxiety disorders can become chronic. Affected individuals require and use many

怪怪

specialized services, and affected men are four times as likely as non-sufferers to be chronically unemployed (Leon, Marzuk, & Portera, 1995). The rates of alcoholism and drug abuse are elevated among sufferers.

The study of anxiety has been invigorated by the steady infusion into the subject of cognitive concepts and analyses. One of the earliest and most influential contributions was made by Beck (Beck & Emery, 1985), whose writings on depression in the 1970s were timely and important. Paradoxically, the extension of cognitive ideas into the study of anxiety and its disorders has been more successful and more quickly successful than the original work on depression. The most significant achievement of recent years was the introduction of the cognitive theory of panic, which has already spawned a profusion of new ideas and applications. Most contemporary psychological discussions of anxiety incorporate the cognitive view.

Anxiety is a pervasive and significant negative affect that is now under intense investigation. It is an intriguing and complex phenomenon that lends itself to cognitive analyses: anxiety involves the interplay of vigilance, attention, perception, reasoning, and memory—the very meat of cognitive processing. Moreover, many of these operations take place at a non-conscious level. Small wonder then that clinicians and cognitive scientists are drawn to the subject.

It is probable that the current interest in anxiety will swell and persist for many years. Psychologists have an excellent reason for pursuing their interest in anxiety—it turns out that they are "good at it" and have forged demonstrably effective techniques for reducing unadaptive, distressing anxiety. This is indeed one of the major achievements of modern clinical psychology and it deserves to be recognized as such.

In the next decade we can expect important advances in our understanding of the emotional–cognitive processing of anxiety and some surprising discoveries about the operation of non-conscious processes. On the practical clinical side, the currently successful ideas and methods of cognitive behaviour therapy are being applied to an increasingly wide range of problems and are helping to reshape the scope and methods of all of clinical psychology. Advances in understanding anxiety are also leading to important changes in the larger subject of psychopathology. In all of this, the mighty debate about the relative importance of biological and psychological influences on anxiety will rumble on.

Defining anxiety

Anxiety is the tense, unsettling anticipation of a threatening but vague event; a feeling of uneasy suspense. It is a negative affect so closely related to fear that in many circumstances the two terms are used interchangeably; like anxiety, fear also is a combination of tension and unpleasant anticipation. But distinctions can be made between the causes, duration, and maintenance of fear and of anxiety. Strictly, the term "fear" is used to describe an emotional reaction to a specific, perceived danger, to a threat that is identifiable, such as a poisonous snake. Most fear reactions are intense and have the quality of an emergency. The person's level of arousal is elevated sharply.

Fear has a specific focus. Typically, it is episodic and recedes or ceases when the danger is removed from the person, or the person from the danger. In this sense, fear is controlled or determined by perceivable events or stimuli. The perceived source of the danger might be accurately or inaccurately identified, or correctly identified but wrongly evaluated. The fear might be rational or irrational. Intense but irrational fears are termed *phobias*, as in claustrophobia (intense fear of enclosed spaces), snake-phobia, and so on.

When feeling anxious, the person has difficulty in identifying the cause of the uneasy tension or the nature of the anticipated event or disaster. The emotion can be puzzling for the person experiencing it. In its purest form, anxiety is diffuse, objectless, unpleasant, and persistent. Unlike fear, it is not so obviously determined; it is usually unpredictable and uncontrollable. The rise and decline of fear tends to be limited in time and in space, whereas anxiety tends to be pervasive and persistent, with uncertain points of onset and offset. It seems to be present, as if in the background, almost all of the time: "I constantly feel as if something dreadful is going to happen." Anxiety is a state of heightened vigilance rather than an emergency reaction. Fear and anxiety are marked by elevated arousal, subjective and/or physiological arousal. Fear is more likely to be intense and brief, it is provoked by triggers and is circumscribed. Anxiety tends to be shapeless, grating along at a lower level of intensity. Its onset and offset are difficult to time and it lacks clear borders. Anxiety is not a lesser and pale form of fear and in many ways is more difficult to tolerate than fear. It is unpleasant, unsettling, persistent, pervasive, and draining. Intense and prolonged anxiety can be disabling and even destructive.

The difference between anxiety and fear is illustrated by the following two examples of people suffering from anxiety and the example of a person suffering from a phobia:

Anne complained of being tense, edgy and apprehensive. She awakened each morning with a feeling that something awful but elusive was about to happen. This feeling of dread usually persisted into the late morning, accompanied by uncomfortable bodily sensations such as tremors, nausea, fast pulse, and shallow breathing. It was unsettling and tiring. In the first weeks of her experience of this anxiety, she spent a lot of energy trying to understand why she was feeling so poorly, struggling to identify what was troubling her. The elusive and puzzling quality of her dread was an added source of discomfort.

Anne made a clear distinction between this daily anxiety and the fear she had experienced when encountering a snake in the countryside. Her reaction to the snake was sharp, intense, and focused but quickly declined when the snake scurried away into the undergrowth. She experienced strong bodily sensations, especially a rapidly racing heart but recognized the threat and felt no puzzlement.

Brian worried incessantly about his health, constantly scanning his body for external or internal signs of trouble, and frequently sought medical advice. He dreaded the possibility of illness or injury, and often felt that "something was wrong". Brian was careful to avoid sources of real or imagined infection and lifted or carried objects with deliberate care. Brian recognized that he had an excellent health record and this made him all the more puzzled by this intrusive and disturbing anxiety about his well-being. He was unable to dampen or stifle the continuing feelings of dread. He described episodes of fear, such as his intense but circumscribed and brief reactions to near-accidents on the road, and made a clear distinction between these fearful events and his pervasive anxiety about his health.

A young horticulturalist sought help because her intense, circumscribed fear of spiders was interfering with her work. She was so frightened of encountering spiders that she was unable to work alone in the gardens. The fear was so intense and disabling that it qualified for the term "phobia". She had no other fears, anxiety or psychological problems. The fear had a specific identifiable focus and was episodically evoked by contact with the threatening stimulus.

The existence of these three components of fear, and the fact that they do not always correspond, makes it helpful to specify which component of the fear one is describing.

In everyday exchanges we rely on people telling us of their fears and supplement this information with clues provided by their facial and other bodily expressions. Unfortunately, when our assessments are made in the absence of supporting cues from the context in which the observation is made, the interpretations can be misleading. Moreover, the value of observations of facial and other expressions is limited to certain categories of fear, especially the acute fears. The chronic and diffuse fears are less visible, as is also true for most forms of anxiety. For example, we might without difficulty observe signs of fear in passengers during the descent of an aircraft but fail to recognize fear in a person who is extremely apprehensive about meeting new people. The signs of anxiety are especially difficult to detect because anxiety tends to be relatively formless, pervasive, and puzzling even to the person experiencing this emotion.

In the course of developing effective techniques for reducing fear, some unexpected and complex findings emerged. Perplexing results also emerged in the clinical application of these techniques. Despite the appearance of marked improvements in behaviour, for example a claustrophobic person acquiring the ability to travel on underground trains, some patients deny that they have benefited. In other patients, the physiological reactions to the threatening stimulus diminish after treatment but the person continues to complain of excessive fear. Moreover, the improvements apparent in a patient's behaviour some-times are followed only weeks later by subjective improvements.

Repeated observations of this type led to the recognition that the three components of fear might show desynchrony, that is, different rates of change, either in response to treatment or spontaneously (Rachman, 1990). In general, the order of change in response to therapy is first a decline in physiological reactivity, then improve-ments in behaviour, and finally subjective improvements. The latest form of treatment, cognitive-behavioural therapy, aims first and mainly at the patient's maladaptive cognitions, and here the sub-jective improvements can occur early in the chain.

The low correspondence between some measures of fear also led to difficulties in interpreting laboratory findings on fear reduction. It even produced difficulties at the earliest stage of experiments, in the selection of suitably fearful subjects. Many potential subjects who rate themselves as being fearful display little or no fear when exposed to the fearful object in a specially arranged behavioural avoidance test.

Many of them walk in, approach the snake (for example) and lift it without hesitation, despite having recorded an extreme fear of snakes on the screening questionnaire. There is indeed a strong tendency for people to overpredict their fears, to anticipate that they will be significantly more frightened in specified circumstances than in fact turns out to be the case when they encounter the particular situation.

Discrepancies between different measures of fear have been encountered in different experiments and in clinical settings. For example, in a classic early experiment by Gordon Paul (1966), designed to reduce the circumscribed fear of public speaking among a group of students, the students' fear was assessed by a number of self-report measures, two physiological measures, external ratings, and a behavioural test of public speaking. Paul found a reasonably high correlation between the self-report measures but little relationship between these and physiological indicators of fear. As mentioned earlier, it is common in clinical practice to find that patients with phobias of public transport and public space, such as supermarkets, make considerable advances in overcoming their avoidance of these places but continue to complain of fear for several weeks after these achievements.

Peter Lang, who was responsible for much of the research and theorizing on this subject of fear and fear reduction, expressed the revised view of the fear extremely well. He stated that "fear is not some hard phenomenal lump that lives inside people, that we may palpate more or less successfully" (Lang, 1970). He argued convincingly that the components of fear are related to each other, but imperfectly. The three components are loosely coupled and partially independent.

In an investigation of fear in parachute jumpers, Fenz and Epstein (1967) found evidence of correspondence and lack of correspondence between different measures. The three physiological measures steadily increased during the parachute-jumping sequence but a different pattern was observed in the measure of subjective fear. This component of fear fluctuated at various stages of the sequence, with an early increase in fear followed by a decrease, then a final increment as the jump approached. These observations were made on a group of veteran parachute jumpers and differed from the results subsequently obtained with novice jumpers. Among the inexperienced group there was a closer correspondence between subjective fear and physiological reactions. Both of these measures showed extreme reactivity, which steadily increased and reached a peak shortly before the jump took place. The mean heart rate at the peak point reached 145 beats per minute. Both sets of measures, physiological and subjective, subsided soon after the landing. The veterans experienced only relatively mild increases in heart rate, subjective fear and other measures, whereas the novices displayed extremely strong reactions. These observations support the idea that the correspondence between measures increases at very high levels of fear and that correspondence is also close at the opposite extreme; that is, the measures are concordant during states of calm. The lack of correspondence between the components of fear is most evident during moderate levels of emotional arousal.

In view of the loose coupling between the components of fear, what is the best way to describe and predict fear? After Lang, it is best to avoid relying on a single measure. Self-report measures provide a useful, if crude, basis for the prediction of fear and have some practical advantages over the more elaborate techniques of assessment. The inclusion of a behavioural-approach test is highly desirable in most circumstances and provides accurate information that is not attainable by indirect means. The ratings of fear made by external judges can also be useful but are not free of problems. Some of the physiological measures, that of heart rate in particular, can provide important data. Heart rate acceleration occurs in response to fear stimuli and, at high levels of intensity, is inclined to increase in unison with increases in subjective feelings of fear. The main reason for attempting to measure more than one component of fear whenever possible is that a total reliance on the main measure, self-report, can lead us to overestimate the person's fear and significantly underestimate the degree of courage. Total reliance on observed behaviour in a fear test, however, can lead to an underestimate of the degree of a person's fear. Incidentally, the view of fear as a complex of imperfectly coupled response systems has led to some novel ideas on the nature of courage. A person might be willing to approach a frightening object or situation despite experiencing a high degree of subjective bodily fear and unpleasant bodily reactions. This persistence in the face of subjective and physical sensations of fear leads to a definition of courage that rests on the person's ability to continue despite one's subjective fear. This type of courageous behaviour can be seen as an example of uncoupling of components, in which the person's behaviour advances beyond subjective discomfort (Rachman, 1990).

Few would disagree with the claim that Lang's three components of fear is an advance and that in particular the recognition that fear consists of more than one component, and is not a unitary phenomenon, is enlightening. However, the revised conception might not have escaped the original problem entirely. The three components are loosely coupled and any one of them can predominate as circumstances change. The absence of a physiological response does not prevent us from concluding that the person is frightened. Nor does the absence of avoidance or escape behaviour preclude this conclusion. The experience of fear does not require the presence of all three components but the presence of a physiological response, or of escape or avoidance behaviour (or even their combination), is not sufficient to justify the term "fear". A person might display avoidance behaviour and an elevated heart rate as components of the experience of rage or repugnance. However, in the absence of the appropriate verbal report of fear, the meaning of the avoidance behaviour and the physiological response is uncertain. The behavioural and the physiological components of fear usually are prominent but fear can occur without them. The verbal report is definitional and essential. In this way the problem that prompted the introduction of the three component analysis lingers on in a muted form.

Fear, anxiety, and avoidance

"Fear is a decisive causal factor in avoidance behaviour," according to Mowrer (1960, p. 97). Ever since its introduction in 1939, Mowrer's two-stage theory of anxiety has had a major influence on the way in which psychologists view fear and anxiety (Mowrer used the terms "fear" and "anxiety" interchangeably).

In the original statement of his theory, Mowrer (1939) critically examined the contrasting theories of Freud, Pavlov, and Watson and concluded that anxiety is best construed as a conditioned pain reaction. He argued that anxiety is not merely a reaction to painful stimuli or associations but that it can also energize behaviour. This motivating quality of anxiety is of central importance and Mowrer added that behaviour that leads to a reduction of anxiety is stamped in—the reduction of anxiety acts as a reinforcement. The final part of the theory is the proposition that behaviour motivated by anxiety is avoidant and that, when it is successful, it leads to a reduction of anxiety and thereby to the strengthening of the avoidance behaviour itself. "Fear . . . motivates and reinforces behaviour that tends to avoid or prevent the recurrence of the pain-producing (unconditioned) stimulus" (Mowrer, 1939, p. 554). In an elaboration, Mowrer shifted the emphasis from the cause of fear to its motivating qualities. He claimed that "two causal steps are necessary . . . fear in the case of both active and passive avoidance behaviour is an essential inter-mediate 'cause' or 'variable'" (Mowrer, 1960, p. 48–49).

Abundant empirical support for these ideas was obtained and, for a period, the findings were incorporated successfully into the two-stage theory. For a considerable time Mowrer's theory had a domi-nating influence on the way in which experimental psychologists and clinicians viewed the connection between fear and avoidance and it was incorporated as an important ingredient of the rationale that was presented in support of a novel form of therapy called behaviour therapy.

Excessive and injudicious avoidance behaviour is a common con-sequence of fear and recent investigations of panic disorders provide fresh examples of a seemingly causal connection between episodes of intense fear (panic) and the emergence of excessive avoidance beha-viour. Panic and avoidance are correlated; most patients attribute their avoidance to the episodes of panic and the temporal relations between panic and avoidance are all indicative of a strong connec-tion. Even so, exceptions do occur and panics are not necessarily followed by avoidance. Equally, avoidance behaviour is not always a product of fear. Furthermore, there are significant examples of fear that give rise to approach rather than avoidance behaviour. What, then, is the connection between fear and avoidance?

A great deal of laboratory evidence demonstrates a direct connec-tion between fear and avoidance in animals. If they are shocked in an experimental chamber that physically permits them to avoid further shocks or avoid exposure to stimuli that predict such shocks, then strong and persisting avoidance is quickly established. The evidence is clear and abundant, and it is easy to reproduce the phenomenon; hence, it is not surprising that theorists attach importance to such a consolidated set of data.

In due course, however, problems began to emerge. The first difficulty arose from the observation that laboratory animals con-tinued to engage in avoidance behaviour for hundreds of trials even after the unpleasant stimulus had been withdrawn. The remarkable persistence of acquired avoidance behaviour presents a problem because, in the absence of repeated unpleasant experiences, active avoidance behaviour should gradually weaken until extinguished. The second problem is that the theory incorporates two assumptions that are no longer defensible. It assumes that all fears are acquired by a process of conditioning (see below) and that neutral stimuli are all equally prone to be turned into fear signals. As will be seen presently, the conditioning theory of fear can accommodate a large amount of information but suffers from major weaknesses. The assumptions that all stimuli are potential fear signals, and that they share equal potential, are dubious. The two-stage theory was correctly criticized by Harlow (1954) on the grounds that it exaggerates the motivating role of fear in human behaviour: "The greater part of our energies are motivated by positive goals, not escape from fear and threat" (Harlow, 1954, p. 37).

Most important of all, the claim that fear is a necessary causal stage in the development of avoidance behaviour is mistaken. A wide range of avoidance responses arise, wax, and wane even in the absence of fear. One can provoke, maintain, or modify avoidance behaviour without evoking fear at any stage (e.g. avoiding a noisy party, a muddy pathway, etc.).

In addition, important examples of significant fears are not followed by persistent avoidance behaviour. For example, Craske, Sanderson, and Barlow (1987, p. 153) concluded from their analysis of 57 patients with panic disorder that "panic frequency is not the major determinant of avoidance behaviour". Furthermore, they observed that a long history of repeated panics is not necessarily associated with extensive avoidance. Rather, it appears that the anticipation of a panic emerged as the strongest predictor of this type of avoidance and Telch (1988) argued that cognitive factors played the most important role in its genesis. Other examples of fears that are not followed by avoidance behaviour are abundant in the literature on military psychology.

Weaknesses in Mowrer's theory were identified by Seligman and Johnston (1973). In their persuasive arguments these writers drew attention first to the undue and indeed unpredicted persistence of avoidance behaviour, second to the absence of associated fear during the avoidance behaviour, and third, to what they refer to as the elusiveness of the conditioned stimulus. It is difficult to specify precisely what stimulus the person or the animal is supposed to be avoiding.

Acting on the foundation of the two-stage theory, clinicians took care to advise and encourage patients to refrain from avoiding fearful situations, especially during treatment. It was customary to warn patients that they risked increasing both fear and avoidance if they fled from the fear-provoking situation; they were told that although temporary relief might be obtained it would be purchased at the cost of later difficulties: the reduction of fear that is accomplished by fleeing serves to increase the avoidance behaviour. For a long period many therapists urged patients to remain in the fearful situation until the fear begins to subside. This advice was embodied in the so-called golden rule "Try never to leave a situation until the fear is going down" (Mathews, Gelder, & Johnston, 1981). In many circumstances, clinical and non-clinical, this is a useful rule to follow, even if it is not gold-plated. There are indeed good reasons for agreeing that the reduction of fear can increase avoidance behaviour in many circumstances but it is unlikely that this behaviour is maintained solely by escape from fear.

In an attempt to find out if the presumed connection between fear and avoidance is inflexible and unvarying, a preliminary study was carried out with eight patients suffering from fear of public places and transport (de Silva & Rachman, 1984). Half of the patients were advised to follow the golden rule and avoid leaving the frightening situation until their fear began to subside. The other patients were told to escape as soon as their fear began climbing. Fear and avoidance were assessed by the patient's verbal reports and by behaviour testing before, during, and after the experimental treatment. The patients in both groups made slight progress and, despite encouragement of an escape strategy for the members of one group, neither their fears nor their avoidance behaviour increased significantly, contrary to predictions that flow from the two-stage theory. The study was subsequently replicated on two fresh groups of patients, with a similar outcome (Rachman, Craske, Tallman, & Solyom, 1986). It was observed that patients tended to overestimate the dangerousness of the treatment excursions, especially in the early stages of the programme, and it is possible this was simply an expression of the tendency to overpredict the degree of expected fear (see below). It is striking, however, that in these studies the patients' fear and avoidance declined regardless of the occurrence or non-occurrence of escape behaviour.

In an attempt to understand and anticipate the occurrence and persistence of avoidance behaviour, new explanations were sought. It was soon recognized that other factors such as motivation, the expected level of unpleasantness, and the availability of safety all played a part in determining avoidance behaviour. It also appears that the probability of a person engaging in fearful avoidance is determined mainly by his or her expectation that contact with the object or situation will provoke fear. In other words, it is argued that fearful avoidance behaviour is mainly the product of predicted fear.

It follows that maladaptive avoidance behaviour of potentially fearful situations arises when people overpredict how much fear they will experience in that situation. Moreover, we can expect that the gradual correction of these overpredictions will be followed by a decline in the avoidance behaviour.

Safety signals also play a part in the determination of avoidance behaviour and this influence has to be included. The essence of a safety signal is that it indicates a period of freedom from fear, pain, or aversive threat. In the presence of such a signal the person feels safe and can therefore act with greater freedom. Experimental support for the safety signal hypothesis comes from a study carried out by Carter, Hollon, Carson, and Shelton (1995), who showed that patients with panic disorder had a significantly muted response to a laboratory provocation test when they were accompanied by a safe person. In cases of agoraphobic avoidance, the introduction of a measure of safety, such as the presence of a trusted companion, enables the affected person to travel more widely. The anticipated presence of a safety signal probably modifies predictions of fear, in that they lower the prediction of fear and thereby weaken the fearful avoidance behaviour. However, the withdrawal of an anticipated safety signal will be followed by a prediction of increased fear and hence by stronger avoidance. This is sometimes seen in the surge of anxiety that people with agoraphobic problems experience when they find themselves without the tranquillizing medication they feel they require to cope.

The overprediction of fear

Fearful people have a strong tendency to overestimate how frightened they will be when they encounter the object of their fear (Craske, 1999; Rachman & Bichard, 1988). It is also possible that the tendency to overpredict fear might be part of a more general phenomenon in which we are inclined to overestimate the subjective impact of aversive events of many types, including anticipation of pain. As mentioned previously, the overprediction of fear (and of pain or other aversive events) is linked to avoidance behaviour; we are likely to avoid those events that we predict will be frightening or aversive.

The extensive avoidance behaviour displayed by patients with agoraphobia becomes more intelligible in these terms. Given that patients show the same tendency as people with other types of fear to overpredict, their avoidance behaviour might be a product of these very overpredictions. It is not unusual for such patients to report severe and extensive avoidance and then to be somewhat surprised to find that when it is put to the test, they can move about more widely and with less fear than they had anticipated. They discover that they have been overpredicting the magnitude and intensity of their fear.

When people overpredict their fears, there is a tendency for certain consequences to follow. If their predictions of fear are repeatedly disconfirmed, they tend to make corrections in the predictions of future experiences—they begin to predict that they will have less and less fear. Sequences of repeated disconfirmation of expected fear also tend to be accompanied by steadily decreasing *reports* of fear. In the analysis of overpredictions of fear it is necessary to make place for two other types of predictions: on some occasions people under-predict their fear (that is, the reported fear exceeds their expectations) and it is also possible for people to make correct predictions of their fear; in these instances, the prediction and the report of fear coincide.

A military example of overprediction of fear was observed in a study of the fear experienced by trainees undergoing a course in parachuting. They were asked to anticipate how much fear they would experience during the most difficult final jump of the training course and then report how much fear they actually experienced. It was found that they had overpredicted their fear by roughly 10%. Interestingly, their estimates of the dangerousness of jumping remained unchanged (McMillan & Rachman, 1988).

The effects of underestimating one's fear tend to be immediate and large. Underpredictions are more disruptive than overpredictions. The effects of overestimating one's fear are slower to emerge and it appears that repeated disconfirmation of one's predictions of fear are needed before large and stable corrections are made in subsequent predictions. There is an asymmetry in the effects of overpredictions and underpredictions.

The currently available evidence can be summarized. Fearful subjects tend to overpredict how much fear they will experience. Their predictions of fear tend to decrease after they have made over-predictions and to increase if they have underpredicted their fear. After correct predictions have been made, subsequent predictions remain unaltered. The reports of fear tend to decrease with repeated exposure to the fearful stimulus, regardless of the accuracy of earlier predictions. And it appears that with practice people can learn to predict their fear with increasing accuracy.

As will be seen presently, most of the new information is com-patible with the revised view of conditioning processes; the emphases on the importance of the predictive role of fear stimuli and the tendency for responses to become increasingly precise are common to both phenomena.

These patterns of prediction, and their consequences, have also been observed in research on panic. Predictions of panic tend to decrease after overestimations and tend to increase after under-predictions. Predictions of future panic tend to remain unchanged after a person has made a correct prediction of panic, or a correct prediction of no-panic. It is the erroneous predictions of panic, whether they are overestimations or underestimations, that are followed by changes. The underprediction of panic, equivalent to an unexpected panic, is particularly disruptive. Expected panics can be distressing but are unlikely to be unduly disruptive or to produce major changes. It is partly for this reason, no doubt, that the first one or two panics appear to be the most damaging.

The most common consequences of errors of prediction are as follows: after an overprediction there is a tendency to report reduced fear and a reduction in predictions of future fear. However, the most common consequences of underpredictions are reductions in fear but *increases* in prediction of future fear.

Overpredictions of fear can be quickly established, especially after the person has experienced an unexpected panic or an intensely fearful event, but they are rather slow to decline. Several discon-firmations appear to be required before the overprediction of fear declines. But a single underpredicted fear or panic might be all that is needed to produce a large increment in prediction of subsequent fear. This asymmetry might be one more example of our tendency to overlook experiences that were uneventful and that produced little or no fear, and to give excessive weight to episodes of intense emotion.

The overprediction of fear and of other aversive experiences might be functional, serving to prevent distress insofar as overpredictions promote avoidance of the fear-evoking situations. If this is so, the prevention of fear will be achieved at some cost because avoidance behaviour can become excessive and impose limitations on mobility. It might then preserve the fear. If the overprediction of fear promotes avoidance behaviour, it serves to reduce the opportunities for disconfirming one's expectations. In other words, overpredictions might be functional in the short term but dysfunctional in the long term. The same reasoning has been applied to problems of chronic pain (Philips & Rachman, 1996).

The strong tendency to overpredict fear can even influence social policy. In the period before the outbreak of World War II it was anticipated that the British population would experience severe panic during the expected air raids and special clinics were established to deal with the psychological casualties (Rachman, 1990) but the clinics were little used and closed as unnecessary. Speaking in the House of Commons in 1934, Winston Churchill too warned of mass casualties. The dangers of the effects of continuous air attacks, he said, were material "but no less formidable than those material effects are the reactions which will be produced upon the mind of the civilian population. We expect that . . . at least 3 million or 4 million people would be driven out into the open country around the metropolis" (Jenkins, 2002, p. 476).

Varieties of fear

Fear is an emotional reaction to a perceived threat; generally, there is a strong relationship between the threat encountered and the degree of fear experienced but fear is not determined solely by objective danger. Numerous studies of combat experiences confirm the validity of the relationship between danger and fear but important exceptions occur.

For example, Stouffer et al. (1949) noted that some soldiers experienced considerable fear in the presence of minimal danger and that others had little fear even under the most threatening conditions. At certain periods during World War II, RAF fighter pilots had an extremely high casualty rate but consistently reported less fear than other air-crew who, at the times in question, were in less danger (Rachman, 1990).

Fear is such a common emotion, probably universally experienced, that various attempts have been made to ascertain the range, frequency, and severity of human fears. In one of the earliest attempts to discover the types and degrees of fear that arise in normal populations, Agras and colleagues (1969) interviewed 325 randomly chosen adults in a small town in Vermont. They classified the fear responses into four categories: mild, intense, phobias, and clinical phobias, which were regarded as the most severe form of fear. The most commonly reported type was a fear of snakes, with no less than one in four people expressing intense fear of this reptile. Of the total sample, 39% reported at least a mild fear of snakes. The second most common fear was that of heights. Among the severe fears, the fear and avoidance of public places and transport (often called agoraphobia) was the most common, with the fear of injury or illness a close second. The majority of the fears reached a peak incidence in early adulthood and declined in the following years. Fears of the dark and of animals were examples of this pattern.

The second, but less common, pattern was that of a gradual increase of fear, reaching a peak in middle adulthood (e.g. fears of illness, injury). In a large-scale questionnaire study carried out by Kirkpatrick (1984) these patterns were broadly confirmed and it was also found that with the approach of old age, people began to show an increased fear of heights and of water. With decreasing visual acuity and physical strength, it is not surprising that elderly people begin to fear heights.

The results of a community study of fear carried out by Costello (1982) in Canada produced results comparable to those found in Vermont. Costello reported a high prevalence of mild fears (244 per 1000 of the population) and of phobias (190 per 100,000) in a sample of 449 women. Animal fears were the most common, followed by fears of heights, tunnels, and enclosed spaces, then social fears, fears of injury, and fears of separation.

These findings on the types and distributions of fear, accumulated by interviewing community samples, have been supplemented by numerous questionnaire studies of fear. One of the largest of these studies of self-reported fears was conducted by an international group, which compared the fears of American, British, and Dutch university students (Arrindell, Cox, Van der Ende, & Kwee, 1995). Well over a thousand students were asked to fill in a version of the Fear Survey Schedule, originally constructed by Wolpe and Lang in 1977. They were asked to state whether they experienced any of the 75 fears listed in the schedule and, if so, to give the degree of fear on a 1 to 5 scale, in which 5 was the most extreme fear score. Consistent with earlier research on this scale, five clusters of fear emerged: social fears, agoraphobic fears, fears of injury or illness, fears of sexual and aggressive scenes, and fears of harmless animals. There were some minor differences between the students in three different countries but the overall pattern was consistent across the three samples. The most commonly and strongly endorsed cluster was social fears, followed by fears of injury or illness, then agoraphobic fears, and lastly, fears of sexual/aggressive scenes and fears of harmless animals. Some of these common fears, such as a fear of injury or illness, have a rational basis. However, it is repeatedly found that large numbers of people report that they feel frightened by the sight of small, harmless animals or insects such as spiders. Many of these fears are irrationally disproportionate to the objects that provoke them. At the other extreme, many people are extraordinarily resilient in the face of great danger. Many examples of this type occurred during World War II. Repeated exposure to aerial bombing raids produced far less fear than anticipated (Lewis, 1942) and the pre-war expectations that widespread panic would be caused by such attacks were disconfirmed. Some of the most common fears are irrational, in the sense that the object or situation feared is neither dangerous nor thought even by the affected person to be dangerous; these fears appear to have no biological value or significance. On the other hand, certain rational fears, which might indeed threaten survival, are surprisingly uncommon. Given the great danger of driving at speed, surprisingly few people are frightened to do so. It is highly probable that more people are frightened of small, harmless spiders than of driving at speed.

One of the most evident and most important features of the distribution of human fears is that it is *not* random; some fears are very common and others are extremely rare. This non-random distribution of fears requires an explanation.

Another puzzling feature of the distribution of different types of fear is the occurrence of fears in circumstances where they would not be expected. A remarkable example of this kind is seen in the numbers of people who live in areas that contain few snakes, for example Hawaii, but nevertheless report that they are frightened of snakes. A weaker but relevant example is also provided by the results of Kirkpatrick's survey mentioned earlier. Nearly three-quarters of his subjects reported that they were frightened of snakes even though snakes are too rare in Northern Indiana to account for this fact. This raises the question of whether it is possible to be frightened of an object or situation that one has not encountered. No satisfactory theory of human fear can succeed unless it accommodates the expected and the unexpected distributions of fear, including the fact that the distribution is not random.

The frequent accounts of the fear of insects and harmless animals is an interesting anomaly. Even harmless snakes and spiders are extremely common objects of fear and many people who are frightened of them acknowledge that their fear is indeed senseless. They often experience additional embarrassment from the fact that their fears are so irrational. These irrational fears can be remarkably intense and, as mentioned above, irrational fears can occur even in areas that are virtually free of the insects or reptiles that the subjects fear.

People can develop fears, even intense and persisting fears, of animals or insects that have never harmed them. They can develop fears of animals that are incapable of harming them, and even of animals that they recognize as being incapable of harming them. To add to the puzzle, people can develop intense and lasting fears of insects or animals that they have never encountered. As mentioned above, people who have never left the virtually snake-free island of Hawaii express a fear of snakes, even harmless snakes. Elderly inhabitants of this island say that a fear of snakes was not uncommon even before the introduction of television and movies. Naturally this gives rise to the possibility that people might be inherently pre-disposed to fear certain objects and, if this is so, then snakes and spiders are likely candidates for the "release" of these inherent and deeply rooted tendencies (see the discussion of "prepared" fears, below).

In the case of a fear of snakes, it is possible that people start with an inherent tendency to respond fearfully but learn by various means, especially from harmless encounters, that snakes do not harm them. If so, people who live in areas that allow for many opportunities of this harmless kind should show a lower incidence of snake fears than people who live in areas where there are few or no snakes. The fearful people who live in snake-free areas have fewer opportunities to learn fearlessness by direct encounters.

There is a rational element in some of these fears, in that some spiders and snakes are indeed dangerous. The second rational component is that people who are frightened of snakes or spiders, even the harmless ones, learn to dislike and perhaps even fear their own reactions to the appearance of these creatures. These reactions, which can include trembling and sweating, can be unpleasant in their own right and are regularly provoked by the object in question. It is therefore rational for people to expect and dislike these unpleasant reactions to the appearance of snakes or spiders, but this should not distract attention from the irrationality of the original response.

The boundaries of fear

Fears of snakes and of spiders are so surprisingly common, and many people report that they are frightened of both snakes and spiders, that one is bound to wonder whether we might be dealing with two manifestations of the same fear rather than two distinct fears. Attempts have been made to tease out one fear from another, to determine whether the fears are discrete or interconnected. If two fears, say the fear of snakes and of spiders, are discrete then a deliberate change induced in one of these fears should leave the second fear unaltered. On the other hand, if the fears are connected or perhaps are even a common manifestation of some deeper fear, then a change in one fear should be followed by a comparable change in the second fear. It is argued that if a person responds fearfully to two distinct physical stimuli, when the fear response to one of these stimuli is deliberately reduced, the person's subsequent reaction to the "untreated" remaining fear should provide a measure of the extent to which the two fears are related.

This approach can be illustrated by a study in which 28 volunteers who were frightened of both snakes and spiders were recruited (Rachman & Lopatka, 1986). In some instances, the deliberate reduction of the first fear was followed by a comparable reduction in the second fear but in other instances a deliberate change in one fear left the second fear unaltered. Contrary to expectations, the connections or absence of connections that emerged after the experimental "treatment" did not match the subject's self-estimated judgements of the similarity of their fears. Prior to the deliberate change in one of their fears, each subject was asked to rate the extent to which their fears of spiders and snakes were similar or even identical—this is the self-estimated judgement of similarity. As stated, there was no relationship between their estimations of similarity and the responses of the two fears to experimental manipulation, as measured by behavioural expressions of fear in the presence of the real stimulus (behaviour tests of fear).

Research into the relationship between various types of fears has also included investigations of the effects of encountering more than one fear stimulus at a time. Do fears summate and is a person who has two fears more frightened than a person who has a single fear? If stimulus A (snake) produces fear and stimulus B (spider) also provokes fear, what happens when they are presented simultaneously? In the main, it appears that fears can summate. Summation occurs regardless of whether the two stimuli are presented simultaneously or in succession. If summation takes place, the sheer order of presentation, snake first or spider first, plays no part in the result. There was, however, an interesting variation on the general pattern. If the first stimulus (e.g. snake) produced a stronger fear than the second stimulus (e.g. spider), the simultaneous presentation of both the spider and the snake resulted in a subtraction rather than a summation. The fear reported in the presence of both of the stimuli was weaker than the fear provoked by the first stimulus acting alone. However, if the first stimulus produced a weak fear and the second one a strong fear, summation occurred.

The occurrence of summation probably means that the two fears share important attributes and that therefore, when the two are presented simultaneously, the quantity of these attributes increases, as when we add apples to apples. On the other hand, summation might also mean that the two fears differ on some important attribute—what is being added? If the two fears are very similar then their simultaneous provocation should produce little or no additional fear. The occurrence of subtraction can be explained in a similar way. If the two fears are highly similar and that therefore fear A (say snakes) fully predicts fear B (spiders), then their simultaneous presentation should produce no summation because the "full fear" has already been produced.

The concept of anxiety disorders

Excessive anxiety is a central feature of many psychological disorders. The most widely used classificatory system for psychological and psychiatric disorders, the DSM (*Diagnostic and statistical manual of mental disorders*, now in its fourth edition), recognizes seven types of anxiety disorder (see Table 1.3).

"Panic disorder" is the term used to describe repeated episodes of intense fear of rapid onset (panics); at least some of these episodes are unexpected, they appear to come out of the blue. Panic disorder with agoraphobia, a common association, refers to panics that are followed by pervasive avoidance behaviour, especially of public transport and public places. In a small number of instances, the agoraphobic avoidance behaviour is not preceded by panics.

The term "agoraphobia" strictly means "fear of the marketplace" but is now used to refer to a fear of being in public places from which an escape might be difficult or even a fear of coming to harm when alone in one's own home. Depending on the person's particular fears, the avoidance of "unsafe" situations might be focused on one or a few places or, in severe cases, on virtually any place; they seek the company of a few trusted people, and proximity to hospitals. In these severe cases the person becomes virtually housebound, unable to travel anywhere alone and, even when accompanied by a trusted adult, can travel only for short distances using specific routes, at specific times.

A diagnosis of social phobia could be appropriate if the person complains of intense persistent anxiety about social situations,

TABLE 1.3

The anxiety disorders

- Panic disorder, with or without agoraphobia
- Agoraphobia without a history of panics
- Social phobia
- Specific phobia
- Generalized anxiety disorder (GAD)
- Obsessive-compulsive disorder (OCD)
- Post-traumatic stress disorder ((PTSD) (and acute stress disorder; ASD)

especially if exposed to the scrutiny of others. In specific phobias, the central feature is an extremely intense, persistent, circumscribed fear of a specific object or place (such as an extreme fear of spiders or heights).

Obsessive-compulsive disorder (OCD) consists of repetitive, intentional, stereotyped acts, such as compulsive hand washing and/or repetitive, unwanted, intrusive thoughts of an unacceptable/ repugnant quality that the affected person resists.

Post-traumatic stress disorder (PTSD) consists of many symptoms, including anxiety, disturbances of memory, elevated arousal, avoidance, and fear or horror. These symptoms persist for prolonged periods after an unusually distressing experience, such as a natural disaster, an accident, or a violent attack. Fears associated with this disorder tend to be accompanied by heightened levels of arousal, an involuntary tendency to recall or re-experience the event during dreams or at other times and by strong tendencies to avoid people or places that are associated with the original stress. A full account of PTSD is provided in another volume in this series, *Stress and Trauma* by Patricia Resick.

Generalized anxiety disorder (GAD) is characterized by persistent, excessive, unrealistic anxiety about possible misfortunes, such as financial losses, ill-health, the welfare of one's children, or combinations of these misfortunes.

The entire DSM system of classification, including the category of anxiety disorders, is a great improvement on the diagnostic anarchy that prevailed until the publication of the first edition. It is clearly set out, coherent, based on well-defined criteria, and eminently useable. However, its serious limitations should not be overlooked. The scheme implies that a wide variety of unusual experiences and behaviour are signs of mental illness, the entire system is unacceptably overinclusive, and the despairingly long list of "mental disorders" (now over 400) increases with each new edition. The system is categorical despite the fact that many of the diagnostic items are essentially quantitative and continuous (e.g. How much social anxiety is within the range of normal? How many obsessional ideas are needed for a diagnosis of OCD? How intense need a fear become to warrant a diagnosis of phobia?). Most of the classes included under anxiety disorders do indeed have a common feature, namely excessive anxiety. In obsessional disorders the anxiety might be overshadowed by the presence of unyielding depression. Most of the remaining disorders are, however, justifiably grouped together by the dominance of intense fear or anxiety. The rationale for the DSM is given in the introductory section of the DSM IV and in numerous publications (e.g. Frances, First, & Pincus, 1995; Spitzer, 1991). Critical commentaries are given by Wakefield (1992), Eysenck, Wakefield, and Friedman (1983), and others (Follette, 1996; Follette & Houts, 1996; Kirk & Kutchins, 1992; Schacht & Nathan, 1977).

Summary

Anxiety is one of the most prominent and pervasive emotions. It is a feeling of uneasy suspense, the tense anticipation of a threatening but obscure event. Fear and anxiety share some common features but fears tend to have a specific, usually identifiable focus and to be more intense and episodic.

Fear can be construed as consisting of three loosely coupled components: the subjective sense of dread, associated physiological changes, and behavioural attempts to escape. Fear is both a reaction and a motivating force, usually giving rise to attempts to escape or avoid. Avoidance is promoted by expectations of threat and fearful people tend to overpredict how frightened they will be when they encounter the object of their fear.

Fears of animals are the most common, followed by fears of injury/illness, heights, enclosed spaces, and social fears. The most intense and irrational fears are classified as phobias or anxiety disorders, of which there are seven types: panic disorder, agoraphobia, social phobia, specific phobia, generalized anxiety disorder, obsessive-compulsive disorder, and post-traumatic stress disorder.

Influences on anxiety 2

In this chapter, a model of anxiety is set out and the factors that influence anxiety are described.

A model of anxiety

Many components are involved in the activation and the experience of anxiety; it is a process rather than a categorical event that occurs or does not occur. In an attempt to simplify some of these complexities, a didactic model, which has gaps and at times skirts around the complexities, is set out (see Figure 2.1).

It is assumed that people vary in their proneness to experience anxiety and that the vulnerable ones become hypervigilant when entering a novel or potentially intimidating situation. Their hyper-vigilance promotes rapid and global scanning, which then turns to an intense narrow focus if a threat is detected. The transition from the global scanning stage to narrowly focused attention can be illustrated by the idea of tuning a radio. Initially, one scans fairly rapidly across a wide band until a signal is picked up; one then turns to fine tuning and raises the volume. So the anxious patient entering a potentially threatening situation carries out broad global scanning until a threat signal is detected. The person's attention then focuses narrowly and intensely on the potential threat, with enhanced perceptual sensitivity and even distortion.

Threatening objects appear to be clearer, sharper, even larger. The detection of a threat triggers an inhibition of ongoing behaviour, perhaps seen in the form of attentive stillness and high arousal. The perceived information, whether from an external or internal source, is then interpreted as signifying safety or danger. According to Beck and Emery (1985, p. 56), "when a threat is perceived the relevant cognitive schemas are activated; these are used to evaluate and assign

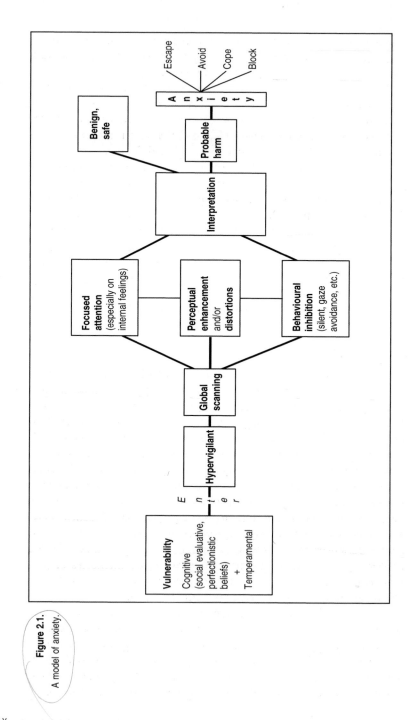

Figure 2.1.
A model of anxiety.

a meaning to the event". If safe, the person can then resume the ongoing behaviour but if there is danger of harm, anxiety arises and might be followed by escape/avoidance/coping.

The early detection of threat is of survival value and appropriately apprehensive anxiety has obvious functional significance. It follows that there should be a selective attentional bias favouring the detection of threats, especially when one is entering circumstances that are unfamiliar or that have a history of threat and danger.

Psychological analyses of the nature of attention have repeatedly produced evidence of important processes of which the person remains unaware. These include the pre-attentive processes (Mathews & MacLeod, 1994; Williams, Watts, MacLeod, & Mathews, 1997), which can be expanded to include the phenomena of perceptual defence, implicit memory, and unaware detection of auditory or visual stimuli. These processes are studied by the use of tasks such as dichotic listening and tachistoscope presentations. In potentially threatening situations, as in other situations, people attend to some stimuli in a non-conscious fashion; they do so without awareness.

Vulnerability

The idea that people vary in the degree to which they are vulnerable to experiencing anxiety (Brewin, 1988) gains support from the clinical and experimental evidence of widespread individual differences in the detection of threat. To begin with, there is evidence of experiential and biological determinants of anxiety proneness, much of it assembled and presented in the theories of H. J. Eysenck (1957, 1967) and in clinical theories such as those propounded by Beck and Emery (1985), and by Clark (1988). In addition to these temperamental vulnerabilities, there is growing evidence of a vulnerability that is largely cognitive in nature [see, for example, Michael Eysenck (1992) and Clark (1988, 1996)]. People are *primed* to detect threat cues by their past experiences and present beliefs. They are prepared, even before entering the potentially threatening situation, by memories of past misfortunes and anxiety, which combine with their current beliefs about the sources of danger that can threaten them.

People who have a temperamental vulnerability tend to have high scores on measures of introversion and neuroticism. The cognitive vulnerability appears to include differences in vigilance, the collection and use of information, perceptual processes, variations in attentional processes, and judgemental biases, among other variables. The components and boundaries of cognitive vulnerability are being determined. Over the years, numerous instruments have been introduced in an attempt to measure vulnerability to anxiety, including the well-used scales designed to measure state and trait anxiety and the Anxiety Sensitivity Index (Reiss & McNally, 1985; Taylor, 1995). As will be seen presently, this self-report scale includes some temperamental factors, some items dealing with interpretation and misinterpretation, and others dealing with levels of arousal.

One of the keenest proponents of the need to distinguish between state anxiety and trait anxiety was Spielberger (1966, 1972, 1983), who employed a down-to-earth approach, emphasizing the practical implications of the concept of anxiety proneness, in developing psychometric instruments for measuring anxiety. Anxiety *states* are said to be transitory; they recur when evoked by threatening stimuli and usually endure for only a limited period after the disappearance of the threat. The *trait* of anxiety, however, refers to a relatively enduring individual difference between people in the way in which they perceive the world and respond to it. People who have high trait anxiety are inclined to react and behave with predictable regularity to perceived threats; they have a low threshold for reacting with anxiety. It follows that the stronger the trait of anxiety, the more probable it is that the person will experience anxiety in a range of situations, with comparatively minimal provocation, and to experience more intense levels of anxiety than people who are low in this trait. Spielberger viewed trait anxiety as a latent disposition to respond anxiously (see also M Eysenck, 1992).

Flowing from his distinction between state and trait anxiety, Spielberger constructed an inventory (the State-Trait Anxiety Inventory; STAI) to measure the two forms of anxiety. The STAI is a self-report inventory of 20 items designed to measure increasing levels of intensity of anxiety, "with low scores indicating states of calmness and serenity . . . and high scores reflecting states of intense apprehension and fearfulness that approach panic" (Spielberger, p. 37, 1972). The items include statements such as, "I lack self-confidence" and the respondent is asked to endorse one of four degrees of agreement ranging from "Almost never", which scores 1, to "Almost always", which scores 4. The anxiety *state* scale also consists of 20 items, similarly ranked from 1 (Not at all) to 4 (Very much so). These items are equally divided between feelings of tension, nervousness, worry, and apprehension on the one hand and 10 items expressing feelings of calmness and contentment on the other. Respondents are asked to state how they feel at the very moment of completing the questionnaire. The maximum score on the state anxiety scale is 80.

The STAI is subject to all the limitations of self-report inventories but is widely used because of its ease of administration and flexibility. It can readily provide an approximate measure of subjective anxiety on repeated occasions for investigations in which fluctuations of anxiety are an important element, and in studies where one wishes to assess the anxiety-provoking effects of particular interventions or experimental manipulations. It has been widely used in investigations of anxiety connected with medical and surgical investigations or procedures and is the most common method used for tracking changes in anxiety during medical/surgical processes such as preparation for surgery and adjustment during the postoperative period (Johnston, 1980; Kincey, Statham, & McFarlane, 1991; Weller & Hener, 1993).

It has been observed, and therefore objected, that trait anxiety and state anxiety are too highly correlated. In some circumstances, this is a limiting factor on the uses of these scales and concepts. However, the correlation between the two concepts is unavoidable and if it did not exist would give rise to suspicion about the psychometric validity of the scales because the occurrence and intensity of episodes of state anxiety is bound to be influenced by the person's pre-existing proneness to anxiety.

Most of these developments in theory and in psychometric research took place before the widespread infusion of cognitive concepts and techniques into clinical psychology generally (Brewin, 1988) and into the field of anxiety disorders in particular. There is no doubt about the importance of cognitive appraisal in anxiety (e.g. Lazarus, 1966) and therefore there is a need to study and measure anxiety cognitions. The need for refined measurements of these cognitions is nowhere clearer than in the successful and influential theory of panic disorder, in which "catastrophic cognitions" play a central role (see Chapter 5).

Although it was not introduced for this particular purpose, the concept of anxiety sensitivity has found a useful place in cognitive approaches to anxiety (Reiss, 1987, 1991; Reiss, Peterson, Gursky, & McNally, 1986; Taylor, 1995). Anxiety sensitivity is a fear of bodily sensations that are interpreted as having potentially harmful physical or psychological consequences, and hence give rise to significant anxiety. The Anxiety Sensitivity Index (ASI, Peterson & Reiss, 1987) is a self-report questionnaire that measures the subject's beliefs about the perceived threat of these bodily sensations and the associated fear of these very sensations. It includes items such as feeling frightened by one's rapidly beating heart, experiencing alarm

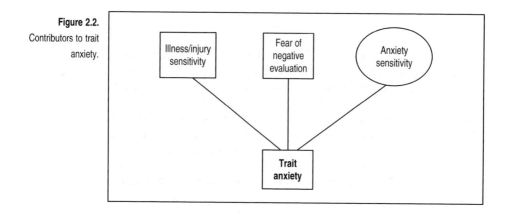

Figure 2.2. Contributors to trait anxiety.

when short of breath, and so on. The ASI results provide evidence that anxiety sensitivity is elevated across all anxiety disorders, especially in panic disorder. The anxiety sensitivity scores of people who have circumscribed phobias are not significantly greater than those that occur in a non-clinical population (Taylor, 1995). The concept is a bridge between the so-called temperamental features of anxiety proneness and the more recently introduced cognitive aspects of anxiety proneness, concentrating as it does on the subject or patient's *interpretations* of the sensations that can contribute to, or signify, anxiety.

It has been said that the notion of anxiety sensitivity is little more than a new version of the concept of trait anxiety, but McNally (1995) has argued that anxiety sensitivity is a specific sensitivity to respond fearfully to one's own sensations, whereas trait anxiety is a broader tendency to respond fearfully to an extensive range of potential threats. In an extensive review, which included his own psychometric investigations, Taylor (1995) concluded that anxiety sensitivity is one of three major factors that contribute to trait anxiety. The three factors, anxiety sensitivity, illness/injury sensitivity, and fear of negative evaluation, all contribute to the general trait of anxiety proneness, and are illustrated in Figure 2.2.

The concept of cognitive vulnerability is important to the cognitive theory of anxiety and, if disconfirmed, would leave a gap in the explanation. In the absence of cognitive vulnerability, the negative cognitions reported by anxious people might better be regarded as parallel effects of anxiety, or even as the results of anxiety, and it would be difficult to press the view that negative cognitions play a causal role in the generation of anxiety.

Vigilance

In the words of Sophocles, "To a man who is afraid everything rustles". A particularly clear account of the nature of anxious hypervigilance is given by Michael Eysenck (1992), who regards this phenomenon as both a reaction to potential threat and as a component of cognitive vulnerability to anxiety (see also Mathews, MacLeod, & Tata, 1987; Williams et al., 1997). According to Eysenck, people who are predisposed to anxiety manifest hypervigilance in the following ways: they engage in a "high rate of environmental scanning which involves numerous rapid eye movements throughout the visual field . . . a propensity to attend selectively to threat-related rather than neutral stimuli; a broadening of attention prior to the detection of such stimuli, and a narrowing of attention when a salient stimulus is being processed" (1992, p. 43).

Michael Eysenck argues that hypervigilance is a vulnerability factor for anxiety disorders and is evident in patients and in non-patient groups who are high in trait anxiety. Hypervigilance is especially obvious under stressful conditions. However, as it is not found in patients who have overcome their anxiety disorders, he concludes that hypervigilance is best regarded as a vulnerability factor. The evidence pertaining to the status of hypervigilance as a vulnerability factor, is far from complete. Be that as it may, in clinical practice with patients suffering from anxiety disorders, the occurrence of hyper-vigilance and selective attention is an obvious and daily occurrence.

In extreme cases, the attentional processes are so distorted that the patients engage in rapid visual scanning in virtually all new or ambiguous situations. For example, a 38-year-old accountant who was suffering from a severe OCD that centred on his fear of disease contamination, and in particular of AIDS, engaged in rapid broad visual scanning whenever he left his home. The scanning was particularly intense and agitated whenever he went into situations in which he thought that the risk of encountering AIDS contaminated material was increased. During one treatment session that took place in the grounds of a large hospital, he carried out vigorous visual scanning of the car park, searching for any signs of discarded hypo-dermics or other medical materials that he regarded as presenting a serious threat to his health. It was extraordinarily difficult to per-suade him to stop scanning the ground around him and instead to look upwards at the buildings ahead of him. Whenever he observed a suspicious object, and this included an astonishingly wide range of perfectly neutral stimuli, he rapidly concentrated his full attention on the suspect object. Where he could risk it, he would then approach very gingerly to make a precise determination of what the object was and whether or not it might constitute a danger. If he was able to satisfy himself that it was indeed a harmless object he would then return to his broad general scanning. However, on those occasions when his narrow, intense focusing of attention on the object led him to conclude that it might be some contaminated medical material, he escaped rapidly and was disinclined to go anywhere near that part of the hospital approach for the remainder of the treatment session. Many months later he was able to recall in detail all of the threatening items he had observed during his therapeutic walk through the hospital grounds.

Another patient with obsessional-compulsive problems who had a severe fear of diseases, including AIDS, was particularly frightened by the prospect of encountering other people's blood, which she felt would constitute a serious threat to her health, even if it was the smallest trace of dried blood, and even if she approached no closer than three or four feet from the spot of dried blood. Her interpretation of the threat emanating from other people's blood, including people who were wearing the smallest piece of elastoplast to cover a minor nick, was a gross—indeed catastrophic—misinterpretation of the probability of harm coming to her and an overestimation of the seriousness of any contact. Nevertheless, her fear of other people's blood was so intense that whenever she went into a public place she would rapidly scan the physical environment and also the people she encountered, looking constantly for evidence of blood, cuts, bandages, adhesive tape, and so forth. She had trained herself so well that she could indeed pick up traces of red spots at a considerable distance and was usually accurate. However, her perception of red spots was grossly in error in overperceiving the occurrence of red spots of blood. She tended to misperceive as blood a wide range of spots of different colours along the colour continuum, so that spots of almost any dark hue were mistaken as evidence of blood (e.g. spots of mud, or small pieces of waste paper, etc.). She was able to recall in detail the innumerable blood or blood-related items that she had encountered in the previous 12 years.

Context and attention

It is assumed that people who are vulnerable to anxiety enter most situations that are novel and/or intimidating with well-formed expectations. They become hypervigilant and carry out global searching scans of the external and also internal environments. They are selectively tuned to attend to stimuli that might be threatening, that is, they display selective attention. If their attentive processes pick up a potential threat signal then the focus narrows. This narrowing of attention is accompanied by elevations of arousal and increased effort. Given that attentional processes are of limited capacity (Kahneman & Triesman, 1983; Kahneman, Triesman, & Burkell, 1983), the narrowed focus of attention, directed at the perceived source of the threat, is accompanied by a relative neglect of other stimuli. In people who suffer from excessively high or persistent levels of anxiety, this can appear as inattentiveness to other people and the appearance, or more than the appearance, of excessive preoccupation with oneself. In addition, the effort involved in the narrowing of the attentional focus "drains away" attention from other tasks, leading affected people to experience and complain of an inability to concentrate on their jobs or other matters. Beck and Emery (1985) reported that 86% of their cases of patients with anxiety disorder complained of impaired concentration.

The liberating effects of reducing hypervigilance are easily observed during the treatment of patients with obsessive-compulsive disorders. A tactic called the "off-duty/on-duty contrast" is often used to good effect. The patients are taught how to instruct themselves to go on-duty or off-duty at will. When they are off-duty they are no longer required to scan and collect threat-related information. As they become skilled at using this self-induced contrast their vigilance is reduced and becomes more specific and controlled. The periods off-duty are a great relief and, even more important, they learn that the burdensome hypervigilance is not a permanent fact of life but an aspect of their daily functioning that is modifiable and reasonably controllable (Rachman, 2003a).

Of course, when people enter novel or potentially threatening situations they do not always become anxious. Even in those circumstances when they enter a novel or potentially threatening situation with high expectations of encountering danger, they might instead find evidence of safety rather than danger. In circumstances of this type the drive to find safety is likely to be heightened. If the search for safety is successful, no anxiety ensues. For example, if a patient suffering from a panic disorder anticipates experiencing palpitations and laboured breathing, which might be symptoms of an impending heart attack, but then notices that he is outside a reputable hospital or clinic, this might be taken as a sign of safety and the anticipated anxiety does not occur.

The signs of anxiety can also be aborted later in the process. If on entering the situation the person becomes hypervigilant, carries out a global scan of the situation, appears to perceive a potential threat but then after giving it his selective attention finds evidence of dependable safety, the anxiety will diminish.

Interpretation and misinterpretation

In a novel or potentially threatening situation, the information the person collects as a result of selective attention and focusing is open to interpretation. If the information is given a benign interpretation, as in the example above but the person interprets his palpitations and laboured breathing as normal expressions of the fact that he has been running, this benign interpretation will be followed by a decline in whatever anxiety had been generated up to this point. If, however, the person misinterprets these bodily sensations as indicators of an impending heart attack, high levels of anxiety, even of panic, can be expected (MacLeod & Cohen, 1993).

In these circumstances, the important misinterpretations tend to have two dimensions. They can be misinterpretations in which the probability of an aversive event occurring is exaggerated, or the mis-interpretation can be an overestimation of the seriousness of the anticipated event (or of course a combination of high probability and high seriousness). We already know that people who suffer from excessive levels of anxiety or of depression are much inclined to overestimate the probability and the seriousness of unfortunate events (Butler & Mathews, 1983) and the research findings of Clark (1988) and of Ehlers (1992) confirm this observation.

In addition to the two by-products of anxiety already mentioned, inattentiveness to other people or stimuli and the impairment of desired concentration, we have to add feelings of fatigue. Much to the bewilderment of friends and relatives, people who suffer from excessive levels of anxiety complain of being extremely tired even though they have spent the entire day housebound and physically inactive. In fact, the hypervigilance, selective attention, and concen-trated attempts to deal with anxiety all require considerable effort and it should not be surprising that people who experience persistent anxiety so often report feeling drained.

Consequences

Anxiety is unpleasant and most people engage in attempts to reduce this aversive state. The methods they employ depend on their previous experiences with anxiety and the success or failure of the methods they adopted in the past. One of the most common reactions to anxiety is to escape from the unpleasant situation and, wherever possible, to avoid coming into contact with it. For example, people who experience excessive anxiety when shopping in a supermarket experience overpowering urges to escape from the situation as soon as possible. After one or two unpleasant experiences in the super-market they quickly adopt a pattern of avoidance, in which they encourage other people to do the shopping for them or make their own shopping expeditions contingent on being accompanied by a trusted person who can care for them if things go wrong, or confining their shopping to very quiet periods when an escape can be made quickly and without impediment should it be necessary to do so. Escape and avoidance behaviour are successful in the short term. For the most part they are followed by reductions in anxiety and hence provide temporary relief. In the long term, however, they serve to strengthen the escape and avoidance behaviour and probably help to conserve the original anxiety (Mowrer, 1960; Rachman, 1990).

Anxiety, attention, perception, and memory

Selective attention

Health anxiety (a strong candidate for inclusion in future versions of the DSM?) can arise from a threat to one's own health or a threat to the health of others and is nowhere more evident than in parental anxiety regarding their children's safety and well-being. For this reason, Parkinson and Rachman (1980) collected evidence of atten-tional selectivity from a group of anxious mothers during the course of a study of the effects of an uncontrived stress on emotional reactions. The reactions of 25 mothers whose children were being admitted to hospital for surgery were compared to those of 25 control group mothers who had children of the same age but who were not receiving medical treatment at the time of the experiment. One of the four tasks given to these mothers consisted of a type of signal detec-tion task. The rationale for this technique was that during periods of anxiety, threat-related stimuli will be detected more sensitively than neutral stimuli.

Accordingly, the experimenters tried to determine the level of volume at which threat-related or neutral words would be detected by the subjects when they were listening to music that was played at a constant easily audible volume selected by each subject to suit herself. The detection rate was assessed by counting the number of correct recognitions of the key words at each of five increasing levels of volume. After setting the volume level at a comfortable level chosen by the subject, music was presented binaurally throughout the task. At random points during the presentation of the musical tape, 30 words were inserted. Of these, 10 were threat-related trigger words (e.g. injection, bleeding, operation, etc.), 10 were words with a different meaning but a similar sound, and 10 were neutral words. The mothers were asked to repeat each word as they heard it. Five trials were given. On the first trial the words were presented at a very low level of volume, on the second trial at a slightly higher level, on the third trial even louder, and so on until the five trials had been completed. The volume of the music was kept constant across all trials. In this way it was possible to determine the level at which the subjects recognized each of the three categories of words while listening to the words.

Evidence of attentional selectivity was obtained. At the lowest volume during trial 1, the mothers in the experimental group reported six times more threat-related words than the mothers in the control group. On the second trial, the experimental mothers reported twice as many trigger words as did the control groups. By trials four and five however, the difference between the groups disappeared. Across all trials there was a significant improvement in detection rate in subjects of both groups, reflecting a combination of practice effects and the ease of recognition at increasing levels of volume.

Medical and surgical procedures are among the most common and most anxiety-provoking experiences that people encounter and it is a pity that this fact is not more widely appreciated and acted upon in clinics and hospitals. It should be mentioned in passing, that the widespread occurrence of health-related anxiety provides many opportunities for uncontrived psychological research. The intensity of this anxiety should go some way to balancing-out the loss of control and precision that is surrendered when moving from laboratory research into the clinic. For example, people experience intense anxiety when waiting for the results of potentially significant medical tests; indeed, some of the highest self-reported scores on anxiety scales have been reported under exactly these conditions (e.g. Kincey et al., 1991; Weller & Hener, 1993).

A prime example of selective attention occurs when new parents bring their baby home. At first they listen for the baby's every breath and the slightest baby noise can arouse them from sleep. Other examples of selective attention are provided by Michael Eysenck (1992), Mathews and MacLeod, (1994), and Williams et al. (1997). The attentional bias that occurs when people become anxious is particularly evident in people who are suffering from panic disorder; they readily perceive threats to their health, threats of social embarrassment, threats of unpleasant mental events, etc. (Ehlers, Margraf, & Roth, 1988).

It has been convincingly demonstrated that attentional selectivity increases in the presence of potential danger but we are dealing with a complex concept. There are different types and levels of attention. Attention can be directed towards external stimuli or, as is important in cases of panic disorder, to internal sensations. Attention can be passive or it can be active, it can be conscious or non-conscious, and so forth. The subject is a full and rather complicated one but fortunately there are a number of excellent analyses of the phenomenon, including Barlow (2002), Craske (1999), M Eysenck (1992), Mathews and MacLeod (1994), McNally (1994, 1995), and Williams et al. (1997), among others.

Self-focused attention

The narrowing of attention that occurs in response to a threat can be directed externally or internally. Attention directed towards internal events—physical sensations such as heart beat, images, thoughts, feelings—is a normal process that, if it becomes excessive, can cause serious difficulties. Self-focused attention can be intense, constricting, and pre-occupying. Excessive self-attention is believed to be the basis for certain kinds of abnormal experience and behaviour. The prevailing theory to account for panic disorder, described in Chapter 5, attributes the cause of episodes of panic to a catastrophic misinterpretation of certain bodily sensations, such as chest pain, sweating, a pounding heart, dizziness, etc. (Clark, 1986). In vulnerable people, excessive monitoring of one's bodily sensations can raise the opportunities for panic. The same is true for other internal events, such as images and memories. In cases of obsessive-compulsive disorder (OCD), it has been argued, serious misinterpretations of one's unwanted intrusive thoughts can generate lasting obsessions (see Chapter 7). Indeed in many instances the person's hypervigilant monitoring of the acceptability of his or her thoughts is the root of the trouble.

Excessive self-focused attention is thought to play a significant part in several of the anxiety disorders. There is evidence of a heightened degree of self-focused attention in test anxiety, social anxiety, sexual anxiety, OCD, and panic disorder. Barlow regards the differences in self-evaluative attention as one of the major distinctions between normal and unadaptive anxiety: "In view of the enormously important role this component (self-evaluative internal focus) seems to play . . . it seems that targeting self-focused attention is essential during therapy" (Barlow, 1988, p. 316).

Some of the earliest and most convincing evidence of heightened self-focusing was collected by Sarason (1980) and colleagues in their protracted research into the nature and causes of test anxiety (see p. 48). One of their major conclusions was that a preoccupation with one's self and one's sensations in the test situation is a major cause of the discomfort and impairment that is observed in affected people. In a classic study by Deffenbacher (1978), subjects worked on anagram problems under conditions of high or low stress. Measures were obtained of the amount of time that they spent thinking about the task itself, thinking about intrusive ideas that were not relevant to the task, and directing attention towards their bodily sensations. The people who were predisposed to anxiety showed a significant reduction in task-relevant thoughts during the stressful condition relative to the comparison subjects. The affected subjects also reported more anxiety, more thought interference, and more thoughts that were directed at monitoring their sensations and thinking about the consequences of their test performance. Broadly speaking, the association between self-focused attention and anxiety that is observed in test situations is a multiple of predisposition to anxiety, initial level of arousal, the nature and significance of the particular task, and the degree of stress produced by the task itself. The more complex and demanding the task, and the more significant the outcome, the greater the likelihood of heightened self-focused attention and associated anxiety.

Evidence of heightened self-focusing has also been found among people who experience anxiety in social situations, and indeed the occurrence of this phenomenon is thought to play a major part in producing social phobias:

> The evidence regarding social and generalized anxiety is also generally supportive of a relation between increased self-focused attention and anxious affect. In individuals with clinical levels of social anxiety, self-focusing does appear to be heightened and related to generalized level of anxiety. (Ingram, 1990, p. 161)

People who have a chronically high level of self-focused attention are at risk for various psychological difficulties (Ingram, 1990, p. 162). In keeping with the importance attached to self-focused attention, significant reductions in such attention are reported after successful treatment (Barlow, 2002).

In passing, it is interesting to notice that alcohol appears to inhibit self-focusing and presumably this is why some people use drink to reduce their anxiety in social or other intimidating situations. The recent interest in using "mindfulness training" for therapy (Teasdale, Segal, & Williams, 1995) might lead to improvements in our capacity to control our attentional focus.

There remain a number of problems about the nature of self-focused attention and these include a lack of clarity about the exact differences between heightened self-focused attention and normal self-focused attention. All of this bears on the nature of attentional processes themselves and it is assumed in all of the theorizing about the role of self-focusing attention that people have a limited attentional capacity and that an excessive concern with self-focused attention will inevitably drain away or detract from the attention that might, or should, be paid to external matters. The concept of limited attentional capacity has been subject to criticism but the general idea is as plausible as its opposite—unlimited attentional capacity—is implausible. It is true, however, that the concept of attention is a complex one and we have to take account of the fact that it varies within the same person throughout the day and can also vary over longer periods, so that one's level of attention can appear to be high for several weeks and then decline in the weeks that follow. We also attend to stimuli that are being perceived by different modalities, as we watch and listen and smell and taste all at the same time. The way in which these attentional resources are allocated, and how the information coming through these different channels is integrated, are fascinating questions. For present purposes, however, the observed association between heightened self-focusing and anxiety, and its probable contribution to anxiety disorders, has useful explanatory value. It should be remembered, however, that the association between self-focused attention and anxiety is not an exclusive one; there is equally good evidence of a relationship between heightened self-focused attention and depression (Ingram, 1990).

The main barrier to elucidating the nature and role of self-focused attention is its elusiveness. Progress is hampered by the technical obstacles to measuring self-focused attention; in most circumstances we are obliged to depend on the person's (retrospective) report of what happened. There is also the embarrassing problem that the act of observing, and later reporting, one's self-focused attention is bound to affect the very process under study. There is no shortage of methodological challenges.

Perceptual factors

In addition to selective attention, there is evidence of selective perception and indeed of distortions of perception. Clinical observations indicate that perceptual distortions can take place during episodes of fear and that the distortions decline after a reduction of the pertinent fear. A patient who experienced increasing apprehension about his ability to control his car experienced acute fear as he approached bridges. As he drove towards a bridge, it appeared to be sloping at a potentially dangerous angle and also seemed to be extremely lengthy. This perceptual distortion occurred only when he was the driver of the vehicle. When the therapist took the wheel, the patient reported perceiving the bridge accurately.

In a second case of driving phobia, the patient had a fear of losing control of the vehicle and reported that when she was particularly frightened the road appeared to tilt sharply to the right, seemingly dragging the car with it. In response, she tended to overcorrect and turn the steering wheel towards the centre of the road, sometimes carrying out this action too abruptly. During episodes of intense fear the surface of the road appeared to deteriorate so that objectively smooth road surfaces were perceived as being corrugated. As in the previous case, she experienced no perceptual distortions whatever when the therapist was driving.

A third patient avoided walking over bridges because he feared he might lose control and either run into the oncoming traffic or jump off the bridge. Whenever he felt extremely fearful, the bridges appeared to be longer and far higher than he knew them to be when he was feeling calm.

A fourth patient who suffered from frequent episodes of panic, dating back to a traumatic incident when she experienced a noxious reaction after taking an illicit drug, reported disturbing distortions of perception during periods of extreme anxiety. During these periods she was inclined to perceive people as being unnaturally thin and tall, just as she had done during the three days following her unfortunate experience with the stimulant drug. She never experienced these distortions, or any others, at any time other than when she was extremely anxious.

The occurrence of fearful distortions was confirmed in an experiment carried out on 60 snake- or spider-fearful volunteer subjects (Rachman & Cuk, 1992). The fearful subjects were asked to describe their perceptions of the feared object during episodes of fear and then again after their fears had been reduced. The snake-phobic and spider-phobic subjects showed evidence of some perceptual distortions in the activity of the pertinent feared object, but no distortions of size. After reduction of the relevant fear, the subjects reported a significant decline in the perceived activity of the fear-provoking creature. The spider-phobic subjects were inclined to perceive the spider as jumping and the snake-phobic subjects perceived more tongue movements in the snake than did the non-fearful comparison subjects.

It is probable that there is a connection between frightening distortions and the narrowing of attention that is observed during fear. Both of these biases appear to serve the same psychological function, namely to select and enhance possible sources of threat, all the better to perceive and deal with them. During periods of apprehensive hypervigilance, people probably concentrate their attention on a narrow focus and also experience a perceptual enhancement of potential sources of threat.

Anxiety and sexual functioning

Disorders of sexual functioning can arise from biological causes, psychological causes, or a combination of both. Erectile dysfunctions, one of the most commonly reported sexual problems, can occur as a result of biological factors or from psychological causes. Similarly, the most commonly reported female sexual problem, low sexual desire, can have biological or psychological origins (Bancroft, 1989).

Barlow (2002) has observed some similarities between sexual anxiety, social anxiety, and test anxiety. In all three examples, he argues, the level of autonomic arousal is only loosely related to the person's performance. Instead, the amount of irrelevant cognitive activity (especially regarding how one is being evaluated and the possibility of failure) is a more reliable predictor of poor performance. Students who are suffering from test anxiety do worse when they focus their attention on self-evaluation than do those students who concentrate on the requirements of the task. In sexual contexts, the perception that one has to perform up to an expected standard, "elicits negative affective responding, including perceptions of lack of control or inability to obtain desired results . . . at this point a critical shift of attention occurs from external focus (on erotic material in this instance) to a more internal self-evaluative focus" (Barlow, 1988, p. 247). According to Barlow, self-focused attention becomes bound up with "negative affect" and this in turn increases the intensity of the self-focused attention. These processes cause disruptions in concentration and often will lead to impaired performance. The impaired performance is interpreted as an indication of impending or actual failure, with a consequent increment in anxiety.

Although it was widely asserted by most clinicians that anxiety is a major contributor to psychosexual dysfunctioning (e.g. Bancroft, 1989; Barlow, 1988; Wolpe, 1958), the evidence collected in laboratory studies is not always consistent with these beliefs. The assumption that anxiety impedes sexual performance was reflected in the considerable efforts made by therapists to reduce their patients' anxiety by techniques such as systematic desensitization (Wolpe, 1958), behavioural rehearsals (Masters & Johnson, 1970), and so on. Masters and Johnson described anxiety as a major obstacle to normal sexual functioning and it was believed to be largely responsible for psychological interferences with sexual arousal, particularly in difficulties that men might experience in gaining or maintaining erections. The results of psychological treatment of these difficulties, particularly the difficulties in sexual arousal experienced by men, were modest but not inconsistent with the beliefs about the connection between anxiety and sexual dysfunction. Recently, however, the emphasis has shifted from anxiety-reducing techniques to the modification of cognitions (Sbrocco & Barlow, 1996). This change is in keeping with the emphasis placed on self-focused attention and maladaptive cognitions in the related disorders of test anxiety and social anxiety.

There is evidence of an association between anxiety and sexual disorders but, as Bancroft (1989) pointed out, anxiety might not play a causal role; the anxiety might be a consequence of some underlying sexual dysfunction or a parallel coeffect. Nevertheless, he went on to list some of the types of anxiety encountered by therapists dealing with sexual problems. These include a fear of failure, a fear of humiliation, a fear of pain or discomfort, anxiety about satisfying one's partner, and a fear of loss of control. To this list we must add the fear of contracting AIDS. Bancroft identified the potential for feeling vulnerable in sexual encounters and the need for both partners to have a degree of trust in each other. In the absence of such trust, vulnerability is increased.

As there are many opportunities for anxiety in sexual encounters, it would be surprising if anxiety were not a factor in disturbed sexual functioning. And for many years it was assumed that anxiety almost always impairs sexual functioning and might well be the major cause of psychosexual problems. It appears, however, that there are exceptions in which anxiety might facilitate rather than decrease sexual arousal and performance (e.g. Barlow, 2002; Palace & Gorzalka, 1990). For example, threats of possible electric shock raise anxiety but can also raise sexual arousal.

We also have abundant evidence that many erectile problems can be dealt with by medications such as Viagra®. As mentioned, the results of psychological treatment of erectile difficulties were modest. Nevertheless, the assumption that anxiety plays a significant causal role in most psychosexual functions remains embedded in contemporary clinical practice. There has, however, been a shift towards explanations that integrate anxiety and maladaptive cognitions.

In the course of studying the relation between anxiety and sexual arousal, it was found that men who appear to have no sexual problems report and show a decrease in sexual arousal under conditions of distraction. On the other hand, men with sexual problems are surprisingly unaffected by the introduction of distractions (Edelmann, 1992; Sbrocco & Barlow, 1996). The laboratory evidence on factors that increase or decrease sexual arousal in women is incomplete and a little confusing at present but there appear to be conditions in which anxiety facilitates rather than inhibits such arousal. A complicating factor is that sexually dysfunctional women report elevated self-focused attention but are poor at "reading" the signs of their own physiological–sexual arousal, generally under-rating it. They tend to be overattentive but inaccurate.

A probable reason for some of the gaps and inconsistencies in the evidence accumulated in the clinic and the laboratory is the inevitable artificiality of the laboratory investigations, including the fact that they are confined to studying sexual arousal and not sexual performance/satisfaction. So far, there is little evidence of the effects of personally relevant cognitions on sexual performance. The fearful cognitions that patients describe to therapists are bound to have a greater effect on sexual performance than the contrived evocation of anxiety by electric shock or other artificial means in the laboratory. The differences between laboratory and clinical reports might arise largely from the meaning of the cognitions that prevail in the two different situations.

The relations between anxiety and sexual arousal/performance are ripe for a fresh approach. The earlier view that anxiety is sexually inhibiting is not wholly correct and an explanation is needed for the facilitatory effects of anxiety on arousal. Clinically, the successful modification of erectile problems is by medications, but the modest effects of psychological treatment, has to be taken into account. The occurrence of excessive self-focusing but inaccurate monitoring of physiological indicators of sexual arousal needs investigation. In all, these unanswered questions and the gap between laboratory and clinic, call for a full reconsideration of the subject of anxiety and sexuality.

Test anxiety

People who experience intense anxiety when carrying out formal tests or other tasks on which are they to be evaluated are said to suffer from "test anxiety". One of the most influential explanations of test anxiety, promoted by Sarason (1980) and others, is that test-anxious people are negatively self-preoccupied and that during the task their attention is inappropriately focused on their bodily feelings, expectations of failure, etc. to the detriment of their test performance. They experience more irrelevant thoughts during the test than people who are relatively free of anxiety in the test conditions:

> Highly test-anxious individuals typically perform more poorly on cognitive tasks than less anxious individuals, especially if the tasks are difficult and are given under situational conditions of evaluative stress . . . the test-anxious individual dividing attention between self-preoccupied worry and task cues and the less anxious person focusing more fully on task-relevant variables. (Wine, 1971)

Although exceptions to this generalization have been recorded, the overall thrust of the evidence indicates that test-anxious people do approach their evaluative tasks with negative cognitions and also devote a good deal of their attentional efforts to irrelevant topics during the test (Sarason, 1980). There is also consistent evidence that test-anxious people are more highly aroused in the test situation than people who are free of anxiety. This difference in level of arousal was taken as a starting point for a number of attempts to treat test anxiety using fear-reducing techniques, such as relaxation and systematic desensitization.

The comparative success of these techniques is consistent with the evidence of increased arousal during test taking but, unfortunately, it does little to explain the causal connection between elevated arousal and misdirection of attention. It is probable that arousal and the misdirected attention are interactive; cognitions can influence the level of arousal, just as the level of arousal can promote an increase in negative cognitions.

The comparative success of the theory introduced to explain test anxiety and the moderate efficacy of treatment techniques derived from this explanation are welcome but should not obscure the fact that in some circumstances mild to moderate increases in anxiety can facilitate rather than impair performance and achievement (Sarason, 1980). From a theoretical point of view, the exact nature of attentional processes remain to be clarified. As with all cognitive explanations of anxiety phenomena, there are methodological obstacles to the definition and measurement of the relevant cognitions, which are of course at the core of all of these explanations. Most investigatory procedures require people to assess their own attention and this inevitably affects the very subject under study—attention. Leaving aside questions of the accuracy of self-assessment and self-report, here we have subjects paying attention to their own attention—a potentially muddling regression.

Anxiety and memory

It seems inevitable that we should remember those places, people, and events that are threatening but, somewhat surprisingly, there is an "absence of a negative bias in explicit memory for patients with generalized anxiety disorder . . . and it is all the more surprising because there is substantial evidence for the existence of such a bias in depressed patients" (Williams, Watts, MacLeod, & Mathews, 1988, p. 96). And again, "anxious patients definitely do not have a negative memory bias in explicit memory, but there are indications that they may possess a negative implicit memory bias" (M Eysenck, 1992, p. 96).

Interestingly, although there is evidence of attentional biases in anxious subjects, for many years there was only weak and contradictory evidence of *memory* biases in these subjects. The studies showing memory biases in depressed subjects were difficult to replicate in people with anxiety:

It appears that different emotions may be more specific in their effects on cognitive processing than was originally thought. One possible interpretation of the data . . . is that anxious subjects, but not depressed subjects, orient their attention towards threat. Depressed subjects (but not generally anxious subjects) may selectively remember negative material. (Williams et al., 1988, p. 168)

The evidence on memory biases is inconsistent (Coles & Heimberg, 2002; Edelmann, 1992; M Eysenck, 1992; Williams et al., 1988). There is evidence of memory bias in one anxiety disorder but not in another. The distinction between implicit and explicit memory is sometimes lost, and results from recall and recognition tasks can differ. Memory bias is particularly difficult to demonstrate in broad, non-focused disorders of anxiety such as generalized anxiety disorder (GAD) but easier to find in focused disorders such as panic disorder and OCD. Memory biases are so evident in post-traumatic disorders that they even feature indirectly in the criteria for making clinical diagnoses.

In 1991, Cloitre and Liebowitz found evidence of a memory advantage regarding threat-related material among patients with panic disorder but in 1992 found no evidence of a comparable bias among patients with social phobia (Cloitre, Heimberg, Holt, & Liebowitz, 1992). A similar failure was reported by Rapee and colleagues in 1992 and by Chambless and Hope (1996). Dalgleish (1994) also failed to find a relationship between anxiety and memory bias.

On the other hand, McNally, Lasko, Macklin, and Pitman (1995) found memory deficits in patients suffering from post-traumatic stress disorder (PTSD), and Sher, Mann, & Frost, (1984) reported that normal subjects who scored highly on a questionnaire of obsessional compulsiveness had poorer memory for prior actions than did control subjects. By contrast, Constans, Foa, Franklin, & Mathews (1995) found that patients with obsessional problems showed recall of recent actions that was, if anything, superior to that of controls. Comparable findings were obtained by Radomsky and Rachman (1999) and by Ceschi et al. (2003). The memory for threatening stimuli was studied in a group of people with OCD who had fears of contamination by showing them 25 clean and 25 contaminated items (Radomsky & Rachman, 1999). Subjects then completed a standard test of memory, after which they were asked to recall the original 50 items. They showed a superior recall of the contaminated items, unlike the participants in the two comparison groups. There were no differences between the groups on the standard test of memory. In a replication of this study, Ceschi et al. (2003) found superior recognition but not recall of the contaminated items.

Bradley, Mogg, and Williams (1995) produced evidence of explicit and implicit memory biases in depressed patients but found no evidence of these biases in anxious patients. These results were consistent with their view that:

> . . . depressives show memory biases in explicit memory tasks . . . such as free recall or recognition . . . there is little evidence that they are biased in early attentional processes. By contrast anxiety is associated with early attentional mood-congruent biases but there is little consistent evidence of such biases in explicit memory tasks. (Bradley et al., 1995, p. 755)

These results and conclusions were consistent with most of the evidence available at the time but, as will be shown, there are reasons to expect that ultimately it will be found that these cognitive biases in attention and memory will be found to operate in depression and in anxiety.

For elaborate reasons, Williams et al. (1988) and Mathews, Mogg, May & Eysenck (1989) argued that clinically anxious people should display a negative bias in implicit memory but not in explicit memory. "The weight of empirical evidence suggests strongly that facilitated ability to recall emotionally negative information is a characteristic of elevated depression, but not of elevated anxiety" (Mathews & MacLeod, 1994, p. 34). Williams et al. (1988, p. 167) report that "repeated attempts to demonstrate a relation between anxiety and recall have failed".

These failures speak to the elusiveness of the phenomenon, rather than its non-existence. The failures were ironic because one of the earliest and prized examples of implicit memory, confirming the operation of non-conscious processes in memory, was provided by Claparede (1911) in a clinical situation in which anxiety might well have been operative.

Claparede carried out a series of investigations into the memorial functioning of a 47-year-old woman, residing at the Bel-Air asylum. Her memory for distant events was intact but she did not know where she was, or even that she had been in the asylum for five years. She did not recognize the physicians whom she saw every day, nor her nurse who had been with her every day for six months. She forgot from one moment to the next what she had been told and knew neither the day nor month, even though she was continually given this information. Interestingly, she knew the position of the toilets, the times for meals, etc., even though she was unable to recognize the asylum or her presence in it.

In a famous demonstration, Claparede pricked her hand with a pin held between his fingers. The pain was as quickly forgotten as all other new information and, seconds after being pricked, she could remember nothing of the event. However, when he brought his hand close to hers a second time, she pulled back her hand without knowing why. When asked why she pulled back, she responded: "Well, don't I have the right to pull my hand away?" or "Maybe there is a pin hidden in your hand?". When asked why she thought about the pin, she replied, "It's just an idea which crossed my mind". She never recognized the idea of being "pricked" as a memory. Her avoidance behaviour indicates that she was responding to the threat of repeated pain even though she could not recall the reason for her fear.

Given that anxiety arises from the detection of a signal of threat, it is inconceivable that dependable and even enhanced memory does not play a major part in this process of detection. The alternative, a threat detection system without a memory, is inconceivable. We would enter every potentially threatening situation fresh and unarmed, as if each situation was novel. Of course we are not so unprepared. There is abundant evidence of the occurrence of acquired anxiety, including the much-studied conditioned form of anxiety that was for many years the foundation on which the entire theory of anxiety was based (Eysenck & Rachman, 1965; Mowrer, 1939, 1960; Wolpe, 1958). Learned anxiety, including conditioned anxiety, is readily re-evoked or recalled. We have memories of fear and anxiety, and many of these are so accessible that they can be recalled with relative ease. In cases of PTSD, however, some important events are relatively inaccessible to the verbal memory system. Brewin (2001) makes a critical distinction between verbally accessible memories and "situational" memories in PTSD (see Chapter 10). The inaccessible memories tend to be vivid and intense (e.g. flashbacks) and are negatively biased for the most part. However, some can be readily evoked by trauma-related cues and, in this sense, are also positively biased. A patient who had been traumatized by a serious accident was unable to recall the details of the event, but the sound of a collision instantly triggered a full, vivid recall of the crash.

For therapeutic purposes, as in the first and best-established of the modern techniques for reducing fear—desensitization (Wolpe, 1958)—past fears are deliberately re-evoked. Subjects and patients are easily capable of recalling the content and qualities of past anxiety and, in most cases, can with almost equal ease re-experience anxiety that resembles past episodes of anxiety if they wish to do so for therapeutic or other reasons. Given the role of memory in anxiety, and the evidence of significant memory biases in disorders such as depression, it is probable that biases of memory are at play in anxiety. Otherwise, we are left to assume that memory in anxiety is uniquely unbiased and peculiarly accurate.

If memories of past episodes of anxiety are essential for the efficient operation of the threat detection system, and if we can easily recall past anxiety, it is certain that we are also influenced by memories of which we are not aware (e.g. as in conditioned fears and in PTSD). Just as non-conscious factors influence the selective attentional processes involved in anxiety, so it is highly probable that non-conscious memorial processes, such as those involved in implicit memory, influence anxiety. The nature and operations of the non-conscious memorial processes involved in anxiety remain to be elucidated. No doubt they too will be found to be subject to bias and also to be of considerable importance.

It is likely that mood-congruent recall occurs in anxious moods. It is certainly the case that the relations between mood and memory, particularly as set out by Bower (1981), have turned out to be more complex and elusive than was originally thought but the occurrence of mood-congruent recall associated with depressive mood is reasonably well established (Eich & Macaulay, 2000). Disappointingly little progress was made in connecting anxious mood and recall but the vivid case histories described by Grinker and Spiegel (1945) provide powerful if inconclusive evidence of anxious-mood-congruent recall of traumatic experiences. PTSD offers a rich test-bed for studying mood-congruent memories.

Memories can be enhanced or impaired by anxiety. In some circumstances anxiety decreases the accessibility of a memory rather than increasing it. For example, McNally et al. (1995) reported reduced accessibility of traumatic memories in combat veterans, and the entire concept of repression, which plays a central part in the theory of psychoanalysis, can be seen as the blocking of memories that arise from intolerable levels of anxiety. Unfortunately, the concept of repression, which was formulated prior to the introduction of rigorous research methods, has defied modern critical evaluation. As

Williams et al. (1988) note, "the psychoanalytical approach was ultimately too unreliable to qualify amongst experimental psychologists as a formal method" (p. 146), and the scientific standing of the psychoanalytic theory has been severely criticized by many writers (e.g. Grunbaum, 1977). Notwithstanding the shortcomings of the analytic concept of repression, there are growing indications from modern research that some memories of anxiety have privileged access and in others, memories coloured by anxiety are frustratingly inaccessible.

The very selectivity of selective attention implies the operation of memorial influences. Certainly, some signals of threat have intrinsically alarming characteristics (e.g. Gray, 1971, 1982) and the entire concept of prepared fears (Seligman, 1971) rests on a similar assumption. However, the leading theorists on the subject of "intrinsic" fear signals, namely Gray and Seligman, also attach considerable importance to the influence of learned signals of threat or danger. These learned signals of threat can be evoked or recalled and are bound to influence the selectivity and focus of one's attention when entering a potentially threatening situation. The selectivity of attention in a threatening situation is likely to be influenced by memories of previous encounters with the particular situation and encounters with other comparable situations. Again, it seems probable that these influential memories are subject to bias. (Given the evidence of memory biases in depression, it seems inevitable that attentional processes in depression are also biased.)

The patients with OCD whose attention was intensely focused on signs of blood or other threatening stimuli (described above, p. 33) were attending to these particular stimuli because of their biased recall of threatening information regarding diseases such as AIDS and because of their past encounters with blood spots and traces. The selectivity of their anxious attention was determined in large part by their particular memories, some of which were definitely skewed. *Their memories were more disturbed (and disturbing) than the original events that were the subject of their recall.* Comparatively mild events had become transformed into remembered catastrophes. But not all of these memories are errors of negative bias. Some of the memories are enhanced, that is, positively biased.

It is evident to clinicians that many patients with OCD have well-developed memorial abilities and can recall precise details of situations and experiences that were disturbing or threatening in the past. As described earlier, a patient who was intensely frightened of disease-related contaminants could recall in detail the types of blood stain or other threatening material that she had encountered in particular places as far back as 12 years ago. The same patient also had a milder fear of making errors and, as a result, engaged in a certain amount of checking behaviour, especially to ensure the stove had been switched off. As is common in compulsive checking, she frequently had difficulty remembering whether or not she had correctly turned off the stove and, on numerous occasions, felt compelled to return to the kitchen to check. So we have a not-uncommon example in this type of disorder of a curious combination of excellent and precisely accurate memory relating to some threats and a patchy and infirm recollection of other activities. (Incidentally this kind of intra-person inconsistency in memorial ability and performance is not easily compatible with assumptions of a biological causation of significant memory and other cognitive impairments in the anxiety disorders.)

Elucidation of the relation between anxiety and memory requires improved methodology. It is essential to ensure the efficacy of the experimental manipulation. In most investigations this will mean ensuring that the participants in the key group, unlike those in the control conditions, report elevated levels of anxiety at the time of the memory task. The effects on memory of levels of anxiety at encoding and recall need to be examined. The items in the memory task should be ecologically valid, in preference to degraded or remote cues. The number of items in the memory task should allow for an error rate in the region of 50%. Both recall and recognition measures of memory require study. In some disorders, notably PTSD, disturbances of memory are of central importance and, for this reason, as well as for general scientific interest, the relation between anxiety and memory is bound to attract growing attention.

Emotional processing

The concept of emotional processing, really a model of emotional processing, was introduced before the shift towards cognitive analyses but retains its significance and, in recent years, has seen use in the evolving analysis of post-traumatic disorders (see Chapter 10). The concepts of emotional processing and cognitive processing are gradually undergoing an integration.

In the face of a potential threat, the experience of anxiety is appropriate. However, there are many instances in which the anxiety is disproportionately great or persists long after the removal of the threat. The model of emotional processing was introduced primarily to tackle the phenomenon of the persistence of unabsorbed emotional experiences, such as excessively persistent anxiety, nightmares, obsessions, and so on. It is assumed that there is a natural tendency for people to absorb emotionally disruptive experiences, including anxiety, and that the failure to do so is an indication of unsatisfactory emotional processing. Broadly speaking, successful emotional processing can be gauged from the person's ability to talk about, see, listen to, or be reminded of emotional events without experiencing stress or disruptions.

The impetus for introducing the concept of emotional processing (Rachman, 1980) came from Lang's (1977) stimulating analysis of fear imagery. He found that fearful subjects who had minimal heart-rate responses to fear-evoking images showed little improvement with desensitization treatment, unlike those who had strong heart-rate responses. He concluded that psychophysiological reactions might be a key to the processing that therapy is designed to accomplish. Lang postulated that the critical requirement for therapeutic change is that at least some components of the emotional state must be evoked if the fear response is to be modified—hence the therapeutic success of techniques that involve exposure to the feared stimulus.

The signs of unsatisfactory processing include unpleasant intrusive thoughts, disturbing dreams, pressure of speech, and persisting anxiety. Satisfactory emotional processing is evident when the anxiety declines, agitated behaviour decreases, concentration improves, and the person returns to "routine" behaviour and thoughts.

Evidence on the factors that promote or impede emotional processing can be summarized in this way. Satisfactory emotional processing is promoted by graded exposures to the threatening situation, calm rehearsals, catharsis, relaxation, and correction of misinterpretations of threat. Some factors that impede emotional processing include excessive avoidance behaviour, unpredicted re-exposures, uncontrollable re-exposure, fatigue, and persisting misinterpretations of the nature and consequences of the perceived threat. Discussions of the nature of emotional processing can be found in Rachman (1980, 1990, 2001), Lang (1977, 1985), and Foa and Kozak (1986). Progressive attempts to integrate emotional and cognitive processing have been undertaken by Teasdale (1999), Teasdale and Barnard (1993), Wells and Mathews (1996), and Salkovskis (1996a), among others. Teasdale (1999) suggests that emotional processing is facilitated by "mindful experiencing", one of three modes of mental functioning.

Affect and cognition

Many accounts of the connections between affect and cognition assume that the cognitions that influence affective experience are essentially conscious and easily accessible. This view has been challenged on many grounds, and the assumption that reasoning always precedes emotional reactions has been criticized. In a famous challenge, Zajonc (1980) asserted that "preferences need no inferences". Although Zajonc (1980) overstated his argument, he nevertheless provided a corrective to writings on the subject of cognition and affect that fail to take into account the influence of non-conscious factors on emotional experiences and manifestations. Critics of Zajonc's work, although correctly drawing attention to weaknesses in the general argument, appeared to attach undue and almost exclusive power to conscious cognitions. In fact, there is evidence that some of the cognitive processes involved in emotional experience are outside of easy awareness and function at an automatic level.

Thoughts and feelings—concepts that have recently been expanded and renamed cognition and affect—commonly combine but it is their opposing pulls that evoke greatest interest. They are so finely intertwined that the task of unravelling them can seem futile. People often need to exert a great deal of effort in attempting to control their fear and anxiety by cognitive means because these emotions can be so dominating. Indeed, *anxiety disorders* can be regarded as examples of such domination. Patients who are persistently anxious about dying of a heart attack, even though they accept medical advice that they are in sound health, can be said to suffer from an imbalance between cognition and affect; to suffer from an imbalance between thoughts and feelings. Patients suffering from OCD can also be said to be suffering from a domination of affect; they are well aware that their intense fears of disease-contagion are excessive and even groundless, and that washing their hands repetitively is futile. Their anxiety is so dominating, however, that it over-rules their rational appraisal.

The concept of irrational behaviour, exquisitely illustrated by OCD, incorporates the idea of a clash between affect and cognition. In addition to conflicts of this character, there are many other opportunities for inconsistencies between cognition and affect. It is common to feel extreme apprehension without a satisfactory explanation of the cause or source of the dread, a disconnection that is embedded in most definitions of anxiety. For example, one might have a conditioned anxiety reaction to stimuli of which one is unaware. It is also possible to attribute one's extreme apprehension to an incorrect cause or source—such misinterpretations are indeed regarded by cognitive-behavioural therapists as the very basis of anxiety disorders (Clark, 1986, 1997; Salkovskis, 1996a).

The relations between cognition and affect are not only intricate but are also in flux. To further complicate matters they can, and do, change at different speeds, making attempts to disentangle their connections extremely difficult. When carrying-out fear reduction techniques it is not uncommon to find that the behavioural manifestations of fear decline hours, days, or even weeks before the person reappraises the level and nature of their anxiety. Direct observation of the person's cognitions about the object of the fear or the nature of the anxiety are not possible and it is difficult and rare for the affected person to be able to pinpoint the exact moment at which his or her cognitions altered. Rather, they tend to become aware of altered cognitions retrospectively and report that the change occurred at some time during the past week or two.

We are intrigued and puzzled by these inconsistencies between affect and cognition, or their conflicts, in part because we tend to assume that they are better integrated than in fact they are. Zajonc (1980) proposed a radically different interpretation of these inconsistencies in his provocative paper, *Feeling and thinking*. He argued that affective judgements:

> . . . may be fairly independent of and precede in time the sorts of perceptual and cognitive operations commonly assumed to be the basis of these affective judgments . . . affective reactions can occur without extensive perceptual and cognitive encoding, are made with greater confidence than cognitive judgments and can be made sooner . . . it is concluded that affect and cognition are under the control of separate and partially independent systems . . . (Zajonc, 1980, p. 151)

He laid great stress on the claim that affect is often, even usually, precognitive. According to Zajonc, the features of a stimulus or set of stimuli that determine affective reactions "might be gross, vague and global . . . thus they might be insufficient as a basis for cognitive judgments . . ." (p. 159). He contrasted affective responses with "cold cognitions" and described affective responses as "effortless, inescapable, irrevocable, holistic, more difficult to verbalize, yet easy to communicate and understand" (p. 169). He also described affective responses as instantaneous, dominant, primary, precognitive, and automatic. For example, we might experience an "instant" liking for a person on first meeting and, more troubling, an "instant" dislike of a new person even though we recognize the absurdity and injustice of our reactions.

Most of Zajonc's supportive evidence was drawn from research in social psychology, with an emphasis on the development of affective preferences, which he argues are largely a matter of familiarity. Preferences need no inferences.

Many of Zajonc's observations can be extended to clinical phenomena but it should not be assumed that the perplexity many patients feel in the face of their irrational, anxious behaviour is confined to people with psychological problems. Disturbing fluctuations of mood are perplexing for all of us. If Zajonc is on the right track, and if affective reactions are indeed precognitive, automatic, dominant, non-verbal, and provoked by stimuli that are gross, vague and global, it is small wonder that we encounter so many inexplicable affective experiences. Rather, it begins to seem remarkable that we ever have a clue about the true source or cause of our feelings.

Given the properties that Zajonc attributes to affective judgements, it is no surprise that the attempts made by psychologists and others to produce substantial attitude changes through direct communication and persuasion can be less than successful. Affect is relatively independent of and often impervious to cognitions.

Most of the examples Zajonc uses to explain why affective reactions are resistant to change by cognitive means describe attempts that have been made to *reduce* affective reactions. But it is easier to find examples in which such reactions were initiated or even increased by cognitive means [see Rachman (1990) for examples]. If anything, we appear to have a lack of symmetry. Cognitive operations might be a weak means of reducing affective reactions but a powerful method for inducing or increasing affective reactions. This asymmetry suggests that the independence of affective and cognitive systems is not as complete as implied by Zajonc.

Zajonc's work is stimulating but there is a risk of overlooking his tendency to overconclude from limited data. There are inconsistencies in his theorizing, some of the key concepts are unsatisfactorily defined or ambiguous, and there is a shortage of supporting evidence. However, his writings are a useful reminder that affect and cognition are indeed relatively independent, that they have some important distinguishing characteristics, and that the assumption of a high degree of integration between affect and cognition is not always warranted. Recent thinking on the subject rests on differences between conscious processing, which is slow and controlled, and non-conscious processing, which is automatic and fast.

Evidence for non-conscious cognitive processing comes from various sources, including subliminal perceptions (Dixon, 1981), selective attention (Broadbent, 1958, 1971; Treisman, 1960), implicit memory (Teasdale & Barnard, 1993; Tulving, 1983), verbal reports of cognitive operations (Nisbett & Wilson, 1977), and the phenomena of automatic cognitive processing (McNally, 1995). Reviews of non-conscious processes involved in anxiety are provided by Michael Eysenck (1992), Williams et al. (1997), and Mathews and MacLeod (1994).

The attentional processes that play so important a part in anxiety are not always in the forefront of awareness (see Mathews & MacLeod, 1994; McNally, 1995; Williams et al., 1997). On a broader level, the implicational meaning of the cognitions that might well contribute to anxiety are not readily accessible (Teasdale & Barnard, 1993). As Michael Eysenck (1992) noted in his analysis of the biological value of anxiety, a system that is "specially adapted for the purpose of threat detection" must include "sensors" that facilitate rapid, early, accurate detection. He suggests that, "Almost certainly, pre-attentive and/or attentional processes are centrally involved," (p. 5). Given that the rapid detection of early warning signs of danger is of survival value, any warning system that depended on a careful, rational appraisal of each threat would forfeit refinement for failure.

Summary

People become highly vigilant when entering a potentially intimidating situation, scanning broadly and then focusing narrowly on any perceived threat. Attention and sensitivity are enhanced and ongoing behaviour is inhibited. If the potential threat is interpreted as dangerous, then anxiety arises and is followed by escape, avoidance, or coping behaviour.

People vary in their vulnerability to anxiety, with the most anxiety-prone inclined to be overly vigilant and to scan rapidly. They are also inclined to misperceive or misinterpret events and/or exaggerate their seriousness.

The narrowing of attention can be directed externally or internally (self-focused attention). Excessive self-focused attention is implicated in various forms of anxiety, notably test anxiety, health anxiety, social anxiety, and sexual anxiety.

Anxiety and memory interact and in turn influence the processing of emotional events or materials. Emotional processing is impeded by excessive arousal, avoidance, fatigue, misperceptions, and misinterpretations. The relations between affect, such as anxiety, and cognition are complex and contain important non-conscious elements.

Theories of anxiety 3

This chapter explores the four main approaches to anxiety: learning theory accounts (including the conditioning theory), cognitive explanations, psychoanalytic theory, and biological explanations.

Anxiety as the product of learning

The idea that fear and anxiety are acquired by a process of learning, most particularly by conditioning, has a long and fruitful history. The idea can be traced back to Pavlov's original discovery of conditioning processes and their relevance to the acquisition of emotional responses. This idea was revised and developed by Watson and Rayner (1920) and Jones (1924), and subsequently elevated to a formal theory by Mowrer (1939) in his classic paper, *A stimulus–response theory of anxiety*. Some of the key ideas were subjected to experimental analysis and later applied to clinical circumstances by Wolpe (1958) and were incorporated (in part) by Eysenck 1957; Eysenck & Rachman, 1965; into his general theory of personality and its application to abnormal psychology. Eysenck's successor at the Institute of Psychiatry, Gray (1971, 1982, 1987) later developed an essentially psychophysiological extension of these ideas and introduced many novel ones. In keeping with the increasing influence of cognitive analyses in psychology in general, the learning theory analysis of anxiety has now been expanded to include important cognitive components. In particular, the writings of Barlow (1988, 2002), Beck and Emery (1985), Beck and D A Clark (1997), D M Clark (1986, 1999), and Salkovskis (1985, 1996a), have strongly influenced the way that anxiety is construed. Historical accounts of these developments are given by Kazdin (1978) and Rachman (1996).

The essence of the learning theory approach is that fears are considered to be acquired by conditioning or other learning processes and that these acquired fear responses in turn generate escape and or avoidance behaviour. The fear-generated behaviour persists because it is at least partly successful—escape or avoidance is typically followed by a significant reduction in fear or anxiety, thereby reinforcing the successful behaviour itself. In one of the original statements of the learning theory of fear, it was believed that any neutral stimulus was potentially capable of being converted through a process of conditioning into a stimulus:

> Phobias are regarded as conditioned anxiety (fear) reactions. Any "neutral" stimulus, simple or complex, that happens to impact on an individual at about the time that a fear reaction is evoked acquires the ability to evoke fear subsequently. (Wolpe & Rachman, 1960, p. 145)

As will be seen, this original statement of the theory has undergone significant revision.

Theories by Eysenck and Wolpe

Eysenck's theory (Eysenck & Rachman, 1965; Eysenck, 1967), and that of Wolpe (1958), had important implications for the psychology of anxiety. Both drew on the early works of Pavlov and Watson and set their theories of neuroses in a learning theory framework, emphasizing the role of conditioning processes. Eysenck was most interested in neuroses and the personality factors that predispose people to develop these disorders. He argued that emotionally unstable introverts are at high risk for acquiring conditioned anxiety responses whereas unstable extroverts are at risk for developing conduct disorders, personality problems, or hysteria. Wolpe's aim was to explain the genesis of neuroses with a view to developing effective methods of treatment. Wolpe was a clinician–researcher, Eysenck a personality theorist who drew clinical implications from his main theory.

Eysenck's (1957) original work on the anxiety neuroses was based on his two-dimensional model of personality. The two dimensions, which can be plotted at right angles to each other (see Figure 3.1) are emotional instability (neuroticism) and introversion/extroversion:

> In our general system introverts are postulated to condition more easily and, therefore, to acquire the conditioned anxieties and fears characteristic of the dysthymic more

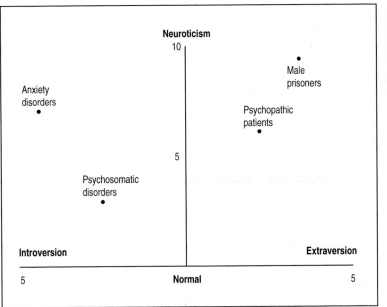

Figure 3.1.
Eysenck's two-
dimensional model of
neurosis. Adapted
from Eysenck and
Rachman (1965).

Neuroticism

10

Anxiety
disorders

Male
prisoners

Psychopathic
patients

5

Psychosomatic
disorders

Introversion

Extraversion

5

Normal

5

easily than other people, whereas psychopaths and prisoners generally are people who condition poorly and who, therefore, fail to acquire the conditioned responses characterizing the socialization process. (Eysenck & Rachman, 1965, p. 24)

Conditioned anxiety responses are the result of single traumatic event, or a series of subtraumatic events, involving strong nervous-system reactions. It was assumed that a previously neutral stimulus becomes connected through association with an unconditioned stimulus giving rise to the traumatic emotional reactions.

From now on it will be found that the conditioned stimulus, as well as the unconditioned stimulus, produces the original maladaptive emotional behaviour. This, it seems to us, is the essential learning process which takes place in the development of a neurosis. (Eysenck & Rachman, 1965, p. 4)

Those conditioned responses that are not reinforced begin to extinguish; this development occurs in conditioned anxiety responses as in all others, giving rise to the clinical phenomenon of "spontaneous remission".

Eysenck relied on Mowrer's (1939, 1960) theory to explain the persistence of anxiety and the associated avoidance behaviour. In brief, anxiety reactions, once established, also take on motivating properties. In an attempt to reduce their anxiety, people engage in escape or avoidance behaviour. To the extent that the escape or avoidance is indeed followed by a reduction in anxiety, this behaviour becomes strengthened and the anxiety reactions are preserved from extinction. The personality theory was supported by a great deal of psychometric and experimental data and the clinical implications were drawn out (Eysenck & Rachman, 1965).

Wolpe's theory (1958) of the neuroses was similarly based on the assumption that the anxiety, which is so characteristic of the neuroses, arises through a process of conditioning. Wolpe's explanation for the maintenance of the conditioned anxiety and other neurotic reactions similarly relied on Mowrer's ideas of reinforcement through the reduction of anxiety. He then went on to develop laboratory techniques for inhibiting the conditioned anxiety reactions, ultimately transferring these to clinical practice (Wolpe, 1958). The best-established of the fear-reducing techniques that he introduced—systematic desensitization—was assumed to operate through a process of reciprocal inhibition. The deliberate and repeated superimposition of an incompatible response on the anxiety reaction steadily gives rise to the development of inhibitory processes that will eventually lead to the elimination of the anxiety pattern. The technique was investigated intensively in the laboratory and widely adopted in clinical practice, laying the foundation for one of the two major streams of what became known as behaviour therapy (Rachman, 1996).

Gray's theory

Gray (1971, 1982, 1987) agreed with several components of Eysenck's theory, including the dimensional approach to the analysis of personality predispositions to anxiety, recognition of the biological contributions to the main dimensions of personality, the role of conditioning, and so forth. Gray's elaboration of the theory is primarily psychophysiological, being based on a formidable assembly of psychopharmacological data and countless experiments on learning in animals. He suggested a rotation of Eysenck's dimensions of introversion and emotional stability to emphasize the importance of impulsivity (Gray, 1987, p. 350). Gray claimed that, contrary to Eysenck's suggestion, extroverts have difficulty in acquiring fear reactions and are not slow at developing conditioned responses in general. According to Gray, neuroticism indicates heightened sensitivity to reinforcing events and introversion represents increasing sensitivity to signals of punishment rather than to signals of reward.

Gray collected convincing evidence that the behavioural effects of punishment and of non-reward are similar and probably mediated by common processes. There is also evidence suggesting a similarity between reward and non-punishment. Signals of punishment or of non-reward trigger the behavioural inhibition system, a psychophysiological system that Gray describes in considerable detail and which has the effect of producing increases in arousal, increased attention, and an inhibition of ongoing behaviour. This behavioural inhibition system can also be triggered by novel stimuli or by stimuli that are innately fear producing. Gray (1986) regards anxiety "as a central state that mediates behavioural responses to stimuli that signal either punishment or non-reward" (p. 220).

This analysis led Gray to reconsider the nature of avoidance conditioning and, in particular, to suggest some improvements to the Mowrer theory. This, it will be recalled, states that stimuli that are followed by punishment come to elicit conditioned fear reactions. Behaviour that produces a reduction in this fear is reinforced. As noted by Seligman and Johnston (1973), Mowrer's theory has difficulty in accounting for the persistence of the avoidance behaviour, among other problems. Gray makes extensive use of the concept of "safety signals" in his reinterpretation of this persistence. These are signals that arise from the omission of an anticipated punishment. Safety signals act as rewards and elicit approach behaviour. They also signal a period and a place of safety, a period and place in which the person or animal can expect freedom from punishment: "Safety signals reduce fear and provide secondary reward for the avoidance response; but at the same time they preserve fear from complete extinction and so ensure their own continued potency" (Gray, 1987, p. 227). As will be seen presently, this elegant analysis of safety signals, the details of which are not necessary for present purposes, is relevant for understanding various aspects of anxiety, including so-called generalized anxiety. It is worth mentioning that safety signals do not necessarily preserve fear; for example, they can facilitate prolonged and therapeutic exposures to fear cues.

Gray's inclusion of "innate fear stimuli" as one of the four triggers of the behavioural inhibition system is consistent with the views of

Seligman, Ohman, and others. According to Seligman, ". . . the great majority of phobias are about objects of natural importance to the survival of the species . . . The theory does not deny that other phobias are possible, it only claims that they should be less frequent, since they are less prepared" (Seligman & Hager, 1972, p. 450). He argued that human phobias are largely restricted to objects that have "threatened survival, potential predators, unfamiliar places, and the dark" (Seligman & Hager, 1972, p. 465). Like Gray, Seligman argues that certain kinds of fears are readily acquired because of an inherent biological preparedness. According to Seligman, prepared fears are easily acquired, selective, resistant to extinction, and probably non-cognitive. The prepared fears can even be acquired by watered-down representations of the actual threat. This idea of selectivity runs contrary to the earlier view of conditioning in which it was assumed that *any* neutral stimulus could be turned into a conditioned signal of fear and that no differences should be anticipated between stimuli.

Seligman's introduction of the concept of preparedness, constructed within the framework of modern learning theory, provoked a good deal of interest, and promising results from the pioneering experiments by Ohman and colleagues (1975) were followed closely. Working in the laboratory, these researchers demonstrated that people respond differently to presentations of prepared stimuli than to unprepared neutral stimuli. For example, fear responses to photographs of snakes differed from those evoked by photographs of flowers or mushrooms. Thus they were able to promote Seligman's ideas and provide a test-bed for further investigations. Regrettably, over the next few years there was a gradual accumulation of disappointing results and interest in the concept of prepared phobias waned (McNally, 1987).

Evidence that the prepared fears generated in the laboratory are easily wiped out by verbal instructions undermined one of the most appealing characteristics of the concept, because these laboratory fears fall far short of the main features of phobias. The laboratory fears are not easily acquired, or stable, or non-cognitive; they bear little resemblance to the concept of prepared phobias as set out by Seligman.

It has been suggested that these disappointing results are attributable to a weak methodology and that more powerful stimuli and more appropriate measures of fear are needed before the theory can be subjected to rigorous testing. The prepared phobias that are the subject of the theory are intense, vivid, resistant, and persisting fears, and it is on such fears that the theory must be assessed, and not on the fragile and fleeting fears that were reproduced in the original laboratory experiments. An excellent research model was provided by Mineka's outstanding experiments on intense and vivid fears in monkeys (Mineka, 1985). She proved that monkeys are indeed predisposed to fear snakes (but not "unprepared" cues) and that their fears can be triggered by observational learning. The broader significance of this research is considered in Chapter 4.

Longitudinal studies, exemplified by the Dunedin cohort study (see Chapter 4), are another source of information about learned and prepared fears. The additional information about the genesis of fears provided by experimental analyses and longitudinal research is an essential supplement to the most direct and common method of interviewing and/or questionnaires because a person's recollections might be incorrect, incomplete, or absent. A total reliance on this direct method is unsatisfactory.

Cognitive analyses of anxiety

The infusion of cognitive concepts into abnormal psychology has promoted an expanded and deeper understanding of anxiety (Brewin, 1996). Beck's work has been particularly influential:

> It is hypothesized that a precipitating event (or series of events) elicits or magnifies an underlying attitude of fear. These events may impinge on the patient's specific vulnerabilities to elicit such danger related ideation. Subsequently, the patient is overly vigilant of danger. He scans internal and external stimuli for "dangerous" properties. When new situations with possibilities of unpleasant outcomes are encountered, they are construed as dangerous. That is, the patient magnifies the possibility and intensity of unpleasant outcomes in his cognition of the situation. (Beck & Rush, 1985, p. 365)

Beck's approach was elaborated by Salkovskis:

> The fundamental idea is that emotions are experienced as a result of the way in which events are interpreted or appraised. It is the meaning of events that triggers emotions rather than the events themselves. The particular

appraisal made will depend on the context in which an event occurs, the mood the person is in at the time it occurs, and the person's past experiences. Particular types of emotions depend upon this specific interpretation. Effectively this means that the same event can evoke a different emotion in different people, or even different emotions in the same person on different occasions. (Salkovskis, 1996a, p. 48)

Significant advances have been made in coming to grips with the nature of panic disorder, social phobias, health anxiety (previously described as hypochondriasis), obsessions, and compulsions. The cognitive analyses of panic set out by Barlow (1988, 2002) and by D M Clark (1986, 1988, 1996, 1999) are broadly similar but were arrived at independently. For purposes of the present account, Clark's theory will be taken as the example. He argued, with some success and subsequent practical applications, that panics are caused by catastrophic misinterpretations of bodily sensations. This idea, the evidence for and against, and a critical evaluation are given in Chapter 5 and, for the present, it suffices to say that it also produced some secondary benefits in the form of fresh re-examinations of a host of anxiety phenomena and disorders (Rachman, 1996).

The theoretical analyses set out by D M Clark (1986, 1997, 1999), Barlow (1988, 2002), Salkovskis (1985), Salkovskis and Warwick (1986), and others were strongly influenced by Beck's ideas and then expanded beyond Beck's theory. Unlike Beck's original ideas, the newer theories are less "pathological" and regard many problems as understandable errors of normal functioning rather than as signs of deep-rooted abnormalities. Emphasis is placed on the continuities between normal and "abnormal" anxiety. In addition, the newer theories attach greater emphasis to the links between cognitions and behaviour than was evident in Beck's original writings. Given their background and training, most of the new theorists moved from a preoccupation with behaviour towards the inclusion of cognitive concepts, whereas Beck began as a "cognitivist" and steadily increased the attention given to the behavioural determinants of anxiety disorders and their treatment. Beck later incorporated information-processing ideas into his construal of anxiety, consistent with the trends in anxiety research generally (e.g. M Eysenck, 1992; Williams et al., 1997), thus bringing his model closer to the theories of D M Clark, Barlow, and Salkovskis. The newest model of anxiety consists of three stages: registration of the threat, "activation of a primal threat mode", and the subsequent evocation of secondary, elaborative checking (Beck & D A Clark, 1997, p. 49). The treatment of anxiety must deactivate the primal threat mode. This revised model is clearly expressed and a stimulating addition to thinking on the subject of anxiety. Of course, much will rest on the nature (and accessibility) of the concept of a primal threat mode.

The cognitive theories make full allowance for the acquisition of fears by the processes of learning, including conditioning, but place greatest emphasis on the affected person's interpretation of the events, whether they are conditioned or not. Moreover, it is argued that the anxiety reactions persist largely as a result of the persisting maladaptive cognitions and that the most effective and lasting way to reduce or remove unadaptive anxiety is to modify or remove the responsible cognitions. At the same time it is recognized that one of the most powerful ways, indeed, in some instances, *the* most powerful way of modifying the responsible cognitions, is by bringing about behavioural changes. It is not always or necessarily the case that behaviour is driven by the cognitions; in many important instances the cognitions appear to be driven and maintained by inappropriate behaviour such as avoidance, physical or mental escape, and so forth. The main propositions of the cognitive theory of anxiety, the evidence for and against, are best illustrated with the example of panic disorder. Similarly, a critical evaluation of the progress and standing of the cognitive theory of anxiety can be approached by considering this particular theory (Austin & Richards, 2001; Clark, 1999; McNally, 1994).

Psychoanalytical explanations

Freud (1948, 1950) was one of the earliest writers to draw attention to the importance of anxiety. He argued that anxiety is a pervasive and critical component of the neuroses; he also distinguished between "objective anxiety" and "neurotic anxiety". By objective anxiety Freud meant fear reactions to the perception of an external danger or in expectation of an injury that is foreseen. He cautioned that objective anxiety is rational and expedient in many cases but that, on deeper consideration, there are many instances in which it is inappropriate or excessive and shades over into neurotic anxiety. Freud regarded neurotic anxiety as inexpedient and excessive, paralyzing actions and even hindering flight. The main characteristic of neurotic anxiety, according to Freud (1949, p. 332), is a general apprehensiveness—"free-floating" anxiety. People who constantly experience this "expectant dread" are tormented and always anticipate the worst outcomes. This tendency—to be overanxious and pessimistic—was regarded as a personality trait.

Freud also described another form of anxiety, a more circumscribed type. This category consists of what would today be called phobias, such as intense fears of closed spaces, snakes, crowds, and so forth. These phobias are not inherently irrational, in that the fear is not entirely groundless, but if it is excessive or inappropriate then it qualifies for the term "phobia". In passing, it is interesting to notice that Freud apparently accepted the view expressed by G. Stanley Hall that "there is a peculiar prepotent quality about some of these fears that suggest such ancient origin . . . (and) their relative intensity fits past conditions far better than it does present ones" (Hall, 1897, p. 245–246); certain fears are innate in the sense that we are predisposed to develop these fears very readily. Freud wrote that some fears, ". . . like the fear of small animals, thunderstorms, etc. might perhaps be accounted for as vestigial traces of the congenital preparedness to meet objective dangers which is so strongly developed in other animals" (Freud, 1953, p. 286). In this way, Hall and Freud anticipated the concept of "prepared phobias" introduced in 1971 by Seligman.

The psychoanalytical approach to anxiety is in keeping with the general theory of psychoanalysis. Anxiety is said to be largely sexual in origin and, for this reason, the unacceptable sexual impulses are repressed into the unconscious. These repressed ideas and impulses are then transformed into symbolic representations. According to Freud, "it remains incontestable that for the average human being anxiety is closely connected with sexual restriction" (Freud, 1949, p. 336). The resultant anxiety is replaced by neurotic symptoms, dream symbols, and so forth. The development of anxiety is said to be the reaction of the ego to danger from the demands of its libido and, in this way, an internal danger is converted into an external one (Freud, 1949, p. 338). When a person's sexual drive cannot be satisfied it is "discharged through being converted into dread" (Freud, 1949, p. 339).

According to Sperling (1971), a fear of spiders is "an indication of unresolved separation conflict and a high degree of ambivalence which intensifies bisexuality and the problem of sexual identification" (p. 493). The development of a fear of spiders, according to Sperling, is a form of defence against more threatening problems or impulses of a sexual kind. Abraham (1927), a close colleague of Freud's, maintained that the fear of spiders is symbolic of an unconscious fear of sexual genitalia: "the penis embedded in the female genitals". It should be said, however, that these complex and colourful explanations of the fear of spiders, as in the cases of fear of snakes and other fears, are difficult to reconcile with modern experimental analyses of these fears. The fears of spiders, as with a fear of snakes and other circumscribed fears or phobias, are relatively simple and readily reduced, typically within three to six sessions or, with the newest methods, even within a single session (Ost, 1996).

The foundation for the psychoanalytical theory of fears was laid by Freud himself in the famous case of a 5-year-old boy, little Hans, who feared horses (Freud, 1905). The case history was celebrated as a major advance and was thought to provide essential support for some of the important concepts of psychoanalysis, including the Oedipus complex, repression, and castration anxiety. In his famous monograph, Freud described and discussed in great detail (covering 140 pages) the events of a few months. The case material on which his analysis was based was collected by the father of the little boy, who kept Freud informed of the developments by regular written reports of his son. The father had several consultations with Freud about the boy's fear (both parents were lay adherents of psychoanalysis). During the analysis, Freud saw the little boy once.

The essence of the case is that, at the age of four, little Hans began to complain of a fear of horses and that this generalized shortly afterwards to animals and to objects that resembled a horse's muzzle. During the period when he complained of the fear, Hans was engaged by his father in repeated conversations and interrogations, and the father then communicated his interpretations to Freud. The material on which Freud's extended account is based, and which provided the raw material for a theory of fear and for other concepts in the general theory of psychoanalysis, was almost entirely third hand. Also the reporter was a central figure emotionally involved in the case.

The little boy's fear of horses was interpreted as a symbol of a more serious latent fear. In him, as in so many others, it was said to be a fear of his father engendered by anticipation of punishment (probably castration) for having experienced sexual desires for his mother. The fear of horses was interpreted as a manifestation of the child's Oedipus complex: little Hans experienced a sexual desire for his mother, followed by a fear of retribution from his father. These thoughts were unacceptable and the fear of the father was transformed into a more acceptable manifest fear of horses.

The interpretation of this case has been subject to criticisms (e.g. Wolpe & Rachman, 1960) and Freud himself conceded that:

It is true that during the analysis Hans had to be told many things which he could not say himself, that he had to be presented with the thoughts that he had so far showed no signs of possessing and that his attention had to be turned in the direction from which his father was expecting something to come. This detracts from the evidential value of the analysis, but the procedure is the same in every case. (Freud, 1905, p. 246)

The little boy's explanation of the origin of his phobia was straightforward. He claimed that it started when he witnessed a street accident in which a horse collapsed. His father added that all of this was confirmed by his wife and by the fact that his anxiety broke out immediately after the accident.

The fascinating psychoanalytical theory of anxiety is ambitious and not without value but the entire psychoanalytical enterprise has withered over the years (Eysenck, 1985; Grunbaum, 1977) and the psychoanalytical theory of fear has been questioned (Rachman, 1990).

The theory of psychoanalysis was constructed on evidence drawn primarily from case histories and suffers from the inevitable deficiencies and limitations of such data (Eysenck, 1985; Wolpe & Rachman, 1960). The paucity of reproducible evidence is one of the major shortcomings of psychoanalysis. The entire enterprise, including the theory of anxiety, is rich in theorizing but lacking in methodological rigour and deficient in facts. The historian Edward Boring (1991) described psychoanalysis as "pre-scientific". On the evidence, bearing in mind the poor methodology, there is little reason to accept Freud's assertion that phobias never occur if the person has a normal sexual adjustment ["the main point in the problem of phobias seems to me that phobias do not occur at all when the vita sexualis is normal" (Freud, 1950, p. 120)]. The assertion remains unproven and is almost certainly incorrect. Many people with anxiety and specific phobias have a satisfactory sexual life and can establish and maintain satisfying sexual relationships. Research collected since the 1980s has expanded our knowledge of human fears and modern methods are capable of significantly reducing these fears with little difficulty, contrary to what would be expected from psychoanalytical theory. Moreover, fears can be reduced without undertaking a major analysis of the person's personality, childhood, sexual life, or other topics that are so important in the psychoanalytical theory. It is perfectly possible to approach the fear directly, to describe and measure it directly, and modify it directly. Phobias can even be treated in a single session (Ost, 1996), and without paying any attention to the person's sexual life.

This does not mean that the psychoanalytical theory is entirely valueless. There is reasonable evidence that some fears have significant symbolic elements in them and that "unconscious" factors influence the emergence and continuation of anxiety. Modern research has shown that cognitive processes of which the person is unaware play an important part in our responses to signs of potential danger. Although it was not an intrinsic part of Freud's theory of anxiety, indeed he regrettably did not develop the idea, the notion that we are predisposed to develop fears to certain kinds of situations or objects is probably correct and it features in the writings of modern theorists such as Gray (1982) and Seligman (1971), and latterly in the work of Poulton and Menzies (2002), who argue the case for non-associative fears such as acrophobia and aquaphobia.

The intense debates for and against psychoanalysis that took place in psychology and in literary criticism in the first half of the twentieth century eventually ran out of steam and the subject became less relevant. Contemporary psychiatry and clinical psychology are firmly based on a comprehensive, detailed classificatory and diagnostic system—the DSM. Psychoanalytical diagnoses, concepts, and even terms play no part in the DSM arena. They simply do not appear and are irrelevant to modern diagnoses, treatment, and research. The diagnostic tests that were constructed to fit into the psychoanalytical scheme, especially the projective tests, whatever their merits and weaknesses, have no bearing on prevailing diagnostic and treatment procedures; they are not relevant. The treatments that are associated with the modern diagnostic sytem are pharmacological and psychological (predominantly cognitive therapy), used separately or in combination.

Biological theories of anxiety

Despite the common wish for a reconciliation between biological and psychological theories of anxiety, and some admirable moves in this direction (such as Gray's, 1971, 1982, 1987), the two approaches tend to proceed independently, occasionally taking time off from their separate pursuits to collide with each other. With few exceptions, the biological theories are explanations for particular disorders rather than broad theories of anxiety; the psychobiological theories of Eysenck (1967) and Gray (1971, 1987) are broad and exceptional.

Two of the most colourful current debates are about the competing explanations for panic disorder and for OCDs. The conflicting explanations for panic are described in detail in Chapter 5; Klein's (1987, 1996) theory is predominantly biological and states that a panic ensues when a physiological suffocation alarm system is triggered by a threat to the supply of useable air. The leading psychological theory states, to the contrary, that panics are caused by catastrophic misinterpretations of certain bodily sensations (Clark, 1986). These competing explanations of panic share some features, and future versions of the two theories might ultimately be reconciled, although at present they lead to different predictions and different treatments. For example, where the psychological theory asserts that a catastrophic misinterpretation is a necessary condition for panic, the biological theory asserts that it is not necessary—rather, that a specific biological dysfunction is the necessary condition for panic. The psychological theory leads to a specific form of (cognitive) treatment and the biological theory leads specifically to medication.

The initial biological theory of OCDs was biochemical and asserted that OCDs resulted from a deficiency of serotonin or a deficiency in serotonin metabolism. Evidence to support this theory is reviewed by Hollander and Liebowitz (1990), Insel (1991), Insel and Winslow (1992), Jenike, Baer, and Greist (1990), Rapoport (1989), and Zohar, Insel, and Rasmussen (1991) among others.

The main evidence in support of the biochemical explanation comes from the therapeutic effects of medications that interfere with the uptake of serotonin. Several of these medications are indeed capable of reducing, but seldom removing, OCD. "At their best [the anti-obsessive drugs] provide only a partial remission for OCD. Most studies report a 50% improvement" (Insel, 1991, p. 15), and many patients derive no benefit. Thus, serotonin dysfunction cannot, even at its best, provide a full explanation of OCD and proponents of the serotonin theory have emphasized the specificity of the selective serotonin reuptake inhibitor (SSRI) drugs, arguing that other types of antidepressants fail to improve OCD. Much of the evidence appears to support this claim but not all of it does so, and some of the supportive studies are flawed. For example, in the studies by Foa and colleagues (1987, 1992), the standard antidepressant (imipramine) used as a comparison with behaviour therapy failed to remove the patients' depression, which remained well within the clinical range. Hence the study fails to test the hypothesis that antidepressant medications help with OCD because they reduce depression. Moreover, the poor effect of the imipramine antidepressant was out of keeping with other studies (e.g. Mavissakalian, 1983).

There is no evidence that patients with OCD have more or less serotonin than non-patients, or more or less serotonin than patients with other forms of anxiety disorders. A great deal of research has been carried out in testing aspects of the serotonin theory of OCD and "the data indicate that the serotonergic system is probably intact in OCD" (Salkovskis, 1996b; 1996c, p. 197). Much of the research involves assessments of cerebrospinal fluid (CSF) and Pigott, Myers, and Williams (1996) also concluded that "recent CSF studies have failed to demonstrate significant differences between OCD patients and controls" (p. 141). There is no convincing evidence of a specific, selective serotonin dysfunction (e.g. Insel, 1991; Insel & Winslow, 1992), nor is there a correspondence between serotonin levels and response to treatment. Different types of SSRI drugs do not "add up" or transfer their effects. The most effective drugs for inhibiting serotonin reuptake are not the best for reducing OCD.

Thus the therapeutic effects of SSRI drugs do not provide an adequate foundation for the biochemical theory, and recall the famous example of the aspirin and the headache: aspirin can remove a headache but should we conclude that this proves the headache was caused by an insufficiency of aspirin? The relief of OCD by SSRIs does not tell us the cause of OCD.

Another problem for the biochemical explanation is raised by the repeatedly confirmed therapeutic effects of purely psychological therapy. This therapy achieves its effects without drugs and leaves the biological account wanting. The claim that psychological treatment might inadvertently produce the exact biochemical changes needed to overcome OCD is far-fetched and lacks confirmation. It will not pass unnoticed that the therapeutic efficacy of psychotherapy presents a problem for any purely biological theory.

Problems with the serotonin theory, and the increasing use of the new neuroimaging diagnostic techniques, gave rise to a second biological theory, which attributes OCD to the presence of a structural and/or functional dysfunction in the central nervous system (CNS)—this abnormality of the CNS probably being in the basal ganglia (Rapoport & Wise, 1988; see also Insel, 1988; McGuire, 1995). Rapoport in particular argued for a dysfunction located in the basal ganglia, the repository of innate psychomotor functions; the idea was that hypersensitivity of the basal ganglia generates repetitive motor behaviour, such as the OCD symptom of compulsive hand-washing. The supporting evidence is patchy, and replication studies are needed (especially of neuroimaging studies, in which masses of data are generated; the statistical problems of data reduction and analysis are formidable). In the study by Aylward, Harris, Hoehn-Saric, Barta, Machlin, and Pearlson (1996), "all structural basal ganglia measures failed to exhibit differences between patients with OCD and matched normal control subjects" (p. 577); this result was consistent with their full review of the existing literature.

By concentrating on explaining the repetitive qualities of some symptoms, Rapoport lost the essence of OCD, which includes a sense of subjective compulsion, purposeful directed behaviour, inflated responsibility, guilt, obsessional thoughts, and so on. Repetitiveness is one feature of OCD but it is neither necessary nor sufficient. Moreover, the repetitive symptoms of OCD are neither mechanical nor automatic. Does psychological treatment inadvertently produce the specific changes in the basal ganglia that reduce OCD?

Recognizing the problems encountered by purely biological explanations, a leading biological theorist concluded that "the link between OCD and serotonin is not a clear one . . . there is a profound mismatch in the time domains of these two events" (rapid uptake inhibition occurs within hours but the clinical response requires many weeks), (Insel, 1991, p. 14). "The importance of serotonin in the pathophysiology of this disorder remains speculative," (Insel, 1991, p. 15) and it is "a bit premature to be proposing a neural lesion in OCD" (Insel, 1991, p. 14). Given the inconsistent and poor quality of the neurophysiological evidence, it might remain premature for some considerable length of time.

Even though the biochemical and the neurophysiological theories have each attracted some support, they do not sit well together. There is no satisfactory connection between these two biological theories and it is unlikely that both can be correct.

It should be mentioned in passing that, just as the therapeutic effects of psychological treatment raise problems for the biological theories, the therapeutic value of antidepressant medications, such as clomipramine, raises difficult problems for the psychological explanations of OCD.

Summary

The essence of learning theory accounts of anxiety is that fears are acquired by conditioning or other learning processes and that these acquired fears in turn generate escape or avoidance behaviour. The explanations put forward by Eysenck and by Wolpe differ in detail but both are based on the assumption that anxiety is essentially learned. Gray's psychophysiological theory expands on these earlier accounts and roots his explanation firmly into physiology.

The psychoanalytical interpretation of anxiety is rooted in general Freudian theory, with an emphasis on sexual motivation and symbolism. Anxiety is said to be closely connected to sexual restriction and is a symbolic transformation of unacceptable sexual feelings.

The biological theories of anxiety are attempts to explain particular anxiety disorders, notably panic disorder and obsessional disorder. They share a common belief in the biological causation of anxiety but differ widely in the details.

a series of + theoretical models accounting the rooting of anxiety differently... perspectives are utilized correspondingly, treatments from different perspectives

② cognitive approaches?

Specific phobias and the conditioning theory of fear 4

In this chapter, the conditioning theory of fear is explained and the supporting evidence assembled. Eight objections to the theory are set out and it is concluded that conditioning is just one of three pathways to fear.

The major postulate of the conditioning theory is that fears are acquired by a process of conditioning. "Neurotic reactions, like all others, are *learned* reactions and must obey the laws of learning" (original emphasis, Eysenck, 1960, p. 5). Neutral stimuli that are associated with a pain-producing or fear-producing state of affairs develop fearful qualities; they become conditioned fear stimuli. The strength of the fear is determined by the number of repetitions of the association between pain/fear experienced and the stimuli, and by the intensity of the fear or pain experienced in the presence of the stimuli. Stimuli resembling the fear-evoking ones also acquire fearful properties; they become secondary conditioned stimuli. The likelihood of fear developing is increased by confinement, by exposure to high-intensity pain and/or fear situations, and by frequent repetitions of the association between the new conditioned stimulus and the pain/fear. It was proposed further that once objects or situations acquire fear-provoking qualities, they develop motivating properties. A secondary fear-drive emerges. Behaviour that successfully reduces fear (e.g. avoidance) will increase in strength.

Wolpe's (1958) explanation of fear-conditioning did not include an account of individual differences in vulnerability but Eysenck attached considerable importance to such differences. It was postulated that (neurotic) introverts condition easily and hence are more likely to develop excessive fears (Eysenck & Rachman, 1965).

Evidence for the conditioning theory

Supporting evidence was drawn from six sources: research on the induction of fear in animals, the development of anxiety states in combat soldiers (and, subsequently, the full concept of post-traumatic disorder), experiments on the induction of fear in a small number of children, clinical observations, incidental findings from the use of aversion therapy, and a few experiments on the effects of traumatic stimulation. The role of individual vulnerability was supported by evidence of ease of conditioning in introverts and by psychometric analyses of samples of neurotic patients.

The strongest and most systematic evidence was drawn from a multitude of experiments on laboratory animals. Evidently it is easy to generate fear reactions in animals by exposing them to a conjunction of neutral and aversive stimuli, usually electric shock. The acquired fear reactions (usually inferred from the emergence of avoidance behaviour, physiological disturbances, and disruptive behaviour, or by some combination of these three indexes) can be produced readily by employing conventional conditioning procedures. There is little doubt about the facility with which fear reactions can be conditioned, at least in animals that are tested under laboratory constraints.

Observations of people under combat conditions show that intense fear can result from traumatic stimulation. Flanagan (1948) reported that the overwhelming majority of combat air crew experienced fear during their missions and, although these reactions were relatively transient, they sometimes presaged the development of combat fatigue that included strong elements of fear. A minority of air crew developed significant and lasting fears. The form and content of these fears, their tendency to generalize, and the conditions under which they arose are consistent with the conditioning theory.

Observations of the traumatic effects of combat were instrumental in the development of the concept of post-traumatic stress disorders (PTSD), for the range of trauma is wide, including natural disasters, abuse, vehicle accidents, and so forth. In a majority of instances, the event(s) that triggered the PTSD are known and, for the most part, the processes involved are partly or wholly conditioning. The fears that so often are the result of trauma are easily construed as conditioned fears and therefore add to the evidence that conditioning is one, important, pathway to fear.

The development of conditioned nausea reactions is commonly observed in patients receiving chemotherapy (Burish & Carey, 1986; Cella, Pratt, & Holland, 1986). The factors that influence conditioning processes in other circumstances (e.g. stimulus strength in laboratory studies), are similarly influential in the emergence of the persisting reactions of nausea. In their review of numerous reports, covering roughly 1700 adult patients, Burish and Carey (1986) calculated that

32% reported anticipatory nausea and/or vomiting. The figures for anticipatory nausea probably are even larger (e.g. 80% of 60 patients in the Cella et al. study). The nausea/vomiting lasted for more than two years in most of their cases (Cella et al., 1986).

Bearing in mind the caution that conditioning of nausea or disgust does not necessarily imply that fear responses are conditionable, we can turn to the clinical accounts of fear acquisition. In clinical practice, it is not uncommon for patients to give an account of the development of their fears that can be construed in conditioning terms. Sometimes they can date the onset of the fear to a specific conditioning experience. Every one of 34 cases of dental phobia reported having had a traumatic dental experience, such as fearing suffocation from an anaesthetic mask, on at least one occasion in childhood (Lautch, 1971). However, these 34 people were found to be generally neurotic and 10 comparison subjects who had experienced comparable traumatic incidents with dentists during their childhood showed little sign of dental fear.

In a study of people who are frightened of dogs, di Nardo, Guzy, and Bak (1988) found that nearly two-thirds had experienced a conditioning event in which a dog featured and that in over half of these instances the animal had inflicted pain. However, two-thirds of a comparable group of subjects who were not frightened of dogs reported that they too had experienced a potentially conditioning event and that in half of the instances the animal had inflicted pain. These reports provide some support for the theory but also illustrate the fact that conditioning experiences, even those of a painful nature, do not necessarily give rise to fear. Here, as in other instances, there was less fear than an unqualified conditioning theory would lead us to predict. Presumably those people who experienced conditioning events, even painful ones, but failed to acquire a fear, placed a different interpretation on the event than did those who became frightened. Di Nardo and his colleagues (1988) note that all of their fearful subjects "believed that fear and physical harm were likely consequences of an encounter with a dog, while very few non-fearful subjects had such expectations . . . an exaggerated expectation of harm appears to be a factor in the maintenance of the fear".

The classic demonstration by Watson and Rayner (1920) of the deliberate genesis of fear in a young child had a considerable influence on early theorists but attempts to reproduce these findings had little success (e.g. Bregman, 1934; Valentine, 1946). The most systematic collection of information on the induction of conditioned fear in humans was carried out by Ohman and colleagues in Sweden

(Ohman, 1987). Stimulated by Seligman's (1971) concept of prepared fears, Ohman and colleagues undertook a lengthy programme of research to discover whether people are "prepared" to acquire fears to particular stimuli. They found that it is possible to produce conditioned fear responses in humans under laboratory conditions but, that the responses tend to be weak, transient, and incomplete. They are incomplete in the sense that the evidence for conditioning is confined largely to changes in electrodermal activity and it has not been possible to obtain dependable, consistent evidence of conditioned heart-rate responses. [Electrodermal activity can be used to index fear but heart rate is a preferable measure (Cook, Melamed, Cuthbert, McNeil, & Lang, 1988; Cuthbert & Lang, 1989; Lang, Melamed, & Hart, 1970; Ost, 1989; Prigatano & Johnson, 1974; Sartory, Rachman, & Grey, 1977; Sartory, 1989).] The conditioned responses were of small magnitude and not readily evoked and, with few exceptions, the electrodermal responses were extinguished within a few trials. Also, the conditioned responses were easily altered or abolished by instructions [see the review by McNally (1987)].

Incidental observations arising out of the use of aversion therapy, a technique explicitly based on the classical conditioning theory, provided some early support for the theory and was supplemented by work carried out by Baker, Cannon, Tiffany, and Gino (1984). After undergoing repeated associations between alcohol and chemically induced nausea, many patients experience nausea when they taste or even smell alcohol. In a famous case reported by Hammersley (1957), a successfully treated patient subsequently changed his mind and decided that abstinence was not the lesser of two evils. He embarked on a "deconditioning" programme and repeatedly drank himself through many episodes of intense nausea until his conditioned reaction to alcohol subsided and finally disappeared.

Another source of support for a conditioning theory of fear acquisition comes from experiments in which subjects were given injections of scoline, which produces a temporary suspension of breathing (Sanderson, Laverty, & Campbell, 1963). Not surprisingly, most of the subjects who underwent this harrowing experience developed intense fears of the stimulus encountered in or connected with the experimental setting. The intensity of their fears tended to increase even in the absence of further unpleasant experiences (providing one of the few examples of fear incubation).

The conditioning theory of fear acquisition does not require single trial or traumatic onsets but fears that arise in an acute manner are more readily accommodated, partly because our conception of conditioned fear is based largely on laboratory experiments in which the aversive stimulus is often traumatic. However, we also have to account for fears that are produced by experiences of a subtraumatic or even of a non-traumatic nature.

Fears that emerge in the absence of any identifiable learning experience present difficulties for the theory. Hence, fears that develop gradually (e.g. social fears) and cannot be traced to specific occurrences are a potential embarrassment. Even more troublesome are those fears that arise even in the absence of any direct contact with the fear stimulus.

The evidence on individual vulnerability was documented by Eysenck (1967). There is little doubt about the association between introversion and anxiety disorders but the putative causal connection was not resolved, especially as it proved difficult to confirm that introverts always are more "conditionable" than extroverts. The existence of individual differences in vulnerability to fear acquisition is evident and the latest approach to the problem emphasizes differences in sensitivity (e.g. the concept of anxiety sensitivity). Certainly, there are high correlations between anxiety sensitivity and total scores on fear questionnaires (Reiss et al., 1986). The overlap between such sensitivity and Eysenck's (1967) concept of "dysthymia" (high introversion and high neuroticism) is likely to be significant.

There is sufficient evidence to support the idea that fears can be acquired by a conditioning process. This conclusion is justified even though some of the evidence is subject to contrary interpretations or is inherently weak. The strongest evidence, both in the sense of its replicability and completeness, comes from the genesis of fear in laboratory animals. This voluminous evidence is supported by some limited findings on the induction of fear reactions in adult humans, but the stimuli were traumatic. The work on the induction of fear in children is inconsistent, based on very small numbers, and all of the experiments have been criticized for errors of contamination and confounding. Clinical observations provide interesting supporting evidence but unfortunately the quality of the information is unsatisfactory, comprising as it almost always does a selected set of observations rarely supported by external confirmatory evidence. This is an unsatisfactory basis for building a theory.

The theory is well supported but is not a satisfactorily comprehensive account of the genesis, or the maintenance, of human fears. The conditioning theory of fear acquisition cannot encompass all of the observed fears. There is more than one pathway to fear.

The conditioning theory: Contrary evidence and arguments

There are eight arguments against acceptance of the conditioning theory as a comprehensive explanation (Rachman, 1978, 1990, 1991). People fail to acquire fears in what should be fear-conditioning situations, such as air raids. It is difficult to produce stable conditioned fear reactions in human subjects, even under controlled laboratory conditions. The conditioning theory rests on the untenable equipotentiality premise. The distribution of fears in normal and neurotic populations is difficult to reconcile with the conditioning theory. A significant number of people with phobias recount histories that cannot be accommodated by the theory. Fears can be acquired indirectly or vicariously. Fears can be acquired even when the causal critical events are temporally separated.

Failures to acquire fear

It would seem that few experiences could be more frightening than undergoing an air raid but the great majority of people endured air raids extraordinarily well during World War II, contrary to the universal expectation of mass panic (Janis, 1951). Exposure to repeated bombing did not produce significant increases in psychiatric disorders. Short-lived fear reactions were common but surprisingly few persistent phobic reactions developed. Few of the civilians who were injured or wounded developed a fear of the situation in which they received the injury (Rachman, 1990).

The observations of comparative fearlessness despite repeated exposures to intense trauma, uncontrollability, uncertainty, and even injury are contrary to the conditioning theory of fear acquisition. People subjected to repeated air raids should acquire multiple, intense, conditioned fear reactions and these should be strengthened by repeated exposures. Civilian reactions to the warlike conditions in Northern Ireland (Cairns & Wilson, 1984) and the Middle East (Saigh, 1984, 1988) are consistent with the findings from World War II. These findings run contrary to prediction.

As stated, the phenomenon of PTSD provides convincing evidence of conditioning onsets of fear but a majority of the people who experience these trauma do *not* develop PTSD. Lesser examples of the failure to acquire fear include people who fail to develop a fear of dogs despite having unpleasant experiences with them, and even having been bitten (di Nardo et al., 1988). Dental fears are fairly common but large numbers of people fail to develop a fear of dental treatment even though they have undergone uncomfortable and even painful experiences when confined in the dentist's chair (e.g. Davey, 1988; Lautch, 1971).

The absence of a direct relationship between injury and subsequent fear runs contrary to conditioning theory. There should be a direct connection between injury and fear, but there is not (Rachman, 1990).

The conditioning of human fears

Deliberate attempts to generate conditioned fears in humans, as in the original attempts to treat alcoholism by establishing a conditioned aversion to alcohol, have had little success.

The equipotentiality premise

The theory assumes that any stimulus can be transformed into a fear signal; the choice of stimulus is a matter of indifference. Seligman (1970, 1971) argued convincingly that this premise is untenable, and hence its incorporation in the theory is a weakness.

The distribution of fears

The corollary of the equipotentiality premise is that all stimuli have an equal chance of being transformed into fear signals. However, this is not borne out by surveys of the distribution of fears, either in a general population or in psychiatric samples (Rachman, 1990).

Subject only to their prominence in the environment, many objects and situations should have an equal probability of provoking fear. What we find instead is that some fears are exceedingly common and certainly far too common for the theory; other fears are far too rare. The fear of snakes is common and the fear of lambs is rare; moreover, a genuine fear of snakes is often reported by people who have not had contact with the reptiles. (Even more surprising is the absence of fears of motor cars and the small incidence of fears of motor travel.) Consequently, one is forced to conclude that the fear of snakes can be acquired even in the absence of direct contact, and this significant concession opens three possibilities: (i) the fear of snakes is innate; (ii) the fear of snakes can be transmitted indirectly; or (iii) the fear of snakes is "lurking" and will appear with only slight provocation. The last two of these three possibilities are compatible.

Patient reports of fear onset

It can be difficult to determine the origin of a patient's phobia and there are phobias in which there was "no apparent trauma to initiate the phobia" (Marks, 1969, p. 42). The absence of a plausible conditioning precipitant in a significant number of phobic patients was demonstrated in the analysis by Ost (1985); 65% of the 183 patients acquired their fears by conditioning, 21% reportedly acquired their phobia indirectly and the remaining 14% were unable to recall the onset. In an expansion of this study, Ost (1987) found an association between the manner in which the phobia was acquired and the age of onset. The indirectly acquired phobias developed at an earlier age than the phobias with a conditioning origin.

The vicarious acquisition of fear

Advances in our understanding of the processes of observational learning and modelling have made it plain that we acquire much of our behaviour, including emotional responses, by vicarious experiences (Bandura, 1969, 1977). It is virtually certain that fears can be acquired either directly or vicariously and that stimuli are likely to develop fearful qualities if they are associated, directly or vicariously, with painful or frightening experiences (Rachman, 1990). To overcome the limitations of retrospective reports by participants, supplementary experimental investigations are needed. Mineka's (1985) research on monkeys showed conclusively that fears can be acquired by observational learning. More recently, Gerull and Rapee (2002) demonstrated the acquisition of a fear of snakes and spiders in 30 toddlers who were shown a rubber spider and snake in alternate pairings with positive, negative, or neutral facial expressions of their mothers. They found "strong observational learning" results, consistent with the view that early fears can be produced vicariously.

Acquisition by transmission of verbal information

It has also been suggested that fears might be acquired by the absorption of verbal information, especially information that conveys a threat (Rachman, 1978). The social transmission of intense fear, even panic, is well illustrated by recurrent epidemics of *koro* in South-east

Asia. *Koro*, derived from the Malay word for "head of a turtle", is a "condition of psychiatric panic characterized by complaints of genital shrinkage coupled with fear of impending death" (Tseng et al., 1988, p. 1538). Episodes of this intense fear, involving hundreds or thousands of people, have occurred in Singapore (1967), Thailand (1976), Assam (1982), and China (1984/1985 and 1987) and mainly affected isolated, poorly educated people who are strongly influenced by folk beliefs. In a survey of 232 victims of the 1984/1985 epidemic in China, Tseng et al. (1988) found that the episodes of *koro* were characterized by panic (intense fear, palpitations, tremor, perspiration, fear of impending death or catastrophe). The Singapore epidemic appears to have been set off by a verbal report that the Viet Cong had poisoned Thai food to produce impotence.

Ollendick and King (1991) found that 89% of children attributed their various fears to negative information, 56% to modelling, and 36% to conditioning. These findings have been replicated twice. Moreover, a prospective study by Field, Argyris, and Knowles (2001) showed that the fears of 7–9-year-old children were significantly increased by negative information. Muris, Bodden, Merckelbach, Ollendick, and King (2003) reported comparable findings; 285 children, aged 4 to 12 years, were given negative or positive information about an imaginary doglike beast. The negative information steeply increased their fear of the beast; the fear was not transient and showed some generalization to dogs and predators. The children who received positive information showed a small reduction in fear.

Acquisition by remote events

At present, there is not sufficient information to include the acquisition of fear by a temporally remote event as an additional argument against acceptance of the conditioning theory. However, convincing proof that fears can be acquired even when the stimulus and response events are separated in time would oppose the original conditioning theory.

In conclusion, the weaknesses of the classical theory are serious but not fatal. One can either search for an entirely new theory to replace it or adopt a reformist view and formulate modifications and extensions of the theory. At its best, the conditioning theory can provide a partial explanation for the genesis of some fears. However, it cannot explain how the common fears are acquired, nor can it explain the observed distribution of fears, the uncertain point of onset of many phobias, the indirect transmission of fears, the ready acquisition of prepared phobias, and the failure of fears to arise in circumstances predicted by the theory. Fears acquired without direct contact with a fearful stimulus are an added problem for the theory and the acquisition of fears when the causal events are temporally separated was considered to be a serious problem until conditioning theory was "liberalized" (see p. 89).

A satisfactorily comprehensive theory of fear acquisition must accommodate all of the above plus the fact that fears can emerge gradually as well as suddenly, the fact that there are individual differences in susceptibility, and the probable acquisition of fears of objects/situations that the person has never encountered. It is also necessary to account for the acquisition of fears by events that are temporally separated. The status of theorizing on the three pathways to fear was reviewed by Merckelbach, de Jong, Muris and van den Hout (1996), and, since then, the additional evidence on vicarious acquisition and transmission by negative information has accumulated. There has also been renewed interest in the fact that many respondents are unable to recall when or how their fears arose.

Influenced by the findings emerging from the remarkable Dunedin longitudinal cohort study, in which all children born between April 1972 and March 1973 were intensively and repeatedly tested over a 20+-year period, Poulton and Menzies (2002) proposed that a fourth pathway to fear should be recognized: "Associative learning producing associations between the relevant stimulus and negative outcomes is not necessary for fears to arise" (p.129). There are non-associative fears, that is, fears that are not acquired by learning processes. Many of the children's fears reported by the children or their parents had no learned onset but rather were present from early in life, notably the fears of water and heights. Moreover, the children with a fear of heights had experienced fewer falls from heights than the non-fearful children. The authors provide a good deal of information about such fears and make a plausible case for non-associative fears. These are reminiscent of the prepared fears discussed earlier (see p. 66), and are a reminder that people do learn certain fears but they also learn to not-fear: "What we learn is how to overcome our existing predispositions . . . in large part we learn to stop responding fearfully to predisposed or prepared stimuli" (Rachman, 1978, p. 255). Poulton and Menzies take this one step further and suggest that we also have to learn to overcome innate fears, such as a fear of water or heights.

Neoconditioning theory

The traditional belief that contiguity of the conditioned stimulus (CS) and the unconditioned stimulus (US) is necessary for the establishment of a conditioned response is mistaken. Recognition of the occurrence of a non-contiguous conditioning removes, in one sweep, most of the objections to the conditioning theory of fear acquisition. Conditioned responses can develop even when the conditioned stimulus and the unconditioned event are separated in time. The most convincing examples of non-contiguous conditioning come from the literature on food aversions. If animals eat a novel food and are made ill minutes or even hours later, they can form a strong aversion to the food. A single experience is sufficient to establish a lasting conditioned aversion.

The troublesome fact that many people cannot trace the onset of their fears to particular conditioning episodes can be absorbed by assuming that non-contiguous conditioning might have taken place. The many failures to acquire fear despite contiguous associations (e.g. dog bites not followed by fear) can be accounted for by blocking (see below), and other failures accounted for by the fact that the stimulus (e.g. dog collar) is not the cause of the significant event. Animals, and people, can learn that a stimulus is irrelevant "as a predictor of anything of significance" (Dickinson, 1987, p. 66). These objections to conditioning theory no longer seem fatal.

Rescorla (1988) observes that, "although conditioning can sometimes be slow, in fact most modern conditioning preparations routinely show rapid learning. One trial learning is not confined to flavor-aversion" (p. 154). Moreover, the associative span of animals "is capable of bridging long temporal intervals" (Mackintosh, 1983, p. 172). However, the learning must be selective, otherwise the animals would collect a "useless clutter of irrelevant associations" (p. 172). According to Mackintosh, the "function of conditioning is to enable organisms to discover probable causes of events of significance" (p. 172).

Additional evidence that conditioning processes are not bound by contiguity comes from research on the *blocking* effect and on the consequences of *random control*. A stimulus will not become a CS even if it is repeatedly presented immediately before a US event, unless it is of some value. If the US event is already well predicted by another stimulus, the addition of a second stimulus is of no value and hence no conditioning occurs. The established CS prevents (blocks) the development of a second CS. If the delivery of the electric shock is already well predicted by a tone (CS) then introducing a visual stimulus (CS?) in addition to the tone will be of no predictive value and the visual stimulus will not develop into a conditioned stimulus; it is redundant and conditioning will not develop even if the visual stimulus is repeatedly presented in contiguity with the electric shock (US). The existing conditioned response is sufficient and blocks the development of the new signal.

The random control effect also demonstrates that mere contiguity is sufficient to produce conditioning. If a stimulus, say a bell, regularly precedes an electric shock, then conditioning will occur. However, if the electric shock also is delivered repeatedly in the *absence* of the bell stimulus, little conditioning will develop. "Temporal contiguity, then, between a CS (or response) and a reinforcer is neither necessary nor sufficient to ensure conditioning" (Mackintosh, 1983, p. 173). The stimulus will not turn into a conditioned stimulus unless it predicts the reinforcer better than other stimuli. The new stimulus is uninformative and "conditioning occurs selectively to good predictors of reinforcement at the expense of worse predictors" (p. 173).

The revised view of conditioning is not merely an exercise in discrediting the classical explanation. Interesting new phenomena have been discovered, fresh predictions are possible, and new explanations of associative learning have been put forward. Simple contiguity is insufficient; information is the key and the prevalent view is that conditioning involves learning about the relations between events. Rescorla (1988, p. 153) argues that "Pavlovian conditioning is not a stupid process by which the organism willy-nilly forms associations between any two stimuli that happen to co-occur." Rather, the organism is better seen as "an information seeker, using logical and perceptual relations among events . . . to form a sophisticated representation of its world" (p. 154). Conditioning is not merely a transfer of power from one stimulus to another.

Contrary to an assumption of the classical theory, stimuli are not equally likely to develop conditioning properties; some are more easily turned into conditioned signals than others. Pain is more readily associated with auditory and visual stimuli than with gustatory stimuli, and gastric distress is more easily associated with taste than with vision. People, certainly adults, do not come fresh to new stimuli; they have a history of associations with the available stimuli. These previous associations influence the occurrence or nonoccurrence of conditioning. So, for example, we all have a history of (benign) associations with dog collars. No one, not even people who have distressing experiences with dogs, ever learns to fear dog collars, despite the contiguous presence of the dog collar during the unpleasant events. Dog collars do not predict distress and they do not become conditioned elicitors of fear. Although many people who have distressing experiences with dogs learn to fear them, comparable numbers of people who have had such experiences fail to acquire the fear (di Nardo et al., 1988). Presumably, a previous history of pleasant and friendly experiences with dogs produces conditioned predictions of harmless exchanges and these predictions are not overturned by one or several unpleasant events. The history of the stimulus influences the conditioning process. Food aversions develop most readily to novel foods (Revusky, 1979). Familiar and especially well-liked familiar foods are relatively immune to conditioned food aversions. Presumably, familiar and well-liked people, places, and animals are also relatively immune to conditioned fears. A relative fear immunity to familiar stimuli and situations might underlie the success of Miller's (1960) "toughening up" exercises as a way of preventing the development of fear.

Animals can be conditioned not only to discrete stimuli but also to the relationships between stimuli, in support of Rescorla's (1988) claim that "conditioning involves the learning of relations among events that are complexly represented" (p. 158). We have come a long way from classical Pavlovian conditioning and the flexibility and range of conditioning is far greater than was previously supposed (Davey, 1988; Mackintosh, 1983; Rescorla, 1980, 1988). Conditioning can occur even when the stimuli are separated in time and in space, and it can occur not only to discrete stimuli but also to abstract relationships between two or more stimuli. Conditioning is a highly flexible and functional process.

The refreshing revival of interest in conditioning has clarified some puzzles but it is not free of problems. The expansion of the scope of the concept of conditioning is welcome but lacks clear limits; there is little that it disallows. Even the revised theory cannot account for fears that arise without any contact between the feared stimulus and an aversive event, and it also has difficulty accommodating some important examples in which fears fail to develop in circumstances in which the theory would predict them (e.g. being subjected to aerial bombing). Fears can be acquired by conditioning, by vicarious means, or by the transmission of verbal information. And it is highly probable that humans are "prepared" readily to acquire fears of particular stimuli, such as snakes (Rachman, 1990).

Specific phobias

Intense and persistent fear of snakes, even harmless snakes, is a common example of a *specific phobia*—one of the anxiety disorders. The specific phobias tend to fall into one of three clusters: social phobias, animal phobias, and phobias of injury/illness (including fear of suffocation). A fear qualifies for the term "phobia" only if it is severe, persistent, and maladaptive. The borderline between fears and phobias is fuzzy and most people with intense fears, or even phobias, endure them or circumvent them. Only a small number of people with phobias seek professional help.

For those who do, psychologists are well able to help. Over the past 30 years, dependably effective and efficient methods of treatment have been developed (Barlow, 2002; Giles, 1993; Marks, 1987). The first of the fear-reducing techniques, desensitization, was developed by Wolpe (1958) and consists of repeatedly exposing the phobic person to the fear-evoking stimulus in a graded and gradual manner, while the person is kept in a state of relaxation. These graded, gradual presentations can be exposures to the actual stimulus (so-called in vivo exposures) or to imaginal representations of the feared stimulus. The former version, in vivo exposure, is more powerful and is the preferred form whenever possible. The supplementary use of "therapeutic modelling", in which the patient is encouraged gradually to imitate the approach behaviour of the therapist, expedites the exposure treatment. In the latest version of exposure treatment, substantial and lasting reductions in a phobia can be achieved within one to six sessions (Ost, 1989, 1996).

For a considerable period cognitive-behavioural therapy (CBT) appeared to have little to offer in the treatment of specific phobias (Last, 1987) but it now appears that in some cases, at least, purely cognitive interventions can reduce phobias. For example, Booth and Rachman (1992) found that cognitive therapy was as effective as the standard exposure treatment of claustrophobia (fear of enclosed spaces). It has also been shown that abrupt and complete reductions of phobias can occasionally be achieved by pure cognitive therapy (Rachman & Whittal, 1989). Nevertheless, the best method at present is repeated, controlled, in vivo exposures to the feared object/situation. Drugs have not proven to be useful in treating phobias. "No psychotropic drug has been demonstrated to be effective in the treatment of simple phobias" (Fyer, 1987, p. 190).

The theories that have been advanced to explain the effects of exposure treatment are: reciprocal inhibition, habituation, and extinction (see Rachman, 1990). Although the sufficient conditions for change (repeated controlled exposure) are now confirmed, the earlier belief that these exposures are also a necessary condition for fear reduction has been discredited. Cognitive interventions without exposure can sometimes do it. Each of the three explanations has some merit but none of them provides a comprehensive explanation for the effects of treatment.

Summary

The main postulate of the conditioning theory is that fears are acquired by a process of conditioning. Fears develop motivating properties and behaviour that successfully reduces fear will increase in strength.

Supporting evidence comes from six sources: laboratory research in inducing fear in animals, fears that arise in combat, clinical observations, studies of fear in children, incidental observations from the use of aversion therapy, and the effects of traumatic stimulation.

The contrary evidence includes the failure of people to develop significant fears in situations that should produce conditioned fear, the difficulty producing fear reactions in human subjects under controlled laboratory conditions, and the clinical reports of people who have phobias but cannot recall relevant conditioning experiences. In addition, the distribution of fears is impossible to reconcile with the conditioning theory.

It appears that fears can be acquired: (i) directly by learning processes, including conditioning; (ii) indirectly by vicarious exposures; or (iii) by the simple transmission of information. Thus there at least three pathways to fear. It is likely that some fears, such as aquaphobia and acrophobia, arise in the absence of learning, and are present from an early age.

Some of the objections to the original conditioning theory can be overcome by reanalysing them in terms of the neoconditioning theory, according to which the function of conditioning is to enable people/animals to discover the probable causes of significant events.

Specific phobias are intense, lasting fears that have an irrational element and are resistant to change, except when established fear-reducing techniques are applied.

Panic and anxiety 5

The nature of panic and its incidence are described in this chapter. The main explanations are set out and evaluated, and the methods of treatment are described.

A panic is an episode of intense fear of sudden onset. The fear, often bordering on terror, is accompanied by disturbing bodily sensations, difficulty in reasoning, and a feeling of imminent catastrophe. There is a close relationship between panic and anxiety, and at times they feed each other. Hence, episodes of panic provide a useful basis for analysing the relationship between fear and anxiety.

Elevated anxiety increases the probable occurrence of an episode of panic (Margraf, Ehlers, & Roth, 1986) and, in turn, a panic is usually followed by prolonged anxiety, a residue of anxiety. In addition to this short-term residue of anxiety, Klein, Zitrin and Woerner (1977, p. 27) observed that "as a result of these panics, they [patients] develop [longer-term] anticipatory anxiety".

In all of the various forms of anxiety disorder, including obsessional-compulsive disorders (OCDs), social phobias, and so on, episodes of panic are common. According to Barlow and Craske (1988), "panic is an ubiquitous problem among patients with anxiety disorders and at least 83% of patients in any diagnostic category reported at least one panic attack," (p. 20). (The term "panic episode" is preferable to the more usual "panic attack", which has misleading connotations, especially with heart attacks. However, the terms used by the original writers are retained throughout this text.) The term "panic" is derived from the Greek god Pan, whose shrill and unexpected noises frightened people.

The feelings of imminent catastrophe are described in various ways. Some people report feeling that "something terrible is happening to me", "I feel that I am in great danger", or "I feel that I am about to completely lose control". During a panic, people commonly fear that they might be dying, losing control, going insane, or losing consciousness. Some of the panics are unexpected and seem to "come out of the blue". However, the majority are provoked by exposure to identifiable stressors and can therefore be anticipated (McNally, 1994). Most people experience an occasional episode of panic in which the cause of the fear is evident. The threat of a serious motor accident can provoke it, as can an attack by a vicious dog. These predictable panics are also distressing and share some features of the unexpected panics, but they are easily understandable. By contrast, episodes of panic that occur unexpectedly can be bewildering and therefore especially troubling. A panic that occurs when at leisure in one's home is difficult to comprehend. In the absence of any apparent psychological stress, it is not surprising that affected people grope for a medical cause of their distress. The panics that occur "out of the blue"—unpredictably and inexplicably—are a central feature of panic *disorder*. On average, episodes of panic last between 5 and 20 minutes, are distressing, and leave the person feeling drained and anxious.

Panics that occur in response to a true threat are appropriate, if at times excessive, and they serve to protect the person from pain, injury, or discomfort. In contrast to these true alarms, episodes of panic that arise in response to threats that are minimal, or entirely misconceived, can be regarded as similar to the triggering of a false alarm. In fact, two of the leading theorists on the subject of panic disorder, Barlow (1988, 2002) and Klein (1987, 1993) construe abnormal episodes of panic as essentially false alarms, although their explanations of the nature and causes of these false alarms differ.

The following are some examples of unexpected panics triggered by unusual and even threatening events that were then catastrophically misinterpreted and resulted in the rapid onset of intense fear, i.e. panic:

A 23-year-old woman described her first unexpected episode of panic in these words: "I was at home one weekend and suddenly had trouble with my breathing. My heart was pounding and I began sweating heavily. I thought that my heart had given in and felt that I was about to die. My husband rushed me to the hospital emergency where they tested my heart and assured me that there was no danger. I gradually calmed down and returned home after an hour or so, feeling shaken but no longer terrified".

A physically fit 32-year-old security guard experienced his first panic while exercising in the gym. During the course of his customary programme of exercises he suddenly became extremely sensitive to his rapid heart beats and interpreted them as a sign that he was about to have a heart attack. He became understandably frightened and, gasping for air, asked a friend to call for an ambulance. He was rushed to the emergency room of the local hospital but during the trip felt that he might die before reaching help. At the hospital he was treated as an emergency and immediately wheeled into the examination room. No evidence of any cardiac irregularity or other problem was found and he was assured that he was healthy and could return home. After resting at the hospital for an hour, during which he felt relieved but exhausted, he returned home. Two weeks later he had another unexpected panic while jogging and again the doctor at the hospital reassured him about his health. A full examination carried out by his family doctor the following day led to the diagnosis of panic disorder and he was referred for psychological treatment.

In these two examples, unusual/unexplained bodily sensations were catastrophically misinterpreted as signs of an imminent heart attack—a rather typical sequence of events in the onset of panic. Other common catastrophic thoughts involved in episodes of panic are the feeling that one is losing control, the fear of going insane, the fear of losing consciousness, and the fear of acting strangely and/or screaming.

A 25-year-old lawyer was walking across a bridge one afternoon when she began to feel extremely dizzy and her heart began to pound. She felt that she might lose consciousness, or worse, lose self-control and run into the road in the face of oncoming traffic. These thoughts terrified her and she fled as fast as she could off the bridge. Thereafter she had a number of repetitions of the episode of panic and in each case the major fear was that she would lose control or act in a bizarre manner or self-destructively. These thoughts in turn led to a further fear that she might go insane and end up in a restrictive ward at a psychiatric hospital.

An anxious young accountant had a long history of worries about her health. On one occasion, she nearly choked when a piece of meat was lodged in her throat. She thought that she was about to choke to death and was terrified. Even after the meat was dislodged, she remained frightened and upset for more than an hour. After this incident she became extremely fearful of choking and limited herself to a very narrow, strict diet of soft and easily swallowed foods. Even so, she occasionally felt that some food had not gone down smoothly and would then feel panicky. Episodes were always provoked by the same, easily recognized event and she was able to predict which foods and situations would provoke a panic, and hence avoided them.

In the DSM classification of disorders, the defining features of a panic disorder are that the person has repeatedly experienced episodes of panic, some of which were unexpected, and at least one of the episodes was followed by persistent worries (lasting one month or more) of having another panic. During the episodes, at least four of the following sensations/feelings are experienced: shortness of breath, dizziness or faintness, increased heart rate, trembling or shaking, choking, sweating, stomach distress or nausea, feeling that one's surroundings or self are not quite real, feelings of numbness, hot flashes or chills, chest pain or discomfort, a fear of dying or losing control or going crazy. In cases of panic disorder, the episodes might occur daily or several times a week. Typically, after the first episode of unexpected and inexplicable panic, medical reassurance is sufficient to provide temporary relief and a state of calm. However, when the second or subsequent episodes occur, conventional reassurance is of limited value. The person begins to fear that more episodes will take place, and at unpredictable times and in any setting. He or she becomes anxious and apprehensive, develops a pattern of avoidance, and rarely achieves a satisfactory sense of safety.

In a majority of cases, the occurrence of repeated panics is followed by restrictions of mobility. People tend to avoid situations in which they feel that a panic may occur and/or situations from which a rapid escape might be difficult. They plan in advance a particular route, time of the journey, and escape exits. Places and activities that are commonly avoided include supermarkets, theatres, cinemas, public transport, driving unaccompanied, bridges, and tunnels. Being caught in a traffic jam or standing in a long queue are common causes of anxiety. In many instances, the affected person becomes fearful of being alone at home and needs the reassuring presence of a trusted person who can provide safety or take actions to provide safety (e.g.

calling a doctor or ambulance) if a catastrophe threatens. If these fears and the consequent avoidance of "unsafe" places becomes excessive, the diagnosis of panic disorder is expanded to panic disorder with agoraphobia.

The experience of panic

The average duration of an episode of panic is between 5 and 20 minutes, but at the time it seems to be endless. It is a distressing episode of intense fear during which the person feels that a catastrophe is about to happen. During the episodes, ordinary processes of reasoning are somewhat impaired (i.e. "My mind goes blank", "I can't think straight"); it is like a mental dust-storm. At the time of the panic the person is convinced of a realistic and imminent danger. The most commonly reported intense bodily sensations include rapid heart beat, sweating, dizziness, shortness of breath, and shaking. The most commonly reported thoughts experienced during panic include: "I am having a heart attack", "I am losing control", "I am going to faint", "I am going to scream", "I am going to choke", "I am going to suffocate".

One young woman patient had such intense sensations of a pounding heart during panic that she sometimes felt her heart would actually burst right through her ribs. During one panic episode, her heart rate was observed to increase by 25 beats per minute. It is not unusual to see an increase of 20 or more heart beats per minute during a panic, although in some episodes little or no increase in heart rate occurs. In a typical episode, people experience at least some of these bodily sensations and, during the most intense panics, they tend to report an increasing number of the sensations. In a particularly bad episode they report feeling flooded by a rush of these disturbing sensations, which intensify the threat of losing control and of imminent danger. The sensations are intense and intrusive and are probably one of the causes of irrational thinking described earlier. After being buffeted by these disturbing sensations and frightening thoughts, the person is likely to be left feeling anxious, shaken and tired, even exhausted for between 30 minutes and several hours. As mentioned earlier, episodes of panic leave a residue of anxiety.

During panics, most people experience a feeling of being trapped and their main and overwhelming thought and need is to escape. This powerful urge to flee can lead to irrational and risky behaviour, such as driving too fast or recklessly, or running blindly out of a building.

One patient who had experienced many panics became so apprehensive about losing control when driving her car that she restricted herself to driving very slowly, only in the slow lane, and only in the early or late hours of the day. When she sensed the possible onset of a panic, she brought her vehicle to an abrupt halt, almost regardless of the following traffic. In severe cases, patients keep adding to their list of places to avoid, with each new panic adding another dangerous setting to the list, so that, in the most extreme cases, the affected person ends up being restricted to his or her own home.

Roughly one-third of the initial panics occur in public places, about one-quarter while in a car, and approximately one-third begin at home. In most cases it is possible to trace the occurrence of the major stress after or shortly before the first panic (personal conflicts, stress at work, loss or grief, etc.). The person's interpretation of and reaction to that first panic depends on the accompanying bodily sensations and the circumstances of the panic. As was evident in the first two case illustrations above, it is common for an unexpected panic to occur when a person notices rapid heart beats, shortness of breath, and a sense of danger. If this is interpreted as the start of a heart attack or other medical catastrophe, the person searches for emergency medical help, expecting treatment for heart condition or some related medical problem. When the doctors conclude from the tests that the person's cardiac system is functioning normally, this produces a great sense of relief but also leaves unexplained the nature and the cause of the discomfort and the distress. This absence of a satisfactory explanation can become a breeding ground of anxiety.

When a second episode occurs and the absence of cardiac or other medical problems is confirmed, the possibility of an anxiety disorder is considered. Once the person is persuaded by repeated medical reassurance and testing that there is no danger of a medical catastrophe, the fear might change from a worry about illness to an intense fear of having another panic. The person begins to fear the panic itself: the fear of fear.

The incidence of panic

Contemporary estimates of the incidence and prevalence of panic disorder, and other psychological and psychiatric problems, are strongly influenced by the results of a large epidemiological study carried out on nearly 20,000 people in five districts of the United States—the Epidemiological Catchment Area (ECA) study (Klerman,

1985). The information was collected by trained but lay interviewers, who administered a standardized interview to all of the respondents. Their findings, which have since been criticized on a number of grounds, apparently showed disturbing evidence of widespread mental illness, with an upper estimate that 20% of American adults suffer from mental illness at some point in their life and that, among these, anxiety disorders appeared to represent the single largest mental health problem in the country. It was estimated that women have a 2.1% lifetime prevalence rate for panic disorder; the rate for men was 1.0%. The disorder was found to be most common among people in middle adulthood and uncommon among people over the age of 65; in these latter cases it appeared to arise after significant illness or injury. These estimates were contested by other workers, some of whom reported a combined rate for men and women of 3.8% and others who thought that the ECA study greatly exaggerated the presence of these disorders. The ECA study produced some other surprising and contested results. For example, the interviewers identified a large number of people with agoraphobia but found that a mere 7% of them also had a panic disorder. By contrast, a study of 300 anxiety patients assessed in the course of a large-scale colla-borative study on the treatment of panic (Ballenger et al., 1988) did not find a single person whose agoraphobia had not been preceded by panic episodes. In an attempt to reconcile these conflicting find-ings, Horwath, Lish, Johnson, Hornig, and Weismann (1993) reinterviewed 22 of the subjects who were classified in the ECA study as having agoraphobia without panic, and found that this conclusion was justified in only two cases.

For these reasons, and a number of methodological limitations, the estimates arising out of the ECA study are best regarded with caution. However, the discovery that anxiety disorders are extremely common in the general population is broadly consistent with other modern information on the subject. In addition, the ECA findings regarding the age of onset (median age of 24) and the peak incidence (in middle adulthood) are consistent with other findings, as is the determination that the ratio of panic disorder among women is 2 to 3 times that in men.

The debate about panic

Panic disorder has replaced agoraphobia as the anxiety disorder of greatest interest. Agoraphobia is now regarded as a secondary manifestation of panics: "almost all agoraphobia . . . is initiated by spontaneous panics" according to Klein and Klein (1989). Klein argues that panic disorder is a distinctive type of anxiety disorder and that it is essentially biological in nature. His views gave rise to fruitful discussions about the nature of panic, and arguments for and against the biological and the psychological explanations are the substance of one of the most interesting debates in the whole field of abnormal psychology. The opposing points of view were summarized in this way: "One model, biomedical, claims essentially that panic is a disorder of the body, is biochemical, with a genetic vulnerability, and appropriately treated by drug therapy. The other, cognitive–behavioral, claims that it is a disorder of the mind based on misinterpretation, with a cognitive diathesis, and suitable for psychotherapy" (Seligman, 1988, p. 321).

Klein based his claim for the distinctiveness and importance of panic disorder on two main arguments. First, patients with a history of panic attacks do not respond to the drugs that produce improvements in patients with other types of anxiety disorders but they respond well to imipramine, an antidepressant drug (Klein & Klein, 1989, p. 20). Klein accidentally discovered the antipanic effects of imipramine in 1959. While carrying out research on the newly introduced antidepressant medication imipramine, he decided to test its effects on those patients who were not deriving benefit from anti-anxiety medications such as benzodiazepines. "The logic behind this was not exactly coercive: it was more a case of our not knowing what else to do for them, and thinking that perhaps this strange, new, safe agent with peculiar tranquilizing powers might work. Several patients volunteered for a pilot trial, primarily because anything was better than being sent home unimproved" (Klein, 1987, p. 4). Their unexpectedly positive response to antidepressant medication set them apart from patients with other types of anxiety disorder.

The second piece of evidence on which Klein based his claim for the distinctiveness of panic arose from the fact that panic attacks can be induced in the laboratory by the infusion of lactate into patients who have a history of panic episodes.

These two pieces of evidence were combined to reach the conclusion that panic disorders are distinctive, panic patients respond differentially to drug treatment, and panics can be provoked in these patients by a specific drug that leaves other patients unaffected. The concept of panic disorder was established on these two main pillars.

The connection between the two pillars is strengthened by the fact that the induction of a panic by an infusion of lactate can be blocked by the prior administration of imipramine. Additional arguments were introduced later but they are secondary in importance and timing to the two main arguments. It then became apparent that there is a close connection between episodes of panic and agoraphobia, with a high proportion of agoraphobic patients recalling experiences of panic episodes.

Klein originally left the precise nature of the putative biological dysfunction unidentified, but later introduced the idea that the episodes of spontaneous panic are "due to the pathological central discharge of an evolved alarm mechanism, possibly linked to separation anxiety or asphyxia" (Klein & Klein, 1989, p. 37). Still later, Klein homed-in on the nature of the dysfunction and argued that spontaneous panics are the result of false firings of a suffocation alarm system (see below).

Klein assembled a good deal of evidence to support his arguments and his original observation that imipramine does have antipanic effects has been confirmed. It is also true that a proportion of people with a history of panic attacks respond positively to the lactate infusion laboratory test. However, Klein and others are now attaching less significance to the results of the lactate tests (see McNally, 1994). It was originally claimed that the overwhelming majority of panic patients respond positively, but the latest figures are slightly above 50%. Moreover, it is clear that people who are not sufferers from panic disorder can respond positively to the test and, most interestingly, the response to the infusion of lactate has been shown to be partly dependent on psychological factors (Clark, Salkovskis, & Anastasiades, 1990). Klein's claim that episodes of panic initiate agoraphobia has received considerable support and nowadays is disputed by very few. In six surveys and studies it was found that the percentage of people with agoraphobia who said that their panics had occurred *prior* to the development of their phobia never reached less than 80%, and in one study it went as high as 97%.

The biological theory has been subjected to four types of criticism: (i) the numerous attempts to find a biological substrate for the disorder have been unsuccessful; (ii) the revised theory provides significantly more detail than the original proposal but remains unclear on critical points; (iii) there is positive evidence that contradicts the theory or its implications; and (iv) some critics consider the whole enterprise to be misguided.

The basis for the original argument, the two main pillars, has been challenged. The biological interpretation of the induction of panics by lactate infusions has come under criticism. It turns out that these responses are not specific to panic-disorder patients, as was originally suggested. For example, the panic rates for patients with depression, those with generalized anxiety, and those with panic, do not differ (Ehlers et al., 1988). Barlow (2002) and others have shown that panics are commonly reported by all categories of anxiety-disorder patient; patients with panic disorder are not as distinctly different as Klein had originally postulated. As conceded by Klein, a large number of panic-disorder patients do not respond positively. The response to the infusion test lacks specificity and sensitivity. Noting that so many different chemical agents have been shown to produce panic effect, Gorman (1987) questioned whether there was "any active agent that does not cause a panic". Moreover, as Clark (1988) comments, these active agents do not have a common chemical property. If panic disorder is indeed a biological dysfunction, it is one that is easily provoked by diverse chemical agents. The evidence on lactate infusion has also been criticized on the grounds of methodological shortcomings, including failure to control for baseline responding (i.e. ensuring comparable levels of baseline responding in the panic-disorder and comparison patients before the lactate is infused).

The original observation that led Klein to separate out panic disorder from other types of anxiety disorder has also been criticized. Contrary to what was originally believed, the claim that imipramine (and related antidepressant drugs) has a specific action on spontaneous panics has not been confirmed. According to Tyrer (1986), imipramine produces broad effects and, in addition, several classes of medication are capable of blocking spontaneous panic attacks. These include antidepressant medications of two main types, and certain types of benzodiazepines. A similar view was expressed by collaborators of Klein, who pointed out that at least three classes of medication effectively blocked panics. The claim of an exclusive connection between imipramine and panics has not been confirmed.

Throughout the development of this concept, Klein has emphasized the distinction between spontaneous and situational panics, laying greatest emphasis on the former type. Spontaneous attacks are those that are said by the patients to more or less come out of the blue and differ from the situational panics in which a probable external threat can be identified. However, the distinction between spontaneous and situational panics can be difficult to maintain (see Barlow & Craske, 1988: Turner, Beidel, & Jacob, 1988).

Some positive evidence that the biological theory has difficulty in accommodating includes the fact that panics can be induced by purely psychological procedures (Rachman, 1990). Psychological treatments are followed by significant reductions in the frequency of panics (Marks, 1987) and there is good evidence that cognitive-behavioural therapy is particularly effective in reducing panics (Barlow, 2002; Clark, 1999; Clark, Salkovskis, Hackmann, Middleton, Anastasiades, & Gelder, 1994; Margraf et al, 1986; McNally, 1995). There is no reason why psychological treatment should not be effective in modifying panic disorders, even if they are essentially biological in character, but these treatment results are not deducible from Klein's theory.

The major demographic features of panic disorders remain unexplained. There is nothing in the biological theory to explain why women are so much more vulnerable to this putative biological disorder, and there is no reason to explain why it should occur most frequently in early adulthood. The argument that panic disorders are distinctive has come under challenge because episodes of panic are common to all anxiety disorders, and indeed are experienced by members of the general population. The decreasing likelihood of a panic being induced by a lactate or other infusion after repeated inductions, a sort of adaptation effect, is not consistent with a biological dysfunction and, if it is such a dysfunction, it has the unusual quality of diminishing with repeated tests.

Klein's revised theory

After delineating panic disorder as a separable disorder, Klein then went on to analyse the implications of this distinction, demonstrating its connection with agoraphobia, and setting out treatment possi-bilities. At a later stage, he set forward a bold explanatory theory, proposing that "many spontaneous panics occur when the brain's suffocation monitor erroneously signals a lack of useful air, thereby maladaptively triggering an evolved suffocation alarm system" (Klein, 1993, p. 306). He postulated that the suffocation alarm is primarily biological in nature and consists of physiological mech-anisms that detect increasing carbon dioxide and brain lactate levels. According to Klein, the suffocation alarm is activated by increasing levels of carbon dioxide, which produce sudden respiratory distress (sensations of smothering), which promote brief hyperventilation, panic, and an urge to flee. Obviously such a monitor would be of survival value; when our breathing becomes difficult, nothing else matters.

Klein also proposed that the alarm can be activated by psycho-logical cues to suffocation. "A no-exit situation or one where stuffy, stale air implies no exit, where there are crowded, immobilized people or someone appears to be smothering, might all elicit panic if the suffocation alarm threshold is pathologically lowered or if the cues are particularly salient" (1993, p. 306). False alarms, the triggering of the suffocation monitoring system by inappropriate or insufficient stimuli, can then occur. Unexpected panic attacks are the result of a false firing of the suffocation alarm system and are particularly likely to occur in people who have an abnormally low threshold for activation (hypersensitive alarms), as this causes the alarm to misfire in a seemingly irregular and unpredictable manner. It can be seen that Klein's theory, with its allowance for biological and psychological triggers of the alarm system and consequent panic, is essentially psychobiological in nature. In the earlier version of his theory, Klein attached seemingly equal importance to breathing problems and to separation anxiety, but that association was never convincing (see Thyer, Nesse, Curtis, & Cameron, 1986) and no longer features in his revised theory.

People who have a hypersensitive suffocation alarm system can be identified by testing their reaction to inhalation of carbon dioxide or by their response to sodium lactate. Rachman and Taylor (1993) demonstrated that suffocation reactions can also be elicited by purely psychological means, in a fashion consistent with Klein's theory. It remains true, however, that Klein places greatest emphasis on the biological causation and nature of the postulated alarm system, and supports his view with a wide range of biochemical and physiological evidence.

There is convincing evidence of widespread and intense fears of suffocation (Rachman, 1990). For example, fear of suffocation is prominent in dental fears, as demonstrated in the experiment by Sanderson et al. (1963) where the interruption of breathing gave rise to extremely intense and prolonged disturbances.

Klein also attaches importance to the significance of a medical condition known as congenital hypoventilation syndrome ("Ondine's curse"), which he regards as exactly converse to the problem that arises from an excessively sensitive suffocation detector. Among a very small number of infants, the hypoventilation syndrome can have fatal consequences. Children who cease breathing during sleep, hence becoming hypoxic, can die. "These children, when grown up, are completely insensitive to carbon monoxide and have no sense of suffocation under asphyxiating circumstances. Can there be any clearer proof of the existence of a suffocation detector than the demonstration of subjects who do not have one?" (Klein, 1996).

If this is correct, it should follow that children who survive Ondine's curse, that is the overwhelming majority of such children, should be relatively immune to the development of panic disorder in adulthood (except perhaps if they have had the misfortune to experience a traumatic experience that induces the disorder). To be precise, these unfortunate infants are not suffering from the absence of a postulated suffocation alarm monitor but from a seriously deficient one. For the most part, their breathing during sleep is maintained at a safe level, with very rare failures of the system.

Incidental evidence in support of part of Klein's theory was provided by Rachman and Taylor (1993), who were prompted by the publication of the revised theory to carry out a re-analysis of data collected in an experiment on the nature of claustrophobia that was unrelated to Klein's theory (Taylor & Rachman, 1994). In the course of the study on 179 students, subjects were divided into those with a high fear of suffocation ($N = 49$) and those with little or no such fear, as assessed by a dependable questionnaire. In addition, the subjects completed a number of behavioural tests that included a suffocation challenge of breathing through a narrow straw for two minutes. On re-analysis, it appeared that subjects with a high fear of suffocation reported more panics than those with a low fear of suffocation, namely 18.4% versus 1.5%. After the suffocation challenge test, the subjects completed a brief structured interview pertaining to experiences of anxiety and panic. It was found that, relative to subjects with a low fear of suffocation, the high scorers reported a greater incidence of panic in enclosed spaces (59.2% versus 16.2%) and also in other situations (57.1% versus 20.6%). The subjects with a high fear of suffocation also reported a far greater frequency of unexpected panics (32.7% versus 4.4%). In other words, the subjects with a high fear of suffocation were seven times more likely to report having unexpected panics than those who had little or no fear of suffocation.

In a study that was conducted specifically to test one aspect of Klein's theory, McNally, Hornig, and Donnell (1995) compared the experiences of patients who had experienced panic disorder and community subjects who had experienced episodes of panic but did not have panic disorder. They found three cognitive symptoms that discriminated the clinical from the non-clinical panics: fear of dying, having a heart attack, and loss of control. As suggested by Klein's theory, suffocation symptoms have the largest effect size of any physiological symptom and, as McNally et al. point out, "suffocation sensations may be especially likely to generate the catastrophic thoughts that best discriminate clinical from non-clinical panic" (McNally et al., 1995).

Despite its boldness and several successes, Klein's theory attracted some criticism (e.g. Ley, 1994; McNally, 1994; Schmidt, Telch, & Jaimez, 1996). Among the objections that have been raised are the complaint that the theory is insufficiently detailed to allow for precise evaluation [in an attempt to meet part of this criticism, Klein suggested that the carotid body might house the suffocation monitor (Klein, 1994)]. It has also been pointed out that people die from carbon monoxide asphyxiation and this leaves unexplained why the suffocation alarm monitor failed to trigger and save these people. Klein answers that carbon monoxide and similar agents might "disable the suffocation monitor or alarm system" (Klein, 1996, p. 84). The evaluation of Klein's theory is continuing but the contribution it made to the major debate about the true nature of panic is well recognized. As Seligman (1988) observed, this is an important debate with broad ramifications.

In light of these problems and objections, a word is necessary about the status of Klein's work and the biological theory. It certainly is difficult to defend some of Klein's original arguments but his work is nevertheless of lasting value. Even though the two pillars are best regarded as scaffolding that served a temporary purpose, Klein successfully drew attention to the significance of the occurrence of episodes of panic, their functional relation to agoraphobia, the possible or even probable involvement of an easily triggered suffocation alarm system, and paved the way for the pharmacological treatments. Lastly, Klein's introduction of the concept of panic disorder, and his advocacy of a biological explanation, acted as grist and led to the formulation of competing, psychological explanations.

The cognitive theory of panic

Psychologists, with their long established interest in, and knowledge about, fear and anxiety, were drawn to the new concept of panic disorder but found the essentially biological explanation to be unsatisfactory. Two psychological explanations were developed independently by Barlow (1988) and by D M Clark (1986). These overlap but, for present purposes, the differences between them are not significant. Clark's theory, which has been the subject of a good deal of research will be described and analysed but much of the reasoning in this chapter applies equally well to Barlow's theory.

Clark's theory is stated in an admirably clear and succinct manner: "Panic attacks result from the catastrophic misinterpretation of certain bodily sensations" (Clark, 1986, p. 462–463). Bodily sensations such as rapid heart beat or dizziness are catastrophically misinterpreted as being dangerous. For example, a person might interpret palpitations as evidence of an impending heart attack. Other examples include the misperception of breathlessness as evidence of incipient respiratory arrest or perceiving dizziness as evidence of an imminent loss of control. A wide range of stimuli are capable of producing episodes of panic, and include some external stimuli but, according to Clark (1988), the triggers for panic are almost invariably internal. Barlow (1988) also attaches considerable significance to the misinterpretation of internal stimuli. If the person makes a misinterpretation in which the threat is exaggerated but not imminent, it is more likely to arouse anxiety than an episode of panic. Disturbing misinterpretations of bodily sensations that give rise to anxiety about one's health but pose no immediate threat are the raw material for hypochondriasis, a problem that is increasingly being redescribed as "health anxiety" (e.g. Salkovskis & Warwick, 1986).

The cognitive theory of panic has received research support (Barlow, 2002; Brewin, 1996; Clark, 1999; Craske 1999; McNally, 1994) and provided the rationale for a new form of psychological treatment of panic disorder, cognitive–behavioural therapy (CBT), which is proving to be effective (Acierno, Hersen, & Van Hasselt, 1993; Clark, 1999; Clark & Fairburn, 1997; Clark et al., 1994; Craske, 1999; Margraf, Barlow, Clark, & Telch, 1993; McLean & Woody, 2001). In support of the cognitive theory, there is evidence that patients with panic disorder have a higher frequency of the cognitions that lend themselves to catastrophic misinterpretation (Barlow, 1988; Clark, 1986, 1988; Hibbert, 1984). They are more likely to experience thoughts of impending loss of control, loss of consciousness, heart attack, and so on, than people who have anxiety that is not associated with a panic experience. Reports of specific connections between the catastrophic cognitions and the occurrence of panic are encountered in case after case of patients receiving CBT. In some of the clearest examples, the panics are eliminated shortly after the patient's cognitions have been corrected, and in some other examples the panics were not significantly reduced by established treatments unless and until the cognitions were altered.

Clark (1988) stated that the changes in bodily sensations usually precede an episode of panic. Experimental studies have shown that patients with panic disorder are significantly more likely to interpret their bodily sensations in a mistaken and catastrophic manner than patients who do not experience panics. Furthermore, if a catastrophic misinterpretation is activated, the probability of an experience in panic is increased (Clark, 1987). Much of the research on this topic was reviewed by Ehlers (1992), who reached a number of conclusions: "Panic patients demonstrated an enhanced ability to perceive their heart rate, they tended to shift their attention towards physically threatening cues and they rated bodily symptoms associated with anxiety or panic as more dangerous" (p. 3). The bulk of the experimental findings are consistent with the theory [see Clark (1996) for a review] but a few exceptions have been encountered.

The cognitive theory of panic entails a causal link between bodily sensations and fearful cognitions and, as a first step in locating the presence of such a link, panic episodes were induced in claustrophobic volunteer subjects and in patients with a diagnosis of panic disorder (Rachman, 1990). As deduced from the theory, panic episodes were indeed accompanied by many more bodily sensations and fearful cognitions than were the non-panic episodes, and several understandable links between the sensations and cognitions emerged. The links between combinations of bodily sensations and cognitions were even clearer than the links between single sensations and single cognitions (see also Marks, Basoglu, Alkubaisy, Sengun, & Marks, 1991). For example, when claustrophobic subjects reported bodily sensations of dizziness, choking, and shortness of breath, in association with a cognition of "suffocation", a panic was almost always recorded. Among patients with panic disorder, the combination of palpitations, dizziness, and shortness of breath, accompanied by the cognition of "I am passing out" usually was associated with a panic. As expected, the links observed in the group of patients with panic disorder were different to the links observed in the claustrophobic subjects. It must be said, however, that there were fewer links than might have been expected, although this might simply reflect the stringent criteria that were adopted in the analysis. Among the claustrophobic subjects there were no instances in which a panic was recorded in the absence of a fearful cognition. However, contrary to expectations, a number of panics were recorded by the panic-disorder patients even in the absence of a fearful cognition. For technical reasons, it is premature to draw any definitive conclusions from these "non-cognitive panics" and the subject requires further investigation.

The specificity of the connections between the particular bodily sensations and the associated cognitions is consistent with the theory. So, for example, a combination of breathlessness and dizziness accompanied by a fear of passing out or losing control, was associated with panic on 11 out of 13 occasions, but this combination of sensations was never followed by a panic in the absence of a fearful cognition. The findings certainly do not contradict the biological theory of panic but neither do they offer any support, and it has to be conceded that they are not immediately deducible from the biological theory.

The links are of interest and certainly consistent with the cognitive theory but cannot enlighten us about the claimed causality of the connections. Clark's theory is causal, and it is difficult to demonstrate definitively that the associations between sensations, cognitions and subsequent panic, are more than coeffects. It is possible that the cognitions described by the panic patients are epiphenomena [a view shared by some biological theorists, such as Klein and Klein (1989), and by conditioning theorists, such as Wolpe and Rowan (1988)]. Perhaps they are merely accompaniments of a fundamentally biological disorder or accompaniments of a conditioned panic reaction.

Even though it is difficult to prove the causal connection, there are several arguments to support the view that cognitions do indeed play an important part in the causation of panics. Instructions given to vulnerable subjects or patients can be important determinants of the occurrence or non-occurrence of a panic. For example, when subjects are told that a deliberate provocation, such as the infusion of lactate, might produce a panic, the rate of panic increases (Clark, 1988). To test the hypothesis that the instruction given to the testee influences the likelihood of that person responding positively to a panic provocation challenge, Clark et al. (1990) provided one group of panic patients with instructions designed to reassure them about the sensations they could expect to experience after receiving an infusion of lactate, whereas subjects in the control group were merely told that lactate is safe. All of the subjects knew that they could stop the infusion at any time and, consistent with the hypothesis, the rate of panic in the reassured experimental group was significantly less than it was in the control group. The rate for the experimental group was 30% and that for the control group was 90%.

In addition, important links between bodily sensations, fearful cognitions, and panic have been demonstrated in the experiments on claustrophobic and panic-disorder patients referred to above. Episodes of panic were strongly associated with a significant elevation of fearful cognitions and, in the absence of such cognitions, episodes of panic were uncommon or, in some samples, absent. In an intriguing experiment, Sanderson, Rapee, and Barlow (1989) demonstrated that, by introducing a degree of personal control, it is possible to reduce the probability of the person panicking under the provocation of inhalations of 5.5% carbon dioxide-enriched air that would ordinarily produce panic in a substantial number of subjects. In this experiment, the subjects were given access to a lever, which they were told could control the experimental conditions, and this information succeeded in reducing the rate of panics even though the control was in fact illusory. Carter et al. (1995) also showed the power of psychological factors to moderate the reaction to deliberate provocations of panic.

People can be primed for anxiety or panic by receiving alarming information about their own or other people's health (for example, George had a sudden heart attack) and by adverse life events. The incidence of episodes of panic increases after such events and the onset of panic disorder often is linked to adverse life events. In addition, some people are consistently primed to misinterpret their own bodily sensations. The theories of Clark and of Barlow understandably and correctly emphasize the importance of the misinterpretation of bodily sensations, but there is reason to suppose that misinterpretations of other threatening events can also produce a panic.

Any factors that bring about significant changes in bodily sensations, or in *external* threats, increase the opportunity for catastrophic misinterpretations. The common factors include overbreathing, strenuous exertion, taking stimulants such as caffeine and drugs, and unwanted relaxation. The priming conditions that increase the likelihood of a person misinterpreting these changes in sensation include adverse life events, alarming information, and a consistently negative style of attributions. The eliciting conditions are a threatening context and the absence or withdrawal of safety signals.

The vulnerability to episodes of panic can be reduced by avoiding those actions that provoke excessive bodily sensations (such as high levels of caffeine intake), by adopting or developing safety signals and procedures, and best of all by making correct interpretations of the changes that do take place. The main thrust of CBT, the effective form of therapy derived from the theory, is directed at these very misinterpretations and their replacement by more appropriate and reassuring explanations (see Barlow, 2002; Clark et al., 1994; Craske, 1999; Hawton, Salkovskis, Kirk, & Clark, 1989; Margraf et al., 1993; McNally, 1995; Salkovskis, 1996a).

Brewin (1996) observed that attention has been directed almost solely to the accessible cognitions but that, in time, notice must also be taken of the important non-conscious cognitive processes involved in anxiety (e.g. preattentive processes, memory, and attentional biases).

Cognitive theory has many strengths. It is a coherent theory with successful connections to cognitive psychology, abnormal behaviour and experiences; it also has practical therapeutic applications. Indeed, the therapeutic power of CBT can be explained by no other theory. A less obvious advantage of the cognitive theory of panic is that it enables one to accommodate much of the current information on panic, including the evidence collected and assembled by proponents of the biological theory. The fact that a variety of biochemical and physiological manipulations can induce episodes of panic shows that it is not the specificity of the agent that is important. Rather, the common element should be sought in the person's understanding of the procedure and his or her expectation of the effects of the mani-pulation, especially on bodily sensations. The chemical techniques for inducing panic achieve their effects indirectly and provoke a panic only if the bodily sensations that they induce are interpreted as a sign of immediate threat. As mentioned earlier, the precise instructions given to subjects undergoing the lactate infusion test can cut the episodes of panic from 90% to 30% (leaving the need to explain why the 30% occurred even in the presence of reassuring information). The cognitive theory can provide an explanation for chemically induced panics and easily accommodates the demonstration that panics can be induced by purely psychological methods. The cogni-tive theory, based as it is on the person's appraisal of the threat value of the situation and his or her sensations, has no trouble in accounting for the fact that repetition of the biochemical challenge tests generally leads to a decrease in the frequency of panic episodes (i.e. people learn to adapt to the chemical stimulation without difficulty).

The cognitive theory also accommodates the fact that, in a minority of instances, episodes of panic can be induced by relaxation, an outcome that is not obviously predictable from the biological theory (unless relaxation disarms the suffocation monitor?). Following the cognitive theory, if the induction of relaxation gives rise to a cata-strophic misinterpretation of the changes in bodily sensations that occur during relaxation, a panic can occur. If, for example, the person is frightened of losing consciousness or dying, then the bodily sensations of a slowing in breathing, faintness, and tingling might well be interpreted as threatening and cause a panic. Exactly this chain of events occurred in a patient whose panic disorder had been triggered by an unfortunate experience in which she had had an extremely adverse reaction to taking a street drug. It produced intense feelings of unreality and depersonalization and, at its worse, she felt that she was going insane. Thereafter, whenever she began to feel any unusual sensations or feelings that resembled the trigger event, she became extremely anxious and on occasion panicked. It was not possible to teach her relaxation techniques for the very reason that they produced in her these adverse reactions.

Vulnerability

Clark (1988, 1997) postulates that certain people are vulnerable to panic because they have an enduring tendency to misinterpret bodily symptoms. There are at least three types of vulnerability: (i) the person might be predisposed to experience intense or frequent bodily sensations; (ii) the person might be predisposed to make catastrophic misinterpretations; or (iii) both. The second possibility, the inclination to "catastrophize", has received most attention, and rightly so. Most people experience changes in bodily sensations, even of an intrusive kind, with regularity. Hence, the opportunities for panic are almost limitless but in fact the occurrence of these episodes is extremely rare. We therefore need to ask why and under what circumstances these changes in sensations are catastrophically misinterpreted.

Thus far, the research has succeeded in showing that people with a history of panic episodes do indeed show an enduring tendency to be highly sensitive to changes in bodily sensations, and also to have a tendency to misinterpret them (Clark, 1996). In addition, successfully treated panic-disorder patients showed a marked reduction in their tendency to make these catastrophic misinterpretations (Clark et al., 1994). In some seemingly tame laboratory exercises, even reading a series of statements pertaining to the sensations of discomfort and anxiety have been sufficient to bring people close to a panic (Clark, 1988). For example, in one study, panic patients who were asked to respond to words written on index cards were brought close to a panic by exposure to negative words such as "choking" and "dying". Partly as a result of the research on panic disorder, and for some related reasons, attempts have been made to measure enduring tendencies of this type [see, for example, the construction of a special scale, called the Anxiety Sensitivity Index (Reiss et al., 1986), mentioned earlier].

All theories need to address the question of the timing and context of episodes of panic and in the early formulations of the cognitive theory emphasis was placed on the role of overbreathing. Hyperventilation causes an increase in bodily sensations and was believed to be productive of many instances of panic. Hyperventilation can also be caused by strenuous exercise or by distress and, if the resultant bodily sensations are mistakenly interpreted as signs of an impending medical problem, panic can ensue. Later research on the cognitive theory has led to a de-emphasis on the role of hyperventilation and Margraf (1993) concluded that hyperventilation is related to panic in two ways: "First, it is one of many processes that can lead to the perception of bodily sensations which may trigger positive feedback loops between sensations and anxiety responses. Second, because of the circular nature of such feedback processes, hyperventilation can also be a response to anxiety" (Margraf, 1993, p. 49). It will be recalled that in the revision of his biological theory, Klein (1993) postulated that hyperventilation is a response to a false triggering of the suffocation alarm system. Here, then, is a phenomenon that is differently described by the biological and cognitive theories, and which is open to direct tests. In Klein's view, hyperventilation is an attempt to compensate for the feeling of insufficient usable air but in the cognitive theory, hyperventilation more often is regarded as a precipitant of panic in that it produces bodily sensations that are open to misinterpretation.

Critique

A theory that is bold in conception, extensive in its implications, and successful in generating an effective therapy (Chambless & Gillis, 1993; Giles, 1993), was bound to elicit a great deal of enthusiastic interest, criticism, and research. A number of valuable critiques have already emerged and it is plain that the cognitive theory and its implications will be the subject of continuing research and thought for some time. As mentioned earlier, in addition to its intrinsic interest, the cognitive theory of panic is one side of the mighty debate between predominantly biological and predominantly psychological explanations of many forms of abnormal behaviour.

Criticisms of the theory have been raised by psychologists working within the cognitive framework (e.g. Seligman, 1988; Teasdale, 1988), by advocates of the original conditioning theory of fear and anxiety (e.g. Wolpe & Rowan, 1988), and by advocates of the biological approach (notably Klein & Klein, 1989). Among these objections, it is argued that Clark's theory is loosely specified and inconsistent with some evidence, that the effects of various types of drug on episodes of panic are inconsistent with the theory, that episodes should never occur when patients are relaxed, that nocturnal panics should not occur, and that many circumstances and stimuli increase anxiety but do not lead to panic. Some of these criticisms, such as the occurrence of relaxation-associated episodes of panic, do not raise problems for the cognitive theory and, indeed, can be turned and used in its support. Other criticisms, such as the occurrence of nocturnal panics, gave rise to fresh research (see especially Craske, 1999), and a number of other criticisms can be added. A full account of the biological criticisms and the counterarguments is provided by McNally (1994, p. 110–115).

The main demographic features of panic disorders (onset in early to middle adulthood, female preponderance) remain to be explained. Why should people begin to "catastrophize" in early adulthood? Why are women two to four times more likely to "catastrophize"? Why do so few elderly people develop panic—they certainly have greater reason than young adults to be concerned about their bodily sensations and deteriorating health. Seligman (1988) argues that the concept of "catastrophic misinterpretation" is loose and bears little relationship to conventional cognitive psychology. He also observes that Clark's cognitive theory is not sufficiently different from non-cognitive explanations and seems to overlap the conditioning explanation of panic (see Wolpe & Rowan, 1988). Seligman also reminds us of the persistently troublesome problem of why it is that certain kinds of fear appear to defy disconfirmation. Why, he asks, does a person who has experienced hundreds of episodes of panic fail to learn that his heart is *not* defective? Why does he continue to believe that he is about to have a heart attack? Having received ample disconfirming evidence to prove that what he believed was false, the belief should disappear. However, it is likely that the original fear of an impending heart attack is indeed largely disconfirmed but is then replaced by a strong fear of experiencing a nasty panic. This fearful cognition is not baseless, is intermittently reinforced, and is therefore difficult to disconfirm. Teasdale (1988) raised the important question of why cognitive therapy requires "back-up" by evidence provided by one's own experiences. Even when they do produce changes in thinking, cognitive interventions often need to be supported by direct experience.

A satisfactory explanation is required for nocturnal panics. It is possible that a proportion of these are induced by disturbing dreams and that in other instances the person is awakened and then becomes aware of disturbing bodily sensations. These sensations then trigger a panic in vulnerable people. Collecting the information necessary to test these explanations, with the need for precision and accuracy of reporting and of timing, is no easy task but progress has been made (Craske, 1999). Another potential problem is the occurrence of so-called "non-cognitive panics", in which the person reports having experienced a panic without the accompaniment of a fearful cognition (Rachman, Levitt, & Lopatka, 1987). These might simply be failures to identify the appropriate thought but it should be said that each of the patients who reported a non-cognitive panic had on at least one other occasion reported a so-called cognitive panic. It is not merely a matter of dealing with people who are incapable of recognizing and reporting fearful cognitions.

There are extremely difficult questions of causality and no simple way to determine whether the cognitions are the cause, the consequence, or merely a correlate of the episodes of panic. The decline in cognitions and in bodily sensations observed after successful treatment is open to more than a single interpretation (e.g. Seligman, 1988). The decline in cognitions and/or in bodily sensations might well produce the reduction of the panics but it is also possible that the decline in cognitions and sensations are consequences of the reduced episodes of panic, and not the cause. It is also possible that the decline of cognitions is a correlate of the reduction in the episodes of panic. Some critics have suggested that the cognitions and their decline might be mere epiphenomena (e.g. Wolpe & Rowan, 1988). One reason for giving serious consideration to these alternative explanations arises from the fact that in Margraf et al.'s (1993) study of the treatment of panic disorder, patients who received pure exposure treatment without cognitive interventions showed improvements that were as large and enduring as those patients who received pure cognitive therapy in which exposures were excluded. Moreover, the cognitions declined to the same extent in both groups. It appears, therefore, that negative cognitions can decline after a direct attack or after an indirect attack.

A satisfactory cognitive explanation needs to account for the decline in cognitions that occur after non-direct treatments, such as repeated exposure to the fearful situation. The most obvious possibility is that with each exposure, the patient requires fresh, disconfirmatory evidence (no heart attack, did not lose control, etc.). The accumulation of this personal, direct, disconfirmatory evidence weakens the catastrophic cognitions. However, one is nevertheless left to wonder why the direct assault on cognitions was not significantly more effective than the indirect, incidental effects of exposure in the study by Margraf, and a similar one by Ost and Westling (1995). It is possible that the longer-term effects of CBT are superior, and this advantage can be predicted by the person's cognitions at the end of treatment. Even when differences in cognitions are not evident at post-treatment, CBT might nonetheless provide more durable changes, as has been noted with other disorders (e.g. Cooper & Steere, 1995). In support of the cognitive theory, there is evidence of a relationship between the amount of CBT provided and the extent of change. In the important outcome study by Clark et al. (1994), panic patients who received added cognitive therapy had a superior therapeutic outcome to those who received indirect treatments.

As far as the therapeutic mechanisms of cognitive therapy are concerned, there is a need to determine whether or not the reduction/ elimination of key cognitions is the critical element in this form of therapy. We already know that the direct modification of cognitions can be a sufficient condition for treatment success but we also know that direct modification is not a necessary condition for success (e.g. exposure alone can be effective, medications can produce improvements, and so forth). One of the major obstacles to finding an answer to these questions arises from a need for control over the timing of the events. Reductions in fear are easier to observe and record but they can occur slowly, over weeks rather than minutes. In cases of panic, the measures of change in therapeutic trials typically range over days or, commonly, over weeks (e.g. the number of panics experienced per week or even per month). So if the patient records a decrease in panics, say from four per week to one per week, when exactly did the decline take place? The cognitive changes can be even more difficult to track. Major changes in cognition can occur suddenly (e.g. Ost, 1989; Rachman & Whittal, 1989) and are therefore easy to record. However, in many and perhaps most occurrences—clinical or experimental— the cognitive shifts are slow to develop, changing over weeks rather than minutes [e.g. the cognitive therapy group in the Booth and Rachman (1992) claustrophobia study]. To complicate matters, the changes in fear and in fearful cognitions can, and undoubtedly often do, occur even when the person is separated from and out of context from the fear-provoking stimulus (Rachman, 1990). It is not possible to determine precisely when the change occurred, assuming of course that there is a complete change in the first place. So investigators are left with the difficult task of timing the sequence of changes in the cognitions and in the episodes of panic, knowing that these changes might take place over an extended period and that the determination of a precise point of change will be difficult or impossible. There is also some indication that cognitive shifts can initiate a process of change that becomes evident only some time later.

The fact that medications can significantly reduce panic, even in the absence of CBT (see below), requires a full explanation. The problem is a broad one because similarly therapeutic drug effects have also been obtained in the treatment of social phobia and OCD (Rachman, Cobb, Grey, McDonald, and Sartory, 1979). Are therapeutic effects achieved by CBT or by medications mediated by a common mechanism? It seems unlikely and, in any event, the combination of CBT and drugs is not additive. For reasons that are unclear at present, CBT and medications appear to be independent means of treatment—to the mutual discomfort of proponents of psychological and of biological treatments.

To summarize, the cognitive theory has exceptional explanatory value and has garnered a good deal of support (Austin & Richards, 2000; Barlow, 2002; Clark, 1999; Craske, 1999; Ehlers, 1992). It has also generated a method of therapy that is demonstrably effective. Moreover, there is no satisfactory explanation for the success of this therapy other than the cognitive theory itself. The coherence between the theory and its clinical applications is an added strength. We now have a reasonably good idea of why and when episodes of panic are likely to occur. Any setting or prompt that increases the opportunity for catastrophic misinterpretations, or that increases the probability for a misinterpretation of an internal or external threatening stimulus occurring, will raise the probability that the person will experience an episode of panic. Significant changes in the number and intensity of relevant bodily sensations, and/or a strong tendency to interpret these sensations as indicators of imminent danger, can promote panic. We also know that although everybody experiences bodily sensations of the type that can provide an opportunity for catastrophic misinterpretations, very few people make the misinterpretations that induce a panic. Clark and his colleagues are continuing to map-out the psychological characteristics that predispose people to making these misinterpretations, and this is a step towards learning how to reduce a person's vulnerability.

Treatment

Panic disorder is treated by psychological techniques, by medication, or a combination of both. Until the introduction of CBT, the major method for treating panics and the associated agoraphobic avoidance consisted of controlled, graded exposures to the feared stimulus (Barlow, 1988; Marks, 1987; Mathews et al., 1981; Rachman & Wilson,

1980). This method of behaviour therapy was moderately effective and was supplemented in many cases by training in relaxation, anxiety management skills, and so on. The expansion of this technique to include a large component of cognitive therapy has improved the durability of the treatment (Clark, 1999; Clark et al., 1994; Margraf et al., 1993). The treatment consists of two components: the identification of the maladaptive cognitions and their replacement with accurately benign cognitions, plus the provision of exposure exercises designed to facilitate these cognitive changes (Hawton et al., 1989). The mere fact that in some studies a relatively pure cognitive treatment proved to be as effective as the traditional exposure treatment (e.g. Margraf et al., 1993) means that the existing explanations for the effects of behaviour therapy need to be reconsidered. Equally, the fact that a pure exposure treatment can be as effective as a cognitive treatment raises questions about the underlying cognitive theory (see below). Leaving aside these challenging theoretical questions, the growing potency of CBT is welcome and clinicians are well placed to provide effective help for many people and to do so with well-grounded confidence. In the studies reported over the past seven years, the percentage of patients who were left free of panics ranges from 80 to 90%—an unprecedentedly powerful method (Clark, 1997; Cote & Barlow, 1993). It remains true, however, that the majority of patients receive the alternative treatment, medication. Imipramine in particular, is known to be effective (Clark et al., 1994). This drug, and other similar types of tricyclic antidepressant, can reduce or eliminate panics in many cases. However, these drugs produce side-effects and can be difficult to tolerate (Lader, 1994); there is also a risk of relapse when the medication is withdrawn. In a large study conducted in four sites, 312 patients were given a cognitive therapy (PCT), imipramine, PCT plus placebo, or PCT plus imipramine (Barlow, 2002, p. 373). The groups of patients who received PCT or imipramine were significantly improved. Interestingly, the patients who received PCT plus imipramine did as well as, but no better than, those who received PCT plus placebo. The drug treatment and the psychological treatment were both independently effective but, when they were combined, no advantage accrued. The effects of the psychological treatment were lasting but there were many relapses after drug treatment (40% to 50% within six months); the psychological and drug treatments had a high-scoring tie but the psychological method won comfortably in overtime.

The risk of relapse is also high (50% or more) with another class of medication, the well-established and widely used anti-anxiety benzodiazepine drugs (e.g. alprazolam). Lader (1994) noted that up to 15% of patients attending general practitioners seek treatment for anxiety, in one or other of its forms, and that the standard treatment is anxiolytic medication (especially benzodiazepine). "Anti-anxiety drugs suppress the symptoms of anxiety to some extent, sometimes quite effectively, but they do not deal with the root causes of the disorder" (Lader, 1994, p. 323).

Even when the provision of psychological treatment might be the preferred alternative, practical or financial limitations might rule this option out. There are many instances in which a combination of psychological and drug treatments will be considered.

As psychological treatment and medication are both at least moderately effective in reducing anxiety disorders, it was reasonable to anticipate that a combination of the two should be superior to either method used independently; surprisingly, this is not the case. The majority of studies in which a combination of the two was matched against medication only and psychotherapy only, failed to demonstrate a superiority for the combination of methods (e.g. Otto, Pollack, & Sabatino, 1996). For example, in an early comparative investigation of the therapeutic effects of behaviour-therapy-only versus medication-only (clomipramine) in 40 patients with severe and chronic OCD, both treatments were shown to be moderately effective (Rachman et al., 1979). A comparison group of patients who received a combination of the two treatments did only as well as did the patients who received either the medication or the behaviour therapy. There was no additive effect [see also Foa et al. (1992), "imipramine did not potentiate the effects of behavior therapy" (p. 279) and numerous other instances (Otto et al., 1996; Marks, 1987)]. At the time that the OCD study was completed (Rachman et al., 1979), it was suggested that clomipramine achieves its effects secondarily, as a consequence of a reduction in depression (clomipramine being an antidepressant medication). The clomipramine reduces the depression, which then relieves the OCD. Some investigators failed to confirm this suggestion and the matter remains to be resolved. Regardless of the explanation for the surprising absence of additive effects, the later comparisons of psychological treatment alone or in combination with medication tend to give the same answer—additive effects are rarely found (Otto et al., 1996). We appear to have stumbled onto a peculiar therapeutic arithmetic in which $2 + 2 = 2$.

Despite the absence of convincing evidence of its value, the combination of psychological treatment with medication continues to be the method of first choice in many clinical facilities. Indeed, in day-to-day clinical practice it often seems to be in the patient's interest to receive both treatments. However, there are signs that in some combinations at least the addition of certain medications might interfere with psychological treatment (Marks et al., 1993) and/or increase the risk of relapse. Otto, Pollack, and Sabatino (1996) reported that 69% of panic-disorder patients who took no medication after cognitive therapy remained well for up to two years, whereas only 24% of those who continued to take medication after cognitive therapy remained well in the follow-up period (see also Otto, Pollack, Meltzer-Brody, & Rosenbaum, 1992).

Summary

Panic is an episode of intense fear of sudden onset and generally lasts between 5 and 20 minutes, only to be followed by a residue of anxiety. Panics are commonly experienced by people with an anxiety disorder but, if the repeated occurrence of panics is the major or only problem, it is diagnosed as a panic disorder.

The original theory of panic disorder states that it is essentially a biological disorder and is appropriately dealt with by medication. The revised theory is more specific and traces the problem to an oversensitivity of the body's alarm system; panics are false alarms that occur when the alarm system is triggered in the absence of a true threat to the supply of useable air. The theory is supported by some evidence but does not account for important aspects of the phenomena, which the competing psychological theory attempts to address.

The cognitive theory states that panics result from a catastrophic misinterpretation of certain bodily sensations and it follows that a correction or elimination of these misinterpretations should prevent recurrent episodes of panic. The theory has attracted considerable support and the deduced therapy is effective, but several problems remain to be solved.

Agoraphobia 6

The original concept of agoraphobia, a fear and avoidance of public places, has been revised and is now connected to the theory of panic disorder. This chapter explores current views of agoraphobia and describes contemporary treatment.

The concept of agoraphobia, the prototypical modern neurosis because it is so common and because its features contain the essence of neurotic behaviour, has been criticized in the past few years and, in a sense, demoted. For over 30 years, agoraphobia was regarded as the prototype and theories of neurosis that were unable to provide a plausible explanation of agoraphobia attracted little interest. The main features of agoraphobia are a fear and avoidance of public places and of travelling, especially in public transport. These features sometimes are associated with a fear of being alone, even at home. Affected people report that they are frightened of passing out, having a heart attack, being trapped, losing control, or undergoing some other distressing event. They describe unpleasant bodily sensations in anticipation of and during excursions from safety, which is in most cases their own home. In serious cases the person is immobilized unless accompanied by some trusted companion, and even then their mobility is constricted. A severely affected patient described his state in these words: "Everything outside my front door is Vietnam."

The disorder usually emerges in early adulthood and is at least twice as common in women as in men. It is often associated with other psychological problems, notably panic disorder, claustrophobia, and depression.

People who have agoraphobia tend to have high levels of general anxiety. Nevertheless, their levels of fear and avoidance do show some daily and weekly fluctuations, but the essential fear and avoidance can persist for many years. Agoraphobia sometimes declines spontaneously and the problem does respond moderately well to treatment (Rachman, 1990). Repeated practice in which the person methodically enters those situations that provoke the fear—the so-called exposure treatment method—is a dependable way of achieving improvements but tends to leave the patients with residual fear.

The subject of agoraphobia rose to prominence in the early 1950s because of its common appearance in clinics. The fear was well-suited for treatments by the emerging methods of behaviour therapy, and learning theorists such as Eysenck (1957, 1967) and Wolpe (1958) insisted on the importance of studying observable behaviour. They were quick to recognize that agoraphobia could provide a testing ground for their fresh ideas on the subject of neuroses.

As unadaptive avoidance *behaviour* is a central, major, and accessible feature of agoraphobia, it was well suited as a test-bed for the emerging explanations of neurosis that concentrated on observable behaviour. By concentrating on the avoidance, indeed by even defining the problem as one of avoidance behaviour, theorists hoped to develop therapeutic techniques for modifying the unadaptive conduct. As such, they were guided in their approach by a considerable store of information that had been collected on the behaviour of small animals studied under laboratory conditions. A great deal was already known about the generation and maintenance of avoidance behaviour in animals. The advocates of the application of learning theory to abnormal behaviour were familiar with the concepts and methods of studying avoidance and they readily construed agoraphobia in these terms.

Conditioned fear was thought to be a central component of most neuroses, including agoraphobia. In this disorder, it was argued, the conditioned stimuli that evoke the fear consist of public places, public transport, and so on. It was argued, furthermore, that the conditioned fear gives rise to avoidance behaviour because people learn to avoid those places in which they have experienced fear or pain. For a period this theory was valuable, supported as it was by the laboratory evidence and encouraged by the successful development of treatment techniques that were derived from the theory.

Among the reports that provided support for this approach was a study of 88 agoraphobic patients by Ost and Hugdahl (1983), who found that 81% of the patients attributed the onset of their agoraphobia to a conditioning experience. Thorpe and Burns (1983) obtained a lower figure in their survey of agoraphobics but one that certainly gave no grounds for dismissing the theory; 70% of their respondents reported having experienced a precipitating event, although only 38% of the total described it in a way that was consistent with a conditioning explanation. The nature of the precipitating event remained unclear and, even at its most successful, the conditioning theory of agoraphobia was silent on a number of important questions. As a result of the increasing reliance on cognitive explanations of abnormal behaviour, psychologists began to question whether people with agoraphobia are truly frightened of public places. It was argued instead that people are frightened of *what might happen to them in these places* rather than the places themselves—just as people who feel claustrophobic when travelling in a lift are not frightened of the lift as such but rather of what will happen to them in the lift (e.g. panic).

In addition, a substantially different explanation was gradually introduced from a different quarter. As described in Chapter 5, Klein (1987) introduced the alternative idea that agoraphobia is merely a by-product of a more fundamental problem, panic disorder. He argued that people develop agoraphobic avoidance because they are fearful of experiencing episodes of panic, and it is for this reason that they are apprehensive about using public transport, going to public places, sitting in restricted sections of theatres, and so on. It is now widely accepted that the most common sequence is episodes of panic followed by the development of agoraphobic avoidance. As a result, there has been a shift away from regarding public places and public transport as contributing to the core of the problem. Instead they are seen as providing the *context* in which the panic-related fears are made manifest. Given this change of view, attention shifted from the causes and consequences of agoraphobia to the causes and consequences of panic.

The construal of agoraphobia as persistent avoidance behaviour that arises as a result of the establishment of a conditioned fear reaction has useful explanatory value and, for a considerable period, provided the basis for an effective treatment for agoraphobia. However, it left unexplained a number of phenomena and in an attempt to address these problems it was suggested that agoraphobia might more usefully be seen as a balance that the person strives to achieve between signals of threat and signals of safety. In addition, many people who suffer from agoraphobia describe their main feeling as one of being trapped and their most intense motive in these circumstances is to flee to safety. Three of the most important difficulties encountered by the original construal of agoraphobia as fear-generated avoidance behaviour are: (i) the undue persistence of the avoidance behaviour; (ii) the fact that in a significant minority of cases agoraphobia emerges after non-fearful events, such as recent bereavements; and (iii) the therapeutic effectiveness of treatments that do not involve exposure to the feared stimulus and could not therefore be predicted or accounted for by the original theory. The idea of introducing a safety signal component into an explanation of agoraphobia was based on critiques of Mowrer's two-stage theory of fear and avoidance set out by Gray (1971) and by Seligman and Johnston (1973).

The emergence of agoraphobic behaviour after someone has undergone a frightening or painful experience in a public place or when travelling presents few problems for the formerly dominant (conditioning) theory. But the onset of agoraphobic avoidance after loss or bereavement, in which there is no convincing evidence of a fearful experience in the place subsequently feared, could not be accounted for in conditioning terms. There is some debate about the proportion of agoraphobic avoidance problems having their onset after a specific fearful experience (Mathews et al., 1981) but little dispute about the fact that, in a significant proportion of instances, no specific trigger experience can be detected (e.g. Thorpe & Burns, 1983). These latter authors carried out a national survey of 900 agoraphobic respondents and found that no less than 23% stated that their agoraphobic avoidance emerged after the death of a relative or friend; another 13% reported the onset after they had experienced an illness. In the national survey, 89% of the agoraphobic subjects reported daily fluctuations in their avoidance behaviour, and these fluctuations argue against any interpretation that adheres too rigidly to a conditioning account of agoraphobia. Hallam (1978) argued that we should not regard "agoraphobia as fear of discrete cues such as streets, shops, and crowds . . ." (p. 314). Instead, it is preferable to consider exactly what it is that people with agoraphobia actually fear. Fears of illness and death are unusually prominent in this group (Hallam, 1978; Thorpe & Burns, 1983) and the survey respondents said that their most common fear was that of having a panic attack. Closely related are fears of fainting or collapsing. In light of this information, namely that people with agoraphobia fear fainting/ panics, collapsing, illness, death, and so on, it follows that they should be most apprehensive about those situations in which they would need assistance if these feared events occurred. Indeed, they are most apprehensive about situations in which they feel trapped, increasing distance from home or other safety, waiting in a queue, being in the centre of a row in the theatre or cinema, travelling unaccompanied, and so forth.

If we pursue the idea that agoraphobic avoidance is determined by a balance between danger and access to safety, it is possible to rethink why these problems can arise after a loss or bereavement. The loss of a relative or friend can seriously undermine one's sense of safety. This is particularly likely among people who are generally anxious and who have developed dependent styles of behaving. Broadly speaking, any important event that threatens one's sense of safety or general sense of security is capable of tilting the balance between danger and safety.

It follows that any therapeutic or naturally occurring event that increases the person's sense of safety will be followed by a decline in fear and avoidance (e.g. Carter et al., 1995). A sense of safety can be promoted by the development of self-help safety procedures that include such familiar techniques as relaxation, cognitive restructuring, planning of safety procedures, and a range of other plans and activities that increase one's sense of efficacious independence. From a therapeutic point of view, the greatest benefits can be expected from a sense of safety that is based on the development of satisfactory coping skills because this enables the person to ensure his or her own safety, to widen mobility, and to reduce the dependency on other people, which sometimes brings in its train unwanted problems.

On the contrary side, an important cause of the reduction in one's sense of safety is the experience of threat, the experience of failure, or other aversive events. Indeed, a single aversive experience appears to have the power to undermine for lasting periods the sense of safety that has developed over long periods. The second contributor to the decreased sense of safety is the loss of protection, especially in the form of a trusted companion. A diminished sense of safety can also occur when the protection loses some of its dependability. In the case of a companion, it requires only one or two instances of unreliability to undermine the sense of security. As far as other safety devices are concerned, people with agoraphobia understandably attach importance to the dependability of not only people but also motor vehicles, telephones, and other forms of safety or access to them. A sense of safety is nurtured by dependability and predictability (Rachman, 1984).

Treatment

The traditional treatment of agoraphobia, dating back to the introduction of behaviour therapy, consists of planned, controlled excursions into the patient's feared places:

An impressive collection of outcome studies provide compelling evidence that having agoraphobics confront the situations they fear is sometimes sufficient, frequently necessary, and usually beneficial. Approximately 60–70% of patients treated with in vivo exposure experience moderate or greater reductions in symptoms.

(Shapiro, Pollard, & Carmin, 1993, p. 187)

However, it is now accepted that the majority of cases of agoraphobia arise from episodic panics and, consequently, the treatment of agoraphobic avoidance tends to be secondary to the treatment of panic. Tackling the panic disorder first and then "mopping up" the agoraphobic avoidance has become the preferred approach to treatment (Clark & Fairburn, 1997; Hawton et al., 1989).

Summary

The main features of agoraphobia are a fear and avoidance of public places and transport. It was originally regarded as a prime instance of a conditioned fear pattern and analyses of case material supported this view. The affected person underwent an unpleasant conditioning experience in public that gave rise to a persisting conditioned fear. The motivating properties of fear then came into operation and led to the reinforcement of escape and avoidance behaviour—agoraphobia.

Later, it was argued that people with agoraphobia are not actually frightened of public places as such but, rather, of what might happen to them in these places. This re-analysis led to the introduction of the role of a search for safety or signals of safety. Agoraphobic avoidance is seen as a balance between a sense of danger and access to safety.

The traditional treatment of this problem by planned, controlled excursions into the very places the person fears to enter, is at least moderately effective. Tackling the cause of the fear and/or the associated episodes of panic has become the preferred choice of treatment.

Obsessions and compulsions 7

This chapter describes the main features of obsessions and compulsions; their relation to anxiety, as evident in clinical material and experimental analyses, is noted. The methods of treatment are psychological, pharmacological, or both.

The compulsive behaviour that is characteristic of many people who suffer from obsessive-compulsive disorders (OCDs) is in many ways the purest example of abnormal behaviour. For these people, the repetitive execution of essentially irrational actions, such as washing their hands over and over again, can be a source of considerable distress. People whose behaviour is in most respects well within rational borders carry out acts that they recognize to be senseless; this is irrational behaviour. To a considerable extent they are executing urges against their rational inclinations; their compulsion is relatively out of control. Obsessions are recurrent, unwanted, intrusive thoughts that generally have a repugnant quality and that the affected person tries to resist. The main themes of obsessions are unacceptable religious thoughts/images, unacceptable sexual thoughts/impulses, and unacceptable thoughts of harming other people.

Obsessive-compulsive disorders are uncommon but can be disabling and distressing for the affected person and also for friends and relatives, who rarely escape the adverse consequences of this problem. Obsessions and compulsions are strongly associated with anxiety, and even driven by anxiety (because of this association, OCDs are classified under anxiety disorders in the DSM system). Obsessions and compulsions are also closely associated with depression.

The classic examples of compulsive behaviour are repetitive, excessive, stereotyped *cleaning* and, comparably, stereotyped and repetitive *checking*, especially to ensure safety in the home and at work (e.g. repeatedly checking the safety of the stove, doors, windows). For example:

A 36-year-old salesman developed an intense fear of disease contamination, especially AIDS, and began washing his hands, his body, and his clothing over and over again each day. At its worst, he was having eight showers a day, none of them entirely reassuring because of his pervasive fear of contracting the disease through any contact with "unclean" people, objects, or places. He vigorously avoided any people or places that he felt were potential sources of contamination. Whenever he went out in public he was frightened of possible contacts with sources of contamination and was especially frightened by the prospect of encountering used condoms. As a result, he vigorously scanned the environment for any evidence of these signs of danger. So, for example, when walking in a public park, he constantly scanned the area for signs of condoms, often mistaking even the slightest trace of white, such as a discarded tissue, as a used condom. His general level of anxiety was high and his intense fear of contamination was the peak. Even though he recognized that the chances of contracting AIDS or other serious diseases by casual contacts in his everyday life were exceedingly remote, and that in any event, repeatedly washing himself would provide no protection, he had an overwhelming urge to repeatedly clean himself. Despite the exaggerated and admittedly senseless quality of his actions, the driving force of the anxiety dominated his behaviour.

Compulsive checking of the security of the electrical appliances, stoves, doors, and windows of her house became such a problem for a young clerk that she was spending up to two hours carrying out these checking activities before she was able to leave her home each morning. She recognized that the chances of a mishap occurring at her home were exceedingly unlikely but the anxiety she experienced as she was about to leave her home was so intense that it could be dampened only by repeatedly checking each potential source of danger over and over again.

The difficulty that compulsive checkers experience in trying to convince themselves of safety is remarkable, and the sheer repetitiveness of their actions can seem to be bewildering, even to the affected person: "I have to do it again and again to make sure". They seem to have a problem remembering if they have checked adequately but this is a lack of confidence in memory rather than a deficit; they repeatedly strive to achieve a "precise and liberating memory" (Proust, 1981, p. 55).

A third patient was intensely anxious about the possibility that she might have inadvertently injured someone when driving her vehicle. Any unusual events, such as sights or sounds encountered during a drive would spike up her anxiety and force her to retrace her entire journey, carefully searching for any signs of an accident or an injured person.

A devout young man was tormented by blasphemous thoughts and images whenever he attended church services. He felt urges to shout obscenities during prayers, had aggressive sexual images of the Virgin Mary, and was prevented from praying by the intrusion of blasphemous satanic phrases. He interpreted these obsessions as signs that he was a vile hypocrite and unable to control himself. He became increasingly miserable and isolated.

The experience of anxiety and its consequences is well described in the following account given by a patient:

The thought is that something awful is going to happen, not to me, but to my family. It happens dozens of times a day—on some days over 50 times. It can happen at any time, but more when I am on my own. Sometimes it is an accident, sometimes a certain illness, sometimes even death; it is not always clear which. What is clear is that something terrible is going to happen. It comes into my mind sharply, all of a sudden, and when it comes I cannot get rid of it. Whatever I might be doing at the time, say, reading a book, has to stop. The thought dominates everything else. It makes me quite anxious, and very tense. I *know* [original emphasis] that it is irrational to worry about my family simply because of a silly thought but when the thought comes, I do worry. I then have to somehow put it right: I have to cancel-out the thought. I don't remember how it began, but what I do now when I get this thought is to imagine certain things. It is a very fixed sequence (of visualizing pictures of family, friends, religious figures—always in the same sequence). (de Silva and Rachman, 1992, p. 37)

Another patient felt compelled to ensure that "everything was right" and therefore engaged in extensive checking behaviour. He repeated almost every action that he carried out. His most serious doubts were about the doors, windows, and gas taps in his house, which he checked many times before leaving home and before retiring to bed. He could relate some of his checking behaviour to particular threats, such as the possibility of his house being burgled, but for the rest he had only a vague notion why it was necessary to carry out these repetitive checks—to avoid some unspecified and unspecifiable disaster. All of us are familiar with the feeling that some of our completed tasks seem "just right" but others leave us with the feeling that they are "not just right". Numbers of people with OCD are tormented by an overwhelming need to ensure that whatever they do, however trivial, must be "just right" and they labour long and hard to achieve that release, repeating their actions over and over again. It can lead to immobilizing procrastination and avoidance, typified by perfectionist students who are seldom satisfied with their work and tend to turn assignments in late or not at all.

The main features of OCDs are easily recognized. The classic definition set out by Jaspers (1963) is representative and comprehensive:

> In a strict sense of the term, compulsive thoughts, impulses, etc. should be confined to anxieties or impulses which can be experienced by the individual as an incessant preoccupation, though he is convinced of the *groundlessness* of the anxiety, the *senselessness* of the impulse, and the *impossibility* of the notion. Thus, the compulsive events, strictly speaking, are all such events the existence of which is strongly resisted by the individual in the first place, and the *content* of which appears to him as groundless, meaningless or relatively incomprehensible. (Jaspers, 1963, p. 134, original emphases)

An *obsession* is an intrusive, repetitive thought, image, or impulse that is unacceptable or unwanted and gives rise to subjective resistance. It is generally regarded by the person as being repugnant and produces distress. It is characteristically difficult to control or remove. The person generally acknowledges the senselessness of the impulse or idea. The content of an obsession is repugnant, worrying, threatening, blasphemous, obscene, nonsensical, or all of these. The major themes of obsessions are unacceptable sexual, aggressive, or blasphemous ideas. Affected people devote sustained attention and effort to suppress the obsessions and/or to neutralize the anticipated consequences of these intrusive thoughts.

Compulsions are repetitive stereotyped acts. They can be wholly unacceptable, or more often partly acceptable, but are regarded by the person as being excessive or exaggerated. They are preceded or accompanied by a subjective sense of compulsion and generally provoke subjective resistance. They usually produce distress and the person can acknowledge the senselessness of the activity, especially when judging it in calmer moments. Although the particular activities are within the person's voluntary control (that is, they can be delayed, extended, postponed, or reduced—or even carried out by other people), the urge to perform the acts can be extremely powerful. The person experiences a sense of reduced volition.

OCD is not as rare as it was once thought to be. Most of the original estimates were based on figures collected on patients whose disorder was sufficiently severe to warrant admission to hospital. These early estimates were that less than 1% of the population was affected by OCD. Recent findings suggest that the figure could be higher. From surveys carried out in selected cities in the US, it is estimated that between 2 and 3% of the population have significant OCD at some point in their lives. These figures probably err on the side of overestimation but, even allowing for this, the data show that OCD is more common in the general population than had been suspected (de Silva & Rachman, 2004).

It should also be remembered that many people have obsessions and/or compulsions that do not cause distress and disablement. Moreover, even among those whose problems are of clinical severity, a significant proportion never seek professional help. In many instances they take positive steps to conceal their problems. Overall, there is no clear preponderance of either males or females who are affected with OCD but there are some gender differences in the types of OCD (e.g. there is a preponderance of females in the subgroup of compulsive cleaners). The disorder usually begins in adolescence or early adulthood and, in most cases, has emerged before the age of 25. By the age of 30, nearly three-quarters of all cases will have come to

TABLE 7.1

Distinctive features of obsessions and compulsions

Obsessions are intrusive thoughts that:
- are repugnant
- are unwanted
- have aggressive/sexual/blasphemous themes
- provoke internal resistance
- cause distress
- are recognized to be of internal origin
- are recognized to be senseless (insight)
- are ego-alien
- are associated with depression

Compulsions are repetitive, stereotyped activities that:
- are preceded or accompanied by a sense of compulsion that is recognized to be of internal origin
- provoke internal resistance
- are recognized to be senseless or excessive
- can cause embarrassment or distress
- are difficult to control over the long term
- are purposeful and directed

People with organic impairments can engage in repetitive acts that:
- lack intellectual content
- lack intentionality
- have a mechanical and/or primitive quality
- are associated with related organic dysfunctions

be diagnosed. In many instances a considerable time elapses before the affected person comes to a clinic but this unnecessary delay is becoming less common as public education on the subject of OCD improves. It certainly is true that the problem is more readily recognized than it was three decades ago. In roughly half of all cases the problems develop gradually. Among those with a sudden onset there is an excess of cleaners over compulsive checkers.

There is a close and probably causal relationship between compulsive urges and compulsive acts, with the former producing the latter. Obsessions and compulsions are closely related and a study by Akhtar and colleagues (1975) found that only 25% of the patients had obsessions that were not associated with overt acts. In a study of 150 obsessional patients, Wilner, Reich, Robins, Fishman, and van Doren (1976) reported that 69% of the patients complained of both obsessions and compulsions, 25% had obsessions only, and 6% had compulsions only.

The necessary and sufficient conditions for describing repetitive behaviour as *compulsive* are an experienced sense of pressure to act and attributing this pressure to internal sources. The occurrence of resistance is an important confirmatory feature but is not necessary or sufficient.

The necessary and sufficient features for defining a repetitive thought, impulse, or image as *obsessional* are intrusiveness, internal attribution, unwantedness, and difficulty of control. The confirmatory indicators are resistance and an alien quality. An obsessional-compulsive disorder is one in which the person's major complaint is of distress and/or disablement caused by obsessions or compulsions. The overt indicators are repetitive, stereotyped behaviour and a degree of psychological and social impairment associated with the complaints.

Types of compulsive behaviour

A broad division can be drawn between the two main types of compulsive behaviour—compulsive cleaning and compulsive checking. This division arose from clinical observation and was confirmed by psychometric studies (Rachman & Hodgson, 1980) but many people with obsessional compulsive problems have elements of both these forms of compulsion.

Checking compulsions are intended to prevent harm from coming to someone and are almost invariably oriented towards the future. For the most part they can be construed as a form of preventive behaviour (actively avoiding the prospect of some adverse event). Cleaning compulsions share some of these properties but have in addition a significant element of passive avoidance, that is, taking steps to avoid coming into contact with the stimulus or situation that might provoke the urge to clean (as in the case of the salesman, described on p. 130, avoiding contact with any person or places that might have an association in his mind with contamination by the AIDS virus). When these acts of passive avoidance fail, the person feels obliged to escape. The immediate purpose of carrying out cleaning compulsions is restorative, plus a longer-term preventive aim. Cleaning compulsions are characterized by high levels of anxiety and share some similarities with phobias. They are generally driven by fears of contamination, with fears of dirt or disease prominent. In threats of contamination by AIDS or syphilis there are elements of disease and dirt. In a further complication certain feelings of contamination are acquired by mental processes (memory, criticism, etc.)

in the absence of any physical contact with a contaminant. This form of contamination, called mental pollution, shares some of the features of ordinary contamination but is distinctive in several ways. In addition to usual feelings of contamination, the person has a sense of internal dirtiness that fails to respond to ordinary cleaning: "I look clean but feel dirty". Mental pollution can emerge without physical contact with a contaminant and is responsive to memories and social influences, including criticism; it appears to be particularly common after sexual assaults.

Checking compulsions more often than cleaning compulsions are associated with doubting and indecisiveness, take a long time to complete, have a slow onset, evoke internal resistance, and tend to be accompanied by feelings of anger or tension.

Persistence

One of the most puzzling aspects of obsessive-compulsive behaviour is its persistence. There is no obvious reason for people to engage in this repetitive, tiring, embarrassing, unwanted, and self-defeating behaviour. Even more puzzling is the persistent recurrence of intrusive, unacceptable, and distressing thoughts. The persistence of these abnormal experiences and behaviour is the core of the problem.

The most favoured answer is that compulsive behaviour persists because it reduces anxiety. Although this view was proposed in one form or another before the development of modern behaviour theory and therapy, it received support from most psychologists who attempted to explain this type of abnormal behaviour. For many years Mowrer's (1939, 1960) two-stage theory of fear and avoidance, stating that successful avoidance behaviour paradoxically preserves fear, was incorporated into many accounts of obsessional-compulsive behaviour and had a profound influence in the way in which we construe this problem. The reports given by people who have obsessional-compulsive disorders can be accommodated with ease into Mowrer's view and the theory served well for a period. However, the inadequacies of the theory (described earlier, see p. 13) gradually became apparent and the theory can no longer provide a comprehensive account of obsessional-compulsive behaviour. Patients commonly say that they have to carry out their compulsive acts to achieve relief from anxiety or tension. However, this kind of information is not conclusive and there is a difficulty at source because a few patients report

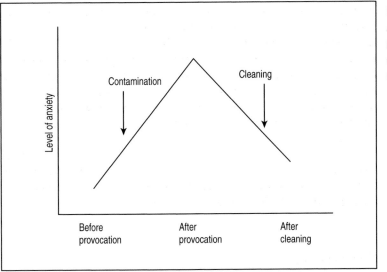

Figure 7.1.
Anxiety increases after provocation and decreases after compulsive cleaning.

that the completion of their compulsive behaviour is not followed by a sense of relief (Beech, 1971, 1974). A combination of clinical investigations, psychometric studies, and experimental analyses has introduced a measure of clarity into the nature and functions of compulsive acts.

In a number of experiments it was found that when patients with obsessive-compulsive disorders are deliberately stimulated by contact with one of their provocative stimuli (e.g. touching dirt) they almost invariably report a steep increase in anxiety and an accompanying urge to carry out the relevant compulsive act (e.g. cleaning). If the compulsive act is carried out, the anxiety declines promptly.

If in other experimental conditions they are asked to delay carrying out the compulsive activity (such as cleaning) their anxiety level tends to persist for a while, then gradually declines. In other words, the execution of the relevant compulsive act is followed by large and prompt decline in anxiety. An illustration of this relationship is given in Figure 7.1.

The direct prediction that compulsive activities are followed by a reduction in anxiety was the subject of a series of connected experiments (see Rachman & Hodgson, 1980) in which a simple procedure was used. The patients were relaxed as far as possible and then asked to carry out some "prohibited" activity (such as touching a dirty carpet) that would give rise to an increase in anxiety and an accompanying urge to carry out the checking or cleaning compulsion that was relevant for them. Once the anxiety and the associated urge were evoked, the patients were asked to carry out the appropriate compulsive act (such as washing) and report on the strength of the compulsive urges and the amount of anxiety experienced at each stage of the experiment. In the majority of these cases the completion of the compulsive activity was indeed followed by a reduction in anxiety and in the strength of the accompanying urge. Among patients with cleaning compulsions, very few exceptions were encountered. Among patients with checking compulsions, however, a small number of exceptions occurred in which the completion of the compulsive checking either left the anxiety unchanged or, in exceptional circumstances, was followed by a slight increment in anxiety. Notably, the amount of anxiety that could be provoked under these experimental conditions was larger (and easier) among patients with cleaning compulsions than among those who engaged predominantly in checking compulsions.

Using the same experimental methods, an attempt was made to collect information about the nature and the course of compulsive urges. For purposes of the experiments, compulsive urges were defined as impelling forces directed towards a goal and it was implied that the source of the prompting was internal, even if the urge itself was partially evoked by an external event. In a psychological sense the compulsive urges are the psychological activity that lies between an obsessional thought and the execution of a compulsive action.

As in the experiments on investigating the persistence of compulsive behaviour, each patient was first exposed to a provoking situation that led to a significant increase in anxiety and compulsive urges. Again it was found that the anxiety and urges can be provoked regularly, reliably and without difficulty.

The natural course of these compulsive urges, their relation to anxiety, and the extent to which they can be modified were analysed in two experiments. It was found that completion of the appropriate compulsion promptly reduced the anxiety and the urges, leaving only a minimal amount of residual anxiety. After the anxiety and urges had been provoked, a 3-hour observation period was used to trace the time course of the so-called spontaneous decay of anxiety and urges. In most cases, the anxiety and urges underwent a significant decline at the end of the first hour of the observation period and, by 3 hours at the outside, almost complete dissipation occurred (Figure 7.2). When the person was allowed to carry out the compulsive action, a rapid and steep decline in the urges was reported. It

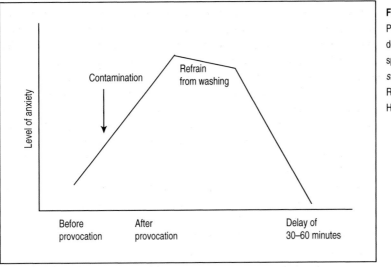

Figure 7.2.
Provoked anxiety decreases spontaneously but *slowly*. Adapted from Rachman and Hodgson (1980).

became evident that the completion of the relevant compulsion serves a function in the sense that it produces *quicker* relief. In view of the relative slowness with which compulsive urges and anxiety decay under spontaneous conditions, it is understandable why compulsive behaviour develops in the first place. It produces quicker relief from intense anxiety.

Therapeutic experience revealed that when patients learn that they can expect relief from their anxiety and compulsive urges, even if they refrain from carrying out the appropriate compulsion, the compulsions begin to weaken. After repeated experiences of the natural, spontaneous decay of anxiety and compulsive urges a lasting decrement in the anxiety and compulsive urges takes place.

It has been suggested that compulsive checking occurs when people who believe that they have a special responsibilty for preventing harm feel unsure that the perceived threat has been removed or adequately reduced (Rachman, 2003b). In their attempts to achieve certainty that all is safe, they check repeatedly. Paradoxically, these attempts to check for safety can produce adverse effects, which fuel a self-perpetuating mechanism: checking increases the urge to check again. The first element of the mechanism arises from the person's inability to achieve assured safety because the checking can have no natural terminus, as it is rarely possible to achieve certainty that future threats have been eliminated. The second element is a deficit of memory, actually a deficit in the confidence one has in one's memory.

With repeated checking confidence in memory declines (van den Hout & Kindt, 2003). The third element is a cognitive bias in which people feel that the probability of a misfortune occurring increases when they are responsible. The fourth element is another bias in which the person's sense of responsibility increases after checking for safety.

Obsessions

The intrusive, unwanted, repetitive thoughts that give rise to subjective resistance—obsessions—are fascinating and, for a long while, were puzzling. What is the origin of these unacceptable thoughts? What function if any do they play? Why are they so difficult to control? Little progress in addressing these questions was made until it was assumed, and later demonstrated, that most people experience unwanted intrusive thoughts which bear a qualitative similarity to obsessions, even though there are considerable differences in intensity and frequency.

Examples of obsessions include repetitive blasphemous thoughts, such as obscene ideas in church, or aggressive thoughts about harming elderly or infirm people, or having intrusive thoughts about unacceptable sexual acts. To make matters worse, there is a tendency for people who are afflicted by these unwanted intrusions to believe that by having the thought they actually increase the likelihood of the feared event occurring. An example of this phenomenon, called "thought action fusion", was given by a student who was tormented by repetitive thoughts that his family might be involved in a serious motor accident (Shafran & Rachman, 2004). He felt that every time he had this thought and the accompanying horrific image, he increased the probability that his family would indeed be involved in such an accident. Naturally this raised his sense of responsibility and ensuing guilt, as well as inflating his anxiety.

Unwanted repugnant thoughts can become recurrent or protracted and are therefore extremely distressing. People who experience obsessions often engage in behaviour that is comparable to escape and avoidance behaviour, including the obvious forms of avoidance but also the less obvious mental neutralizing types of behaviour ("undoing" the thought) and repeated requests for reassurance. The person is not actually seeking information (he or she knows the answers) but is attempting to cope with his or her anxiety. The effects of reassurance in OCD, and other disorders such as health anxiety, are transient; the reassurance quickly evaporates.

Many of the tactics that people use in their attempts to cope with recurrent obsessions are equivalent to overt compulsions. The majority of naturally occurring obsessions are generated internally, although they can also be provoked promptly and with ease by external stimulation, such as the sight of a sharp object that is then incorporated into an unacceptable aggressive obsession. For example, a fond mother was tortured by thoughts that she might stab her young children and, as a result, was terrified of being left alone near knives or other sharp objects.

Horowitz (1975) demonstrated that after being exposed to stressful events people tend to experience intrusive and repetitive thoughts. Evidence to support this view was collected by Parkinson and Rachman (1980), who studied the experiences of a group of mothers whose children were being admitted to hospital for elective surgery. The mothers experienced extremely high levels of anxiety accompanied by a steep increase in unwanted and distressing thoughts. Reassuringly, the high level of anxiety and distressing thoughts decreased rapidly when the parents were informed that their children were safe again.

There are grounds for believing that there is an important connection between the intrusive unwanted thoughts of everyday life and certain aspects of clinical obsessions. Obsessions in the form of thoughts, images, or impulses certainly are a common experience. The large majority of non-clinical respondents report experiencing unwanted intrusive thoughts of the type that bare a strong similarity to obsessions. The form of the content of obsessions reported by non-clinical respondents and by obsessional patients are similar but those experienced by the patients are more intense, more vivid, and longer lasting. They also provoke significantly higher levels of anxiety, are difficult to resist, and difficult to dismiss. It is precisely the anxiety-provoking and distressing obsessions that are most difficult to control. The "normal obsessions" reported by the non-clinical respondents can be dismissed, blocked, or diverted with little effort or difficulty.

It is entirely possible that the observed connection between the distressing effects of the thought and its consequent adhesiveness are connected. There is a limited amount of evidence of a correlation between disturbed mood and the difficulty in dismissing an intrusive and unwanted thought (e.g. Sutherland, Newman, & Rachman, 1982). We also have evidence that the frequency of obsessions is significantly increased by increments in anxiety, even if the anxiety is not directly related to the content of the obsession. In a valuable cognitive re-analysis of this and related questions, Salkovskis (1985) suggested that the distress and adhesiveness of obsessions arises from the person's overinterpretation or total misinterpretation of the significance of the relevant thoughts. Insofar as they interpret these unwanted thoughts as being of great significance (for example, if they interpret the thoughts as revealing some utterly repugnant but important aspect of their true personality), they will experience a significant increase in anxiety and other adverse emotions. These emotional disturbances in turn will interfere with the person's ability to deal with these thoughts. Instead, the person is inclined to engage in ultimately futile neutralizing behaviour, which in most instances is functionally equivalent to compulsive behaviour. At best, these neutralizing activities will provide a temporary relief but in the long run they serve to confirm the significance of the intrusive thoughts. Hence they contribute to the persistence of the problem.

The following are some example of obsessions described by patients (de Silva & Rachman, 1992):

- the thought of causing harm to children or elderly people
- blasphemous thoughts during prayers
- the thought of 'unnatural' sexual acts
- the impulse to violently attack and kill a dog
- the impulse to disrupt the peace at a gathering (for example, shout or throw things).

The cognitive theory proposes that obsessions are caused by a catastrophic misinterpretation of the personal significance of one's intrusive thoughts (Rachman, 1997, 2003a). Everyone has streams of thoughts every day and a proportion of these are unwanted, uninvited, intrusive. Among these uninvited thoughts some are objectionable, repugnant, even horrifying. If the person interprets these unacceptable thoughts as being of important personal significance— of being revealing—it can cause distress: "The thoughts reveal that I am mad, bad, dangerous."

Attempts to suppress the thoughts often produce a paradoxical increase in their frequency ("Think of anything, but not elephants. Definitely do *not* think of elephants!"). Other attempts at control can be equally futile. Ideally, the obsessions are best dealt with by altering the significance attached to the uninvited thoughts. Virtually everyone has these experiences and deals with them by dismissing the thoughts as insignificant, mere noise.

Compulsive hoarding

Hoarding compulsions resemble other compulsions but have some distinctive features [see the comprehensive review by Frost and Hartl (2003)]. Hoarding is most often associated with OCD but also occurs in association with some mental illnesses and in dementia. Patients who engage in hoarding and have other symptoms of OCD tend to be significantly more anxious, and depressed, than other people with OCD. The nature of the link between OCD hoarding and anxiety is not yet clear but it has been suggested that the hoarded items and the site of the hoarding provide a sense of safety: "Possessions come to be associated with feelings of safety and disposing of them feels like a violation of that safety. The safety signal value of their posssessions adds to the emotional turmoil associated with the disposal" (Frost & Hartl, 2003, p. 174). Presumably, the removal of the safety signals arouses anxiety.

Relationship to anxiety

There is a connection between most forms of obsessional-compulsive problems and fear/anxiety. The relationship between cleaning compulsions and anxiety is particularly close but the connection between obsessional slowness and anxiety is slender. The psychophysiological responses to presentations of phobic or to obsessional stimuli appear to be similar. In both instances the stimuli produce an increase in autonomic responsiveness and this responsiveness tends to diminish after successful treatment. The subjective responses to obsessional and anxiety-provoking material also involve a similar increment in subjective distress. These subjective responses, like the physiological reactions, tend to diminish after successful treatment. Obsessional-compulsive reactions and anxiety reactions frequently are associated with extensive avoidance behaviour and this too is diminished after successful treatment. Obsessional patients give retrospective reports of having experienced excessive anxiety during childhood and there is an elevated incidence of anxiety neuroses among the relatives of obsessional patients (Rachman, 1985).

Treatment

Given the association between certain kinds of obsessional-compulsive phenomena and anxiety, it is to be expected that those psychological techniques that can successfully reduce anxiety should prove to be useful in dealing with obsessional problems. This indeed is the case (Barlow, 2002; Clark, 2003; Freeston et al., 1997; M P Marks, 2003; Menzies & de Silva, 2003; Stanley & Turner, 1995; Swinson et al., 1998; van Balkom, van Oppen, Vermeulen, van Dyck, Nanta, & Vorst, 1994). For certain types of problem, notably those characterized by observable compulsive behaviour, the established techniques of fear reduction are effective. Until the comparatively recent introduction of cognitive analyses of the nature of obsessions, the existing fear-reducing techniques, with their emphasis on direct behavioural exercises, were so ineffective that OCD patients whose obsessions were not accompanied by observable compulsive behaviour were routinely excluded from treatment trials. It is too early to reach a conclusion about the therapeutic value of the new analyses of obsessions but the preliminary results are encouraging (Freeston et al., 1997). The introduction of cognitive analyses has introduced content into the previously threadbare behavioural analyses. Prior to this change, obsessions were simply obsessions and their actual content was of no interest.

Detailed accounts of the nature and treatment of obsessional compulsive disorders are provided in Hawton et al. (1989), McLean and Woody (2001), Menzies and de Silva (2003), Steketee and Lam (1993), and Swinson et al. (1998). The favoured treatment is a combination of planned, controlled exposures to the situation/stimuli that evoke the fear or discomfort (e.g. repeated, controlled contacts with perceived sources of contamination) followed by response prevention, that is, the inhibition of any consequent or associated compulsive behaviour (e.g. hand washing). These exercises of exposure and response prevention are planned with care by the patient and therapist and carried out repeatedly and systematically. The treatment is effective in a majority of cases (Barlow, 2002; Menzies & de Silva, 2003; Rachman & Hodgson, 1980; Swinson et al., 1998; Tallis, 1995). The infusion of cognitive analyses and procedures (Salkovskis, 1985) met with early success (Salkovskis & Kirk, 1997; Tallis, 1995) and there is a strong probability that a *cognitive* behaviour therapy will expand the range of problems that can be dealt with (e.g. the pure obsessions that have presented major difficulties) and also increase the power of the treatment.

At present, the majority of patients with OCD receive medication, usually one of the antidepressants of the selective serotonin reuptake inhibitors (SSRI) class. As with the treatment of panic disorder, even if psychological treatment is the preferred option, practical and financial limitations might rule-out this choice. There is sound evidence that this class of drugs is clinically effective in a proportion of cases (Insel, 1991; Insel & Winslow, 1992; Stanley & Turner, 1995; Swinson et al., 1998; Zohar et al., 1991) but side-effects are common and there is a risk of relapse in coming off the medication. In clinical practice a combination of medication and psychological therapy is frequently recommended, and in particular cases is the preferred course but, as mentioned earlier, the uncomfortable fact is that the research data rarely show that a combination of the two treatments is additive (Rachman et al., 1979).

Depression is evident in most cases of OCD and might require pharmacological treatment prior to or instead of psychological treatment.

Summary

Obsessions are repetitive, intrusive, unwanted thoughts that the person finds repugnant and attempts to resist, at least in the early stages. The main themes of these unacceptable thoughts are sexual, aggressive or blasphemous. Compulsions are repetitive, stereotyped acts that the person feels driven to carry out, even though they are recognized to be irrational or at least, excessive. They are intentional, directed acts that are carried out to reduce anxiety or discomfort or to reduce the likelihood of some anticipated distress/event. The two most common forms are compulsive cleaning and compulsive checking. In addition to the association with feelings of anxiety, a large majority of people have current or past episodes of depression. Increasingly, specific theories are being advanced to account for compulsive checking, obsessions, and compulsive hoarding.

The two competing explanations for OCD are psychological and biological and each theory has an associated form of treatment—medication or cognitive-behavioural therapy. Each type of treatment is at least moderately effective.

Social anxiety 8

Social anxiety is defined and described in this chapter. The extensivity of this type of anxiety is difficult to determine but is often associated with other psychological problems. The cognitive theory of social anxiety is described and evaluated.

Social anxiety, the apprehensiveness that people feel when entering novel or troublesome social situations, is familiar to most of us. There will be few people who are unfamiliar with this experience. Clinicians and clinical researchers, however, focus on the most extreme forms of social anxiety, often referred to as social phobia, a condition that is defined categorically in the DSM classificatory system.

The definition of social anxiety

The terms "social anxiety" and "social phobia" are used interchangeably and, in the DSM IV classification system, the term "social phobia" (300.23) is followed by the term "social anxiety disorder" in parentheses. In this classification, the essential feature of the disorder is an intense and persistent fear of social or performance situations. Entry into one of these situations "almost invariably provokes an immediate anxiety response" (DSM IV, p. 411) but a formal diagnosis is appropriate only if the anxiety interferes significantly with the person's life or causes extreme distress.

Social anxiety can manifest in a variety of forms. It can appear as a reluctance or inability to speak in public, stage fright, an inability to write or eat in public, excessive blushing, sweating or trembling in public. As is implied in the DSM definition, social phobia, or for that matter social anxiety, is described as *social* because the anxiety is experienced in social situations or in anticipation of entering such situations. It is also implicit in the definition of social phobia that the affected people are fearful of possible scrutiny and also anxious that they might behave in a manner that is embarrassing, inept, unacceptable, or all of these. It is a source of distress, concern, and shame.

Some people report that they fear and avoid a range of different social situations but for others the fear is circumscribed and is evoked in a specific context (Rapee, 1995). The most commonly feared specific situations include, in descending order, fear of public speaking, attendance at parties, meetings, and speaking to figures in authority. In recognition of the difference between multiple and circumscribed fears, it is now common to distinguish between generalized social anxiety and specific social anxiety. Thus far, few important causal or treatment implications of this distinction have been teased out but there are indications that generalized social anxiety is associated with wider psychological problems and that the circumscribed social phobias are more often preceded by specific traumatic experiences (Sternberger, Turner, Beidel, & Calhoun, 1995).

Socially phobic people tend to engage in considerable avoidance behaviour but some social interactions are unavoidable and hence a cause of anticipatory anxiety as well as situational anxiety. Because of the variety of manifestations of social anxiety, and the possibility of confusing it with other overlapping disorders (see below), it is difficult to reach reliable estimates of the prevalence of social phobia, with figures ranging from as low as 1% of the population to as high as 22% (see Barlow, 1988, 2002; Edelmann, 1992). For specific manifestations of social anxiety, such as a fear of public speaking, the prevalence can go as high as 70% (Pollard & Henderson, 1988). Mannuzza, Schneier, Chapman, Liebowitz, Klein, and Fyer (1995) estimated that social phobia might affect more than 10% of the population and that more than 20% of the population experience significant irrational fears of social situations, although these do not meet all of the criteria for social phobia. Social phobias tend to emerge in late adolescence and early adulthood: 15–25 years of age (Schneier & Johnson, 1992). Survey data collected by Weiller, Bisserbe, Boyer, Lepine, and Lecrubier (1996) suggest that social phobia is common, under-recognized and costly, and that affected people could be at risk for later depression and/or alcoholism; one-quarter of social phobics had alcohol-related problems.

The connection can be illustrated by a lawyer who sought treatment for his social anxiety, which was making court appearances a torment. He attempted to control his anxiety by drinking increasing amounts of alcohol before appearances, as a form of "self-medication". On some occasions he needed so much alcohol that his speech was slurred.

It is widely believed that alcohol reduces anxiety, and there is persuasive evidence that this can happen. However, there are exceptions, when drinking alcohol is followed by an increase in anxiety, and several moderating factors have to be taken into account when assessing the relation between alcohol and anxiety. These include the social setting in which the drinking takes place, the person's previous history of drinking, the interpretation the drinker places on bodily and psychological changes that occur during drinking, and so forth. It is also possible that the same episode of drinking can have anxiety-reducing effects and, later, anxiety-elevating effects. This sequence is not uncommonly reported by patients with anxiety disorders who describe an initial period of reduced anxiety during the drinking episode itself, only to be followed the following day by uncomfortable jittery feelings that resemble anxiety.

This pattern of early relief and later jitters is illustrated by a patient who had social anxiety and agoraphobia. In the early stages of a course of behavioural treatment he made slow, steady progress in overcoming his social anxiety and in regaining the ability to walk about freely. However, he continued to have troublesome weekends, when he frequently experienced a return of anxiety and an inability to venture through those parts of the city that he was able to manage on most days. It turned out that he celebrated the end of the working week, in tried and tested tradition, by drinking on Friday night, only to wake up on Saturday morning feeling agitated and fearful. He subsequently decided to curtail his drinking and this was followed by a decline in his weekend anxiety.

The distinction between the social phobics and the so-called avoidant personality disorder was teased out by Heimberg (1996). When there is a viable distinction, it is that social phobics recognize that their anxiety constitutes a problem and ideally would like to overcome it. The person with an avoidant disorder expresses no wish to have a more active social life and adopts an isolated life by choice. Perhaps even more than people with other types of anxiety disorders, those who suffer from persistent social anxiety frequently complain of the unpleasant intrusiveness of the bodily manifestations accompanying these problems, especially blushing, twitching, palpitations, and sweating.

Social phobics tend to rate their social skills as deficient. There is, however, some debate as to whether some or most people who suffer from intense social anxiety do indeed lack the appropriate social skills, whether they have the skills but have difficulty in deploying them, or whether they deploy the skills appropriately but *feel* that they have not done so. The present consensus appears to be that a significant minority of people with intense social anxiety do indeed have deficits in social skills but the extent of these deficits and the exact role that they play in social anxiety remains to be determined. Undoubtedly, the phobic person's appraisal of their social skills and conduct are of critical importance.

The general finding that people with anxiety disorders tend to have multiple problems (Barlow, 2002) is evident in social phobia (Rapee, 1995). According to Rapee's estimate, approximately 50% of those people with intense social anxiety also suffer from related disorders, two of the most common being depression and substance abuse. Among social phobics one commonly encounters agoraphobia, generalized anxiety disorder, and obsessional-compulsive problems. Or, to put it the other way around, people who suffer from anxiety disorders such as obsessional problems, agoraphobia, etc. have a high chance of suffering from concomitant social anxiety. Similarly, a high proportion of people who have significant depression also experience excessive social anxiety.

Because of the difficulties involved in carrying out experimental analyses of social behaviour, most researchers have resorted to administering self-report questionnaires. These instruments provide useful information but inevitably assume that the respondents have greater self-knowledge than is justified [see Nisbett & Ross (1980) for a description of how people tend to tell more than they can know]. Assessment of the personal beliefs that are given such an important place in the cognitive theory of social phobia rests on similar assumptions about self-knowledge, and also tends to assume that there is greater generality of these beliefs than is the case. Many of these beliefs are idiosyncratic and difficult to capture on standardized questionnaires.

Cognitive theory of social anxiety

The cognitive theory of panic proposed by D M Clark (1986) was used as a springboard for a theory of social anxiety. Starting with the basic premise of the theory of panic, Clark and Wells (1995) amassed and analysed clinical and experimental evidence pertaining to social phobia. There is a good deal of such evidence but some of it is piecemeal and scattered (Spurr & Stopa, 2002). Given the earlier success of the cognitive theory of panic, and the clarity of thought and exposition that made that original theory so accessible, the cognitive theory of social phobia, despite some gaps and weaknesses, provided a theoretical backbone that is promoting fresh thinking and research on the subject. It gives structure and direction to this previously amorphous subject:

> The core of social phobia appears to be a strong desire to convey a particular favourable impression of oneself to others and marked insecurity about one's ability to do so . . . In particular they believe that when they [social phobics] enter social situations, (1) they are in danger of behaving in an inept and unacceptable fashion *and* (2) that such behaviour will have disastrous consequences in terms of loss of status, loss of worth, and rejection. (Clark & Wells, 1995, p. 69)

The authors assume that the cognitive biases described in other types of anxiety disorder are also operating in social phobia, namely that affected people have a strong tendency to overpredict the probability and the seriousness of aversive events.

Social phobics tend to interpret social situations in a threatening fashion because of a series of distorted assumptions they make about themselves and the way in which they should behave in social situations. Clark and Wells (1995) distinguish three main categories of so-called dysfunctional beliefs: (i) unconditional beliefs about the self; (ii) conditional beliefs about social evaluation; and (iii) excessively high standards for social performance. Examples of the first include beliefs such as, "I am stupid" and "I am boring". Examples of the second type include, "If they really knew what I was like they would reject me" and "If I appear to be uncomfortable they will think that I am stupid". Examples of the third type include, "I must make intelligent and witty conversation" and "I must conceal that I am feeling anxious". People with a social phobia also tend have dysfunctional beliefs about other people, in addition to their erroneous self-evaluations. There are at least three clusters of dysfunctional beliefs about other people: (i) the belief that people are closely attentive to and concerned about one's appearance and/or conduct; (ii) the belief that other people can "read" the phobic's emotions; and (iii) the belief that people are quick to reject anyone who appears inept.

When affected people with these cognitive distortions enter a novel or demanding or important social situation, the "anxiety program" is activated and the person begins to experience signs of autonomic arousal, including palpitations, blushing, trembling, and shortness of breath. These intrusive bodily sensations interfere with the person's ability to process the ordinary information that arises in social gatherings, with the further result that negative self-evaluative thoughts are triggered. The person takes the bodily sensations as confirmatory evidence of his or her inadequacy, oddness, and unacceptability. When people begin to feel anxious they tend to behave in a non-friendly manner, which in turn elicits corresponding behaviour from the people they are with, thereby confirming the phobic person's fears.

According to Clark and Wells, interfering processes are activated in these circumstances. There is a significant increase in self-focused attention, initiation of safety behaviour, and the emergence of behavioural deficits that are induced by anxiety. One of the most important components of their model is the idea that social phobics interpret their internal sensations to construct or maintain an impression of themselves, usually negative, which they then assume also reflects what other people are observing. They attach more importance to this internally generated information than to the information provided by the people they are with. This shift in attentional focus occurs directly the person enters the feared situation and the detailed monitoring of their internal sensations has the unfortunate effect of increasing awareness of the anxious feelings. It also interferes with the processing of the behaviour of others. As a result of these changes, the person "equates feeling humiliated with being humiliated, feeling out of control with being observedly out of control, and feeling anxious with being noticeably anxious" (Clark & Wells, 1995, p. 71).

There is evidence that socially anxious people overestimate the extent to which their anxiety is observable (McEwan & Devins, 1983). Because of their preoccupation with their internal sensations and their negative interpretation of these feelings, they are less attentive to what is going on around them and can therefore feel out of touch with other people. To make matters worse, because of their cognitive biases, the words and behaviour of their companions tend to be misinterpreted as being negative and critical.

In an attempt to reduce the risk of receiving a negative evaluation from other people, social phobics are, according to the theory, likely to engage in attempts to create a sense of safety. Unfortunately, these safety actions can serve to prevent the unrealistic beliefs from being disconfirmed. For example, the person might avoid making eye contact to prevent the expected criticism, but by doing so ensures that he or she will never learn that making direct eye contact is not followed by nasty consequences. There is a further difficulty here, not included in the original theory, but that might be consistent with it. Given that much of what troubles socially phobic people arises from their fruitless attempts to guess what other people think of them, almost always negative of course, these pessimistic beliefs are inherently beyond confirmation. It is not possible, except by indirect, difficult, and uncommon means, to learn exactly what other people are thinking about one at a particular time. These types of beliefs are out of the arena and not open to disconfirmation. Clark and Wells make a good case for the untoward effects of certain kinds of safety behaviour but tend to overlook safety behaviour that is constructive and positive. We all engage in mental and physical safety actions in novel or potentially threatening situations, and usually with useful results.

The third process that is activated on entering a potentially threatening situation is a change in performance that is induced by anxiety. The person's preoccupation with his or her internal sensations and their meaning, makes that person relatively inattentive to what is going on in the immediate environment. This is easily interpreted by others as a lack of interest or plain unfriendliness. This, in turn, could make the other people in the situation behave correspondingly, that is, they will feel less friendly towards the affected person and show signs of it. For example, Curtis and Miller (1986) showed that when people were told that the person they had been talking to in a staged experiment disliked them, their subsequent conversation with this person was regarded as less friendly and less warm. If the social phobic's inattentiveness and apparent disinterest evoke a corresponding withdrawal of interest from the other people, the phobic's fears are confirmed.

Clark and Wells also attach importance to the effects of "post-event processing", which refers to the strong tendency for social phobics to spend a good deal of time and effort thinking about past social experiences, analysing their failures, recalling and "reliving" other failures, and so forth. These "post-mortems" might well intensify and consolidate the person's negative experiences, and even undermine formal psychotherapy. If the role of post-event processing in social phobias is confirmed, it will inevitably lead to analyses of post-event processing in all of the anxiety disorders (Rachman, Gruter-Andrew, & Shafran, 2000). Encouragingly, there already is some clinical evidence to support the idea that inhibition of these "post-mortem" examinations provides the patient with some benefit.

The theory is complex and combines maladaptive cognitions, biased information processing, and distorted self-images. The full catalogue of information-processing biases in social phobia was summarized by Clark and McManus (2002, p. 92):

> . . . social phobia is characterized by biases in the following: interpretation of external events, the balance of attention between external and self-processing, the use of internal information to make inferences about how one appears to others, recall of negative information about one's perceived observable self, and by a variety of problematic anticipatory and post-event processing.

There is, in addition, evidence that people who are socially phobic form powerful negative self-images that impair their conduct (Hirsch, Clark, Mathews, & Williams, 2003).

Hackmann and colleagues (2000) have described fascinating and potentially important evidence of recurrent negative images in people with social phobia: "Early unpleasant experiences may lead to the development of excessively negative images of their social selves that are repeatedly activated in subsequent social situations and fail to update" (Hackmann, Clark, & McManus, 2000, p. 601). The triggering events include being harshly criticized, severely embarrassed, and humiliated. The recurrent images are usually self-observer in their form and the content is of oneself appearing to be incompetent, pathetic, bumbling, and pitiful. They are generally accompanied by uncomfortable sensations such as blushing, shaking, and sweating. The persistence and apparent ubiquity of these images is remarkable, and might, in retrospect, go some way to explaining the success of the original fear-reducing technique of systematic desensitization (Wolpe, 1958), which involved the repeated evocation (and hence modification) of fearful images. It was perhaps on target in a way that was not apparent at the time. Needless to add, these early and fixed negative images are likely to be present in anxiety conditions additional to social phobia.

Evidence for the cognitive theory

The evidence is far from complete at present (Barlow, 2002; Spurr and Stopa, 2002), but the cognitive model theory of social anxiety has introduced welcome order and provides a direction for research and clinical innovation. The evidence collected by Clark and Wells (1995) and others (notably, Barlow, 2002; Edelmann, 1992; Heimberg, Liebowitz, Hope, & Schweier, 1995; Rapee, 1995) contains a number of useful pegs and markers. There is evidence that socially anxious people do endorse more negative self-evaluative thoughts than do other people, are inclined to interpret ambiguous social situations as being threatening, underestimate their social performance, and misuse information provided to them about this behaviour [e.g. Newlove and Rachman (1994) found that social phobics systematically discounted the praise that they were given for their social behaviour but readily accepted criticism]. Socially anxious people also are inclined to overestimate the visibility of their anxiety, are inclined to feel criticized, and their belief that others find them boring or dislike them does promote unfriendly behaviour towards these other people. These concerns tend to become self-fulfilling. Rapee (1995) confirmed that social phobics report an excessive number of negative thoughts, particularly related to their perceived inadequacy and to the belief that other people regard them unfavourably.

Beneficial effects can be obtained by redirecting the intense internal focusing of socially phobic patients towards external cues and, after successful treatment, the excessive self-focusing is diminished (Barlow, 2002). This technique and the associated one of discouraging the person's futile attempts to guess what other people are perceiving and thinking about them, are consistent with the cognitive theory. Similarly, useful effects are being reported from the prohibition of post-mortem ruminations about past social events, behavioural experiments to check the assumed visibility of one's own anxiety, and so on. Determination of the therapeutic implications and value of the complex, multifactorial cognitive model of social phobia will require many years of intensive analysis. From the therapeutic point of view, the desirability of redirecting one's self-focused attention when feeling socially anxious is matched by the difficulty of doing so—patients find it difficult to redirect their attention for sustained periods.

The strengths of the cognitive theory are that it provides structure and coherence to a subject that lacked these qualities, it is well integrated with the general cognitive theory of anxiety disorders, and most of it is set out in a way that invites verification. However, it is open to the same criticisms that have been levelled at other cognitive models of anxiety disorders and, as mentioned, there is insufficient evidence at this stage. The interconnectedness between the various components of the theory, such as the relationship between the schema, attentional focusing, negative self-images, dysfunctional beliefs, post-event processing, and so forth, needs to be worked out in detail. There are obstacles that are particular to the study of social anxiety, including the unavailability of experimental techniques that can provide important information about social behaviour without the artificiality that is present in virtually all laboratory experiments on this subject. One should not expect to learn too much from brief, contrived exchanges between specially selected subjects who are fully aware of the artificiality of the situation. Given the importance attached to the role of self-focused attention, the elusiveness of this phenomenon presents an obstinate problem. Techniques for exerting sustained control of the focus of one's attention are in short supply. The remarkable fact is that definite progress has been achieved despite these large obstacles.

Social anxiety within the general framework of anxiety

The cognitive theory can be accommodated within the framework of anxiety set out in Chapter 2. It is possible to substitute for each stage in the anxiety sequence, cues and cognitions that are specific to social phobia. For example, the cognitive vulnerability that is assumed to predispose people to feel anxious can be made specific for social phobia. The three sets of beliefs that are said by cognitive theorists to contribute to the social schemata in social phobics are: (i) perfectionistic standards for social performance; (ii) false beliefs about social evaluation; and (iii) negative views about the self (Clark & Wells, 1995). These beliefs, plus a temperamental predisposition to anxiety, give rise to hypervigilance when the person enters the social situation and starts a process of global scanning that is followed by an intensification of attentional focus. "One of the most significant changes that occurs when a social phobic enters a feared situation is a shift in attentional focus" (Clark & Wells, 1995, p. 70).

In the case of social phobics, much of this attention is focused on internal sensations (and their significance, including whether their emotional state is visible to others). In addition, it is probable that social phobics experience perceptual distortions, particularly in their view of the emotional reactions that they observe in others. If they conclude that their disturbed emotional state is evident to other people, they are likely to interpret it as evidence of their inadequacy, ineptness, and unacceptability. They are likely to interpret the behaviour and gestures of other people as indicating that others are making them the centre of attention and doing so in a critical fashion. Favourable remarks or gestures are discounted and negative ones accepted as confirmatory of the phobic's own beliefs about himself or herself. If, however, the affected person succeeds in making a benign interpretation of his or her own sensations and the behaviour of other people, no anxiety will follow. If the interpretation is predominantly negative, the phobic person will then anticipate a rejection by the people present, and feel likely to be shunned in the future. This sequence culminates in feelings of intense anxiety followed by attempts to escape from the situation. This model of anxiety as applied to the cognitive theory of social anxiety, is illustrated in Figure 8.1.

Treatment

Behavioural–psychological treatment, mainly in the form of controlled exposures to the unsettling social situations, is moderately effective (Heimberg et al., 1995; Hofmann & Barlow, 2002; Juster & Heimberg, 1995; McLean & Woody, 2001) but might need to be supplemented by training in social skills. Given the large cognitive component in social anxiety, it is reasonable to hope and expect that attempts to fashion a fully cognitive form of behaviour therapy (e.g. Chambless & Hope, 1996; Clark & Wells, 1995) will prove fruitful, despite the fact that some initial attempts were less than satisfactory. In particular, it has proved difficult to demonstrate that the results of cognitive therapy surpass those achieved by the existing behavioural methods. (Barlow, 2002). The result of a randomized control trial recently reported by Clark et al. (2003) is a hopeful sign, even though the cognitive therapy was compared to a dilute form of exposure therapy (self-exposure). Sixty patients with generalized social phobia received cognitive therapy, fluoxetine plus self-exposure, or placebo plus self-exposure. The effects of the cognitive therapy were remarkably large and significantly superior to those observed in the two self-exposure groups.

Various medications have been tried in treating social phobia. There have been some successes (e.g. phenelzine; Heimberg et al., 1998) but none has been outstandingly effective and the antidepressants that can be effective have drawbacks (significant relapse rates, food prohibitions, side-effects, etc.):

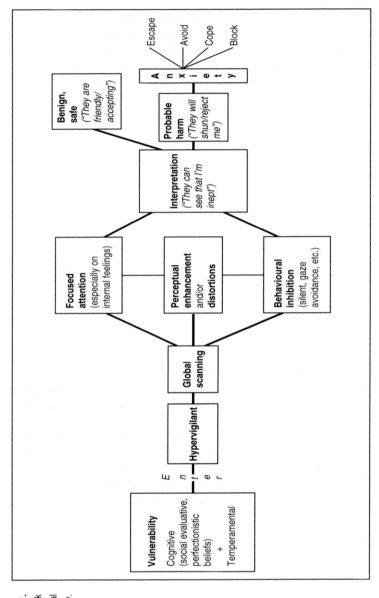

Figure 8.1.
Anxiety framework applied to social anxiety.

Social skills training and exposure (probably with cognitive therapy) appear to be the best first choices for the treatment of social phobia. Given the risks associated with pharmacotherapy and lack of evidence that it is more effective than psychological treatments, medication may best be viewed as a back-up plan under most circumstances. (Hope, Holt, & Heimberg, 1993, p. 247)

Summary

Social anxiety is an intense and persistent fear of social or performance situations; the anxiety is evoked when the person feels under scrutiny or that he or she is being evaluated. The most commonly feared situations are public speaking, attendance at parties, meetings, and talking to people in authority. A distinction can be made between generalized social anxiety and specific, circumscribed social anxiety (e.g. writing in public).

Problems with definition have interfered with attempts to assess the prevalence of social anxiety and estimates range from 1% to 22% of the population. Social anxiety is often associated with depression and/or generalized anxiety.

According to the cognitive theory, the core of social anxiety is a serious lack of confidence in one's ability to convey a favourable impression to others, and catastrophic misinterpretations of actual or perceived failures to succeed in these attempts. Affected people overpredict the probability of such failures and the seriousness of the anticipated consequences. Pertinent evidence is being collected and the early results are broadly consistent with the theory.

Treatment consists of the modification of maladaptive cognitions and controlled exposures to the troubling situations.

Generalized anxiety disorder (GAD) 9

This chapter describes the nature of generalized anxiety and gives estimates of its prevalence. The relation with other problems is noted and the probable role of safety signals is discussed. The approach to treatment is described.

The categorical description of generalized anxiety disorder (GAD) set out in the DSM IV classification is excessive anxiety that occurs on more days than not for a period of at least six months. The anxiety and worry are out of proportion to the probability of an unfortunate event and/or an exaggeration of the seriousness of the event should it occur.

The central feature of GAD is worry—pervasive, persistent, and uncontrollable worry. Misfortunes, accidents, and errors (however insignificant) must be anticipated and prevented. The worry is accompanied by a number of physical signs, notably elevated arousal and muscle tension. Other bodily symptoms, such as nausea, urinary frequency, queasy stomach, and difficulty swallowing, are commonly described. Sufferers complain of restlessness, and do appear to be restless, as if expecting some unfortunate event to occur. They also have difficulty in concentrating, become irritable, and are easily tired:

> A 32-year-old teacher described himself as a chronic worrier. He was persistently anxious about his health and was constantly ruminating about his aches and pains. Any threats to the health of his relatives provoked sharp anxiety; each trip was preceded by anticipatory anxiety, he couldn't rest until his family returned home safely each night, and he felt tense every day of his life.

Barlow (1988) observed that many of the features of GAD are evident in the full range of anxiety disorders and even in disorders of mood. For example, people who are suffering from obsessional-compulsive disorders commonly report prolonged periods of tension and worry, as do many people who are suffering from depression or from social phobia. Roughly half of the people who develop GAD trace its onset to childhood or adolescence, but onset at or after the age of 20 is also common. The lifetime prevalence rate for this disorder is estimated to be 5% (DSM IV) and approximately 12% of patients attending anxiety-disorder clinics are diagnosed as having GAD (Barlow, 2000).

One of the major problems with the concept of GAD is that although the major features of this phenomenon are observed across all types of anxiety disorder, none of the features of GAD is exclusive to or specific to GAD; all occur across the board. There are equivalent amounts of the four main symptoms of GAD (muscle tension, autonomic arousal, vigilance and scanning, and apprehensive expectation) in all forms of anxiety disorder (Barlow, 2002). These findings call into question the value of regarding GAD as a separable problem. Critics object that it is little more than a "residual category", serving as a receptacle for those disorders that cannot be fitted into one of the existing categories. This objection is extreme but, relative to the other anxiety disorders—all of which are well specified and distinctive, GAD is amorphous.

Barlow asserts that GAD is separable because the apprehensiveness displayed by affected people is so general and covers "multiple life circumstances" (Barlow, 2002). People with GAD are the so-called chronic worriers. In addition, Barlow points out that GAD often persists well after the successful treatment of coexisting anxiety disorders and is therefore best regarded as being relatively independent of the original disorder. (It can be argued to the contrary that the persistence of generalized anxiety after the successful treatment of some other clearly defined anxiety disorder is a residual in the truest sense, perhaps similar to the residue of anxiety that is observed after episodes of panic.) It has been claimed that there are important similarities between GAD and social phobia, with the possible exception that people who suffer from the latter disorder manifest their difficulties only, or mainly, when they are in contact with other people. By contrast, the chronic worrier is in play at all times and not bound by his or her social context. It remains true, however, that many of the worries expressed by the people with GAD are social in content (M Eysenck, 1992).

Dugas, Gagnon, Ladouceur, and Freeston (1998) searched for distinctive features of GAD and concluded that an intolerance for uncertainty is conspicuous and might well be the key variable in this disorder, although other factors also play a part. They advanced a complex model of GAD that includes maladaptive cognitions, cognitive avoidance, poor problem orientation, and intolerance of uncertainty, and recruited support from a psychometric study of the disorder. Moreover, they obtained satisfactory results from a treatment trial in which the derived CBT focused on the modification of intolerance of uncertainty (Ladouceur, Dugas, Freeston, Leger, Gagnon, and Thibodeau, 2000). The effects of this treatment were compared to a waiting list control condition in a group of 26 GAD patients. After CBT, the intolerance of uncertainty was reduced and broad clinical gains were recorded. Comparisons with credible alternative psychological treatments are expected.

The intolerance of uncertainty is an interesting concept and could be linked to the striving for safety that is characteristic of anxious people (see below). Uncertainty is no basis for the achievement of safety. Rather, uncertainty is linked to insecurity.

Persistently high levels of arousal are said to be characteristic of people with GAD and Michael Eysenck's (1992) analysis of hypervigilance is particularly relevant to generalized anxiety. Eysenck postulates that people with high levels of anxiety engage in rapid scanning of potential threat stimuli ("everything rustles") followed by a narrowing of attention while the stimuli are being processed (see p. 33). According to Brewin, subjects with generalized anxiety disorder show "attentional biases favouring stimuli that signal threat or danger" (Brewin, 1988, p. 84). Although Eysenck's cogent analysis of hypervigilance is implicitly based on a model of GAD, it is also applicable to other anxiety disorders.

Barlow (1988, 2002) suggests that people with GAD engage in a different kind of avoidance behaviour, including forms that are more subtle than the characteristic flight behaviour associated with intense bursts of fear. This avoidance behaviour can take the form of active as well as passive avoidance. The *active* avoidance includes excessive precautionary behaviour and repeated requests for reassurance.

Michael Eysenck used GAD as the model for constructing his theory of cognitive vulnerability, emphasizing that particular cognitive biases appear under conditions of stress or high state anxiety:

> The main support for a latent vulnerability factor comes from the interactions between trait and state anxiety or stress . . . it appears that cognitive biases in information processing can be obtained most readily in individuals who possess a cognitive vulnerability factor and who are also in

stressed conditions or high in state anxiety. (M Eysenck, 1992, p. 155)

The search for safety

Woody and Rachman (1994) attempted to expand the prevailing explanations of GAD by introducing the role of safety signals to complement the acknowledged role of perceived threats. This description of the proposal draws heavily on their original article. They regard generalized anxiety as an interplay between threatening signals and safety signals, with the failure of safety serving to perpetuate the perception of threat. The behaviour that is typical of GAD is seen as a manifestation of the person's unsuccessful attempts at safety. Affected people consequently engage in persistent, often ill-organized and sometimes frantic searches for safety to enable them to deal with anticipated threats to family, friends, health, and self. GAD is construed as an unsuccessful search for safety.

These multiple and persistent searches for safety seldom provide sufferers with lasting satisfaction and they consult widely, repeatedly seeking reassurance from family and authorities. As in OCD, the relief from reassurance quickly evaporates. Affected people go to great lengths to avoid risks, engage in repeated checking, pursue and recommend cautious behaviour, regulate their diet carefully, practice the most hygienic habits, and generally engage in overprotective behaviour. Despite all these attempts they seldom achieve a sense of safety or of contentment, and remain vigilant and overactive.

A wide range of threats is perceived, many of them involving the possibility of future misfortune, and these cannot be discounted by the worrier. The anxiety is generalized because of the absence or insufficiency of safety procedures or safety signals, and because sufferers overestimate the probability and seriousness of the antici-pated aversive events: "Simply put, the threats are ubiquitous, but there are very few safe places" (Woody & Rachman, 1994, p. 744). The loss, or anticipated loss, of a source of safety, whether it is human or other, will provoke an increase in generalized anxiety and worry, leading to an intensification of the safety-seeking behaviour. The increase in anxiety and vigilance is related to the magnitude of the anticipated or actual loss.

Woody and Rachman argue that to deal with the extraordinary persistence of the anxiety and avoidance behaviour, the addition of this safety signal perspective is necessary. Given that avoidance behaviour, such as that observed in all of the anxiety disorders, can persist even in the absence of fear, Gray (1971) made a strong case for the importance of safety signals, defined as the rewarding properties of stimuli that occur in association with the omission of an anticipated punishment. The safety signals exert a powerful influence on the persisting avoidance behaviour, even in the absence of anxiety. The idea is that anxiety generates escape and avoidance behaviour, and a search for safety. Cues that signal the presence of safety reduce the avoidance behaviour. Safety signals delimit the range and the duration of the threat, and hence of the anxiety. In the presence of an established safety signal the person is assured of safety from threat in that place at that time. Having achieved a sense of safety, the person can rest and reduce vigilance for a time.

A therapeutic example of the operation of safety signals is provided by one of the tactics used in the treatment of OCD (Rachman, 2003a). The patient is trained to take periods "off-duty" in specified circumstances:

> For instance, each evening try to ensure that you are mentally "off-duty" for one hour; during this off-duty period you are not responsible for planning or carrying out any of your preventive behaviour. Imagine that you are an air-traffic controller, and, during your off-duty periods, you are not required to keep scanning the screen for aircraft. There is no need to be super vigilant. You are off duty. (Rachman, 2003a, p. 78)

If a safety signal weakens or disappears, the threats revive or return and hence anxiety follows. This sequence has been illustrated repeatedly in research on laboratory animals that have been subjected to aversive stimulation in a confined space. They engage in vigorous even frantic searches for a safe spot or a safe time. If they succeed in locating safety then their agitated and fearful behaviour subsides; if they fail to achieve safety the frantic search persists. Safe times and safe places are easier to establish if the aversive stimulus is predictable; conversely, if the anticipated aversive event is unpredictable or irregular then the establishment of a dependable safety signal is difficult or impossible. If the search for safety fails then the vigilance and overactivity continue and fatigue ensues, perhaps to be followed by longer-term emotional consequences.

Woody and Rachman give everyday examples of the operation of safety signals that include the behaviour of young children. In the presence of a parent or other safe figure the child will mix and play contentedly. However, if the parent disappears from view or shows sign of leaving, agitated and anxious behaviour is readily evoked. The close connections between a safe figure and contented activity, and the connection between the absence of a safe figure and anxiety, are clearly and constantly present in childhood. These connections are probably more enduring and tighter when the child is excessively dependent.

Following the safety signal perspective, the similarities between GAD and social phobia become particularly evident. In both of these problems it is difficult for the affected people to achieve continuing safety. People with social anxiety can never know for certain that others are not scrutinizing them and/or being covertly critical. Social interactions are impossible to avoid entirely. They can arise when you least expect them, creating unpredictable sources of anxiety. Likewise, because the anxiety in GAD occurs so often in the absence of specific cues, particularly as the content of the worry generally involves future and unknowable events, it is impossible to avoid and difficult to predict. To some extent, the sense of safety provided by interactions with other people is also difficult to predict and control, given the considerable variations in interpersonal interactions. People who are prone to experience persistent generalized anxiety might well be excessively dependent on the sense of security provided by their closest family and friends. If so, interruptions or threats to those relationships are likely to be manifested quickly and prominently in increases in generalized anxiety. Conversely, strengthening of the personal relationships that convey a sense of safety is almost certain to be followed by reductions in the generalized anxiety.

Treatment

As with most of the anxiety disorders, the treatment of GAD can be pharmacological, psychological, or both. Thus far, no specific medication has proved to be of particular value here, nor is there sufficient evidence to support claims for a specifically effective type of therapy. CBT might be shaped up to provide superior treatment (e.g. Borkovec & Costello, 1993; Butler, Fennell, Robson, and Gelder, 1991; Chambless & Gillis, 1993; Clark, 1989; Durham, Murphy, Allan, Richard, Treliving, & Fenton, 1994; Harvey & Rapee, 1995) and the inclusion of tactics to reduce the intolerance of uncertainty might prove to be an effective asset (Ladouceur et al., 2000). It has to be recognised, however, that the effects of CBT and allied methods need to be enhanced. In practice, patients suffering from GAD are likely to receive general counselling and reassurance. If the anxiety is severe or interfering, anxiolytic medication might be added and, failing that, an antidepressant. Traditional behaviour therapy is directed mainly at the identifiable source of the anxiety and, hence, stumbles in the treatment of GAD. A more cognitive form of psychotherapy might be more appropriate (see Wells & Butler, 1997) but the results of a recently completed randomized control study were disappointing. Arntz (2003) found that patients with GAD who received cognitive therapy showed moderate but statistically significant improvements. However, these improvements were equalled by those observed in the comparison treatment group, which received applied relaxation treatment. In both groups, the "recovery rate" was just over 50%. The moderate level of improvement, and the fact that cognitive therapy did not surpass the comparison treatment, indicate the need for enhanced treatments.

Summary

GAD is excessive anxiety in which the probability and the seriousness of aversive events are exaggerated. The anxiety is pervasive, persistent, and usually accompanied by physical signs such as elevated muscle tension, nausea, urinary frequency, and restlessness.

The psychological and physical features of GAD are also encountered in so many other disorders that the distinctiveness of GAD has been challenged. However, GAD can persist even if related anxiety disorders are reduced.

It is suggested that, in addition to the fearful component in GAD, there is an important, counterbalancing search for safety. Multiple and persistent attempts to achieve safety have failed and the restless search continues—the threats are ubiquitous but there are few safe places.

The treatment of GAD can be pharmacological, psychological or both, but no specific and/or powerful treatment has yet been developed.

Post-traumatic stress disorder (PTSD) 10

This chapter describes the main features of PTSD, and looks at the central psychological processes involved. People suffering from PTSD feel under current threat, are disturbed by re-experiencing aspects of the trauma, grapple with disturbances of memory, and are excessively aroused. Approaches to therapy are discussed.

It has long been recognized that traumatic events often produce profound psychological effects that are distressing, damaging, and long lasting. In recent years, the effects of trauma (from the Greek word for "wound") have been fully described and classified as a form of anxiety disorder, namely post-traumatic stress disorder (PTSD). A full description and analysis of the disorder is provided in a companion volume in this series by Patricia Resick entitled *Stress and trauma* (Resick, 2001).

The concept of PTSD arose out of observations of soldiers' reactions to combat—"war neuroses"—and was incorporated into the American Psychiatric Association Classification, the DSM III, in 1980, largely in response to the intense concern aroused by the experiences of veterans of the Vietnam war. Correctly or incorrectly, the concept was classified as one of the seven anxiety disorders, and six diagnostic criteria were set out. The inclusion of PTSD as one of the anxiety disorders was justified because two of the major features of anxiety disorders—fear/anxiety and avoidance—are prominent in PTSD. However, PTSD also includes a number of distinctive features, such as disturbances of memory, and a wide range of associated emotions, such as anger, blame, guilt, detachment, flashbacks, re-experiencing, and numbing. The features and phenomenology of PTSD are numerous and complex, and some of them are unique.

The signs and symptoms of PTSD fall into three broad categories. After experiencing an event that involved actual or threatened death or injury to oneself or others, if the affected person repeatedly "re-experiences" the event and/or has other disturbances of memory, then the description of PTSD is considered. Curiously, sufferers from

PTSD both remember too much and too little. On the one hand, they are inclined to experience extremely unwelcome and disturbing recollections or flashbacks of the trauma but, on the other hand, their ability to recall the details of the event and the aftermath tends to be fragmented and incomplete in a way that can be perplexing and frustrating. These disturbances of memory are distinctive of PTSD.

A second set of signs consists of fear and avoidance of the places or people associated with the trauma, plus intense efforts to avoid thinking about or talking about the trauma or its associations.

Persistently increased arousal (including disturbed sleep, irritability and anger, startle reactions, and extreme vigilance) is a third indicator of PTSD.

Detailed accounts of PTSD are given in a number of texts, including those by Resick (2001), Saigh and Bremner (1999), Yule (1999) and in the advanced text by Barlow (2002). The distressing case of a man who experienced a delayed onset of PTSD illustrates all three features of the disorder:

> An accomplished 52-year-old lawyer had to undergo a series of intrusive and painful medical procedures, but became so anxious that he started to avoid essential treatment.
>
> To his surprise, for he was a resilient person, he felt shaky, trembled uncontrollably, sweated, and felt his heart pounding whenever the subject of his treatment was raised. He began to suffer from recurrent nightmares about his 3-year imprisonment in a Japanese prisoner of war camp nearly 30 years earlier, and woke in a terrified state.
>
> During the intrusive medical diagnostic testing, he experienced vivid flashbacks of his imprisonment and of episodes of the physical torture inflicted on him. His memory of the 3 years of imprisonment was patchy and he was unable to recall large chunks of time. Fortunately, he benefited from psychological therapy and was able to complete the necessary medical treatment.
>
> A young woman who had been injured in a serious motor collision 2 years earlier continued to suffer from frighteningly vivid flashbacks of the vehicle approaching her car in the seconds before the crash. She also had nightmares involving collisions and was so frightened of travelling by

car that she moved home to be close enough to walk to work. She too benefited from treatment, rather more slowly than the lawyer described above; her sleep disturbances came to an end and she was able to resume travelling by car, but not without tension.

PTSD is unique among the anxiety disorders in that the precipitating event—the trigger—is almost always evident. The site, time and nature of the trauma is known to the victim and to others. The connection between the trauma and the fear is evident and fits in well with the conditioning theory of fear acquisition. There are exceptions however, especially if the person has experienced numerous or repeated events, such as sexual abuse over a lengthy period.

The wounding, shocking, damaging, and distressing events that can produce these profound psychological reactions are regrettably wide and diverse, ranging from motor vehicle accidents to combat disasters, floods, bereavements, abuse, financial catastrophes, and medical crises. Thus far, the ones that have been studied most intensively are sexual trauma, vehicle accidents, and combat trauma.

Notwithstanding this disarming list of catastrophes, misfortunes, and disasters, most people cope tolerably well and it is only a small minority who develop PTSD or prolonged adverse psychological effects. Ultimately, a satisfactory psychological explanation of PTSD must explain why the majority of people are able to absorb the effects of "wounding", are able to to cope and persist, and how they succeed in processing the emotions provoked by the trauma.

Explanations for PTSD

A number of attempts have been made to explain the nature, occurrence, and persistence of PTSD but this is no easy task, partly because of the complex mixture of features of the disorder and partly because the precipitants range from motor vehicle accidents, floods, rape, combat, repeated sexual abuse, even to earthquakes. It is therefore a tall order to expect an explanation sufficiently comprehensive to encompass such a wide array of causes and effects.

One of the early attempts to explain the effects of trauma emerged from the experimental work of Pavlov (1941). Having shown that dogs develop disturbed behaviour, even severely disturbed behaviour, after one or more exposures to trauma or to unsolvable conflicts, Pavlov introduced a conception of neurosis that was used in the development of a comprehensive theory. The central idea was that the evolution of neurotic behaviour is best understood as a process of conditioning. As a result of an association with traumatic unconditioned stimuli, the animal or person develops abnormal conditioned reactions to previously neutral stimuli (Eysenck & Rachman, 1965; Wolpe, 1958). These early versions of the conditioning theory of neurosis were essentially theories of traumatic conditioning, somewhat modified by the later inclusion of the possibility that neuroses can be conditioned not only by traumatic events but also by repeated subtraumatic events. This theory of neurosis was influential for a period until it became evident that fear and neurotic behaviour can also be generated by processes additional to conditioning, namely by vicarious experiences and by the transmission of negative information. Aspects of the conditioning theory were later incorporated into the concept of emotional processing, described below.

The current theories of PTSD range from biological to cognitive from conditioning theories to information processing theories and beyond (Brewin & Holmes, 2003). Three prominent explanations are emotional processing, Brewin's dual representation theory, and the Ehlers–Clark cognitive theory.

Emotional processing of traumatic events

The connection between traumatic events and a form of re-experiencing was recognized over a century ago. In one of his famous early papers Freud said that hysterical patients suffer from "reminiscences". He suggested that "their symptoms are the remnants and the memory of symbols of certain traumatic experiences" (Freud, 1910, p. 8). These ideas were richly illustrated by descriptions of the famous case of Anna O, who was treated by Josef Breuer, a colleague of Freud (Jones, 1954). The patient's problems, it was argued:

> . . . originated at the time when she was caring for her sick father and her symptoms could only be regarded as memory symbols of his sickness and death. They corresponded to mourning and a fixation of thoughts of the dead so short a time after death is certainly not pathological but rather corresponds to normal emotional behaviour. (Freud, 1910, p. 8)

While caring for her father the patient had to suppress her strong emotions instead of expressing them in words and actions. As a result of this failure to express appropriate emotions, she was later handicapped by a range of neurotic symptoms and, according to the account given by Breuer and Freud in various versions (Jones, 1954), Anna O derived considerable if transient benefit from talking to Breuer about her symptoms and their origins—the famous talking cure.

The idea that emotional experiences can reverberate for a considerable length of time and continue to disrupt one's behaviour for many years after the event has been freshly revived in a modern form now that PTSD has become a topic of such prominence. Indeed, PTSD can be regarded as a prime example of such long-term reverberation and re-experiencing. For the most part, people absorb their disturbing emotional experiences satisfactorily. Even in these successful instances, however, it is not uncommon to find that the emotions return, at least in part, after an absence and sometimes to the considerable surprise of the person experiencing the return. In cases of PTSD, flashbacks are a vivid example of such unexpected, puzzling, fragmentary returns of emotional experiences.

Emotional processing is a process whereby emotional disturbances are absorbed and decline to the extent that other experiences and behaviour can proceed without disruption (see p. 53). Anna O overcame most of the disturbing symptoms described by Breuer and seemingly resumed a fruitful way of life. If the emotional disturbance is *not* absorbed satisfactorily, some signs become evident. These are likely to recur intermittently and can be direct and obvious, or indirect and subtle. The central and indispensable index of unsatisfactory emotional processing is the persistence or return of intrusive signs of emotional activity such as obsessions, flashbacks, nightmares, pressure of talk, expressions or experiences of emotions that are out of context or out of proportion, and maladaptive avoidance. The indirect signs include an inability to concentrate on the task at hand, restlessness, irritability, and other signs of heightened arousal that is characteristic of PTSD. As noted earlier, it is easier to come to grips with failures of emotional processing than with successes. Successful processing can be gauged from the person's ability to talk about, see, listen to, or be reminded about the significant events without experiencing distress or disruptions. All three of the major features of the present diagnostic basis for PTSD are included in the model of emotional processing, namely heightened arousal, abnormal avoidance, and re-experiencing. The concept of emotional processing addresses the fact that the large majority do cope, do "recover" from trauma. But the model, especially as applied to PTSD, makes insufficient allowance for cognitions and is relatively silent about the memorial disturbances that are a feature of PTSD (Rachman, 2001).

The therapeutic implications of the concept of emotional processing are that the transformation or neutralization of emotion-provoking stimuli or memories is facilitated by promoting adaptive and benign cognitions, by repeated controlled presentations, and by the planned presentation of disturbing stimuli in a progressive way for certain minimal durations, preferably during low levels of arousal. The transformation—the satisfactory processing—will be impeded by the persistence of maladaptive cognitions, negative appraisals, cognitive bias, brief presentations, intense and unpredictable stimulation, or by a state of elevated arousal. The elaborate account and analysis of the therapeutic implications of emotional processing set out by Foa and Kozak (1986) contains many stimulating features but assumes that, if fear reduction is to occur, the putative "fear structures" must be activated. However, fear reductions can occur without such activation. They can be observed after the provision of information, after observation of non-fearful behaviour, after taking placebos, and so on. In most forms of CBT for anxiety disorders, much or most of the effort goes into cognitive analysis and modification; the activation of fear in or between therapy sessions is not uncommon but it is not necessary for fear reduction (e.g. in the treatment of obsessions, panic disorder, etc.). The idea of fear structures is an integral part of their analysis, and is helpful in context, but not free of definitional and conceptual problems.

Dual representation theory

Unlike the model of emotional processing, the centrepiece of Brewin's (2001) original theory of dual representation is memory and its vicissitudes. Brewin argues that the pathological features of PTSD arise when memories of the trauma become dissociated from the ordinary memory system and suggests that "recovery involves transforming them into ordinary or narrative memories" (Brewin & Holmes, 2003, p. 356). There are, it is proposed, at least two systems of memory, and information about trauma is represented primarily in one of the two systems. "Ordinary memories" are mediated by a "verbally accessible memory" (VAM) system but memories of trauma are represented in a different system, called the "situationally accessible memory" (SAM) system. The memories are thought to be represented simultaneously in both systems (C Brewin, personal communication).

The two systems of memory are differentially affected by extreme levels of stress (Brewin, 2001). The SAM system is triggered involuntarily by cues associated with the trauma and is best illustrated by the operation of flashbacks. These memories are more emotional and vivid than ordinary memories but, ordinarily, are not accessible by verbal means. They are poorly integrated into the person's autobiographical knowledge and are difficult for the person to describe. It is argued that the emotions that accompany these SAM memories are confined to the primary emotions that were experienced during the trauma. The ordinary memory system, the VAM, consists of oral or written narratives that can be retrieved deliberately—at will—and are well integrated with the person's autobiographical knowledge. Broadly, the distinction between these two memory systems is that between a conscious memorial system and one that is ordinarily outside conscious manipulation and not easily accessible. Brewin (2001) raises the original idea that flashbacks, re-experiencing, and related phenomena might facilitate the transfer of information from the SAM system to the more accessible VAM system.

SAM memories present an awkward problem because they are extremely disturbing and intrusive but inaccessible. Conscious analysis and re-analysis might be insufficient to reduce the negative emotions that are produced by cognitive appraisals of the trauma and its consequences (the major aim of cognitive therapy). It is implied that a purely cognitive form of therapy would leave the verbally inaccessible but powerful SAM memories relatively untouched.

The emphasis on the important, but as yet inadequately understood, memorial disturbances of PTSD is an original approach and draws strength from its connections with cognitive science and neuropsychology (verbally accessible memories are said to be "hippocampally dependent"). At this stage of its development, the theory is of special interest to academics and research workers, but could pave the way for clinical analyses in due course.

A cognitive theory

The cognitive theory of PTSD proposed by Ehlers and Clark (2000) is ambitious and spans the interests of research workers and clinicians equally well. This stimulating theory opens with the central question of why post-traumatic signs and symptoms persist. In terms of emotional processing, why are these disturbances not processed? The large majority of people satisfactorily adapt to and absorb the effects of traumatic events. Ehlers and Clark address the question of why the important minority fail to do so.

Their answer is that in these instances people's processing of the traumatic experience leaves them with a sense of *current* threat, which can be either an external threat to their safety or an internal threat to themselves or their future. Two mechanisms contribute to this threat: (i) negative appraisals of the event and its consequences; and (ii) the nature of the memory of the trauma itself. "Individual differences in the appraisal of the trauma" and individual differences "in the nature of the memory for the event and its link to other autobiographical memories" combine to produce a sense of current threat (Ehlers & Clark, 2000, p. 320). The feeling of a current threat tends to be accompanied by intrusive images, thoughts or memories; re-experiencing symptoms; and heightened arousal and fear. People interpret a PTSD sign (e.g. an intrusive image, flashback, etc.) as meaning that they are under current threat. Examples of the negative appraisals that can trigger or maintain a feeling of current threat include: "I will never get over this", "My brain has been permanently damaged", "I feel in danger; nowhere is safe", "I will lose my children". Cognitions of this character are so distressing that the person attempts to block the thoughts or images, and even takes steps to avoid any threatening cues, including people, that might evoke or exacerbate the negative appraisals. Attempts to avoid the threatening cues, whether they are internal or external in nature, can sustain the disorder.

Dealing with the paradox of memories, remembering too much and remembering too little, Ehlers and Clark propose that the victim's difficulty in recalling details of the event lies with the frag-mented and poorly organized memory of the trauma. They use the metaphor of trying to remember the contents of a cluttered, muddled mess in one's cupboard. Recall is greatly assisted when the items are tidied, sorted, and arranged in an understandable system. So it is with fragmented, muddled, and poorly connected memories of the trauma.

Involuntarily triggered intrusive memories are so poorly elabor-ated that they are inadequately integrated with normal autobiogra-phical memories, if at all. These fragmented, involuntary memories tend to be vivid, are certainly intrusive, and are often intensely emotional. They also have a puzzling quality because they are so poorly elaborated and loosely connected to the person's normal bank of autobiographical memories. These very qualities are likely to generate or reinforce the person's negative appraisals about the traumatic event: "My disturbed memory is out of control; it means that I have incurred serious and permanent psychological damage."

The theory is skilfully used to account for a number of features of PTSD, such as cases of delayed-onset PTSD, a feeling of being locked into the past, a pervasive sense of doom, and an avoidance of and dislike of talking or thinking about the trauma.

The treatment derived from the theory consists of three elements: first, the trauma memory needs to be elaborated and "integrated into the context of the individual's preceding and subsequent experience in order to reduce intrusive reexperiencing" (Ehlers & Clark, 2000, p. 335). Second, the negative and maladaptive appraisals of the trauma and its consequences need to be analysed and modified. Third, the unadaptive methods that the person has adopted to reduce or avoid the stress need to be identified and extinguished. These include the avoidance of people and places, the many and varied attempts to refrain from thinking about the trauma and its associations, and the unadaptive avoidance of talking about the trauma and its consequences. It is this last tendency that accounts for the fact that patients receiving treatment for PTSD are not always the most dependable and regular attenders at the arranged sessions, some of which can be disturbing. The controlled and graded re-exposure to the trauma or its associations can play an important part in treatment and often this is supplemented by the restorative use of modified images to overcome the vivid, emotional PTSD images.

The value of this newly derived treatment is under investigation and there are grounds for optimism. In the first place, it derives strength from the very fact that it is a derivation from a coherent theory, and second, that the theory and the treatment are the work of Ehlers and Clark, who have made important contributions to the understanding and treatment of a range of anxiety disorders. We also have a considerable amount of evidence of the efficacy of related, earlier forms of this type of treatment in the form of behavioural treatments for PTSD and cognitive-behavioural treatments for other types of anxiety disorder (Barlow, 2002; Foa, Keane, & Friedman, 2000; Harvey, Bryant, & Terrier, 2003; Marks, Lovell, Noshirvani, & Livanou, 1998; Resick, 2001). The behavioural treatment tactics involve repeated, controlled exposures to the traumatic cues. In a comparison between prolonged exposure and a cognitive treatment described as "cognitive processing", equally large improvements were obtained by both methods in the treatment of patients with chronic PTSD (Resick, 2001). The cognitive method developed by Resick and colleagues shares a few common features with the Ehlers–

Clark method but the rationale and strategies of the two differ considerably.

The early evaluations of the CBT derived from the Ehlers–Clark theory are encouraging but full-scale, randomized control trials are so demanding and time-consuming that some years will pass before definitive assessments are possible. A consecutive series of 20 PTSD cases treated by this method demonstrated large improvements (Ehlers, Clark, Hackmann, McManus, & Fennell, 2004). The results from a treatment trial involving 85 victims of vehicle accidents are equally encouraging (Mayou, Ehlers, & Bryant, 2002). Only 11% of the patients who received cognitive therapy still had PTSD at the follow-up assessment; 61% of the patients in the self-help control condition still had PTSD and 55% of the patients who had been given repeated assessments were also diagnosed with PTSD.

In an attempt to translate these ideas and techniques into a community setting, 91 patients who developed PTSD as a result of experiencing the bomb explosion that took place in Omagh, Northern Ireland, in 1998, were treated with an abbreviated form of the treatment. The therapists were given training in these specialist procedures and the patients received an average of eight sessions. Fortunately, "significant and substantial improvements" were achieved and the degree of improvement was comparable to that reported in research trials (Gillespie, Duffy, Hackmann, & Clark, 2002).

The Ehlers–Clark theory overlaps, to some extent, with both of the other two approaches—emotional processing and the dual representation theory. The concept of emotional processing is an attempt to construe the responses to trauma as a normal psychological process that occasionally fails. The signs of PTSD are seen as a disruption of the ordinary, universal way in which people process emotional material. It is intended to assist in understanding how the large majority of people succeed in coping with traumatic events, and to set-out the conditions under which this normal process is disrupted. It implies that any method that promotes the resumption of ordinary emotional processing will be beneficial. The model is weak on the nature of the memory disturbances and is insufficiently cognitive.

The focus of the dual representation theory is on the disturbances of memory and the theory emphasizes the differences between PTSD re-experiencing—flashbacks and all—and the recall of ordinary events. The theory is broadened by making connections with cognitive science and neuropsychology and, in this way, prepares the ground for a far-reaching expansion. However, it does not address the full range of PTSD signs and symptoms and would benefit from an infusion of more clinically relevant cognitive concepts and analyses.

The cognitive theory has wide explanatory value—the widest of any current psychological accounts of PTSD. The introduction of the idea that sufferers feel under current threat is an important addition, and helps to explain why the disorder persists. The links between maladaptive appraisals of the threat and memory disturbances are original and stimulating. The authors also provide a foundation for a coherent, theory-driven form of treatment. Unravelling the nature of the fascinating and even paradoxical memory disturbances, their interplay, and the connections with the maladaptive appraisals, will require a great deal of determined research.

Acute stress disorder (ASD)

In the fourth edition of the DSM, the category of PTSD was expanded by the introduction of acute stress disorders, mainly to acknowledge that dissociative reactions—depersonalization, derealization, amnesia, detachment—can occur within the first month after a trauma. With an emphasis on dissociation, the diagnostic criteria for ASD are dissociation, avoidance, and elevated arousal, the last two of which are also criteria for PTSD. It is postulated that the emergence of ASD reactions is predictive of prolonged psychopathology but the evidence is incomplete (Bryant & Harvey, 1997) and in many cases PTSD ultimately develops despite an absence of the early signs that constitute the diagnosis of ASD. The large overlap between the diagnosis of the two disorders (96% in the study reported by Brewin, Andrews, & Rose, 2003) calls into question the need for the subclass ASD. The justification for introducing this new disorder is not compelling (Harvey & Bryant, 2002) and it might have been preferable to concentrate on dissociation as a phenomenon rather than a diagnosis.

As construed in the DSM diagnosis of acute stress disorder, dissociation is a compound of depersonalization, derealization, amnesia, numbing, and reduced awareness. Each of these fascinating phenomena invites study and their amalgamation as one of the criteria for diagnosing the presence of ASD risks muddying the waters. One of the main reasons for carving out the separate diagnosis of ASD was the hope that it would improve our ability to anticipate the development of post-traumatic stress disorders but, despite some encouraging indications, it remains to be determined whether ASD is a sound predictor of later psychopathology. It is already apparent, however, that other factors have significant predictive power [see, for example, the predictive value of negative appraisals of the trauma (Halligan, Michael, Clark, & Ehlers, 2003) and the theory of Ehlers and Clark (2000)].

Summary

After an actual or threatened death or injury, if the affected person feels under current threat for a prolonged period, repeatedly re-experiences the event, and suffers from disturbances of memory, the possibility of PTSD is considered and is strengthened if accompanied by elevated arousal and by avoidance behaviour. PTSD is psychologically complex and the interplay between the re-experiencing (flashbacks, nightmares, etc.) and the disturbances of memory is of considerable interest and potential importance. Three psychological models of PTSD are described and assessed: emotional processing, dual representation theory and the cognitive theory. The therapeutic protocol derived from the cognitive therapy is under evaluation.

Appendix

Eye movement desensitization and reprocessing

The technique of eye movement desensitization and reprocessing (EMDR) has been promoted as a rapid and effective method for treating PTSD, and several other disorders (Herbert, Lilienfeld, Lohr, Montgomery, O'Donohue, Rosen, & Tolin, 2000). The originator, Shapiro (1995), observed that she was able to overcome some of her troubling thoughts by repeatedly moving her eyes from left to right and, so encouraged, she attempted to use the method of rapid eye movements with some of her patients. She claimed considerable success and the early case descriptions by Shapiro and her trainees aroused attention. There is some evidence for the claims of therapeutic efficacy (e.g. Acierno & Cahill, 1999; Shapiro, 1995) and some evidence against the claims of therapeutic efficacy (e.g. Barlow, 2002; Herbert et al., 2000; Lohr, Tolin, & Lilienfeld, 1998; McNally, 1999). The results of a well-designed randomized controlled trial by Goldstein, de Beurs, Chambless, and Wilson (2000) were disappointing. Their comparison of EMDR with a credible psychological placebo in the treatment of 46 patients with panic disorder and agoraphobia found that the results of EMDR did not differ from those of the placebo condition. Comparably discouraging results were recorded in two controlled trials carried out on people with PTSD; Devilly and Spence (1999) and Taylor, Thordarson, Maxfield, Fedoroff, Lovell, & Ogrodniczuk (2003) obtained superior results with conventional exposure therapy. Moreover, the effects of EMDR were short-lasting.

EMDR has been criticized for lacking a theoretical basis (Barlow, 2002), even of being pseudoscience (Herbert et al., 2000). The element of the treatment that was said to be of critical importance, notably rapid eye movements, has been shown to be dispensable (Herbert et al., 2000; McNally, 1999). In sum, Barlow (2002) concluded that the rationale for EMDR, and the claims made for its value, have not gathered scientific support. McNally's conclusion was more acerbic: "What is effective in EMDR is not new, and what is new (eye movements) is not effective" (McNally, 1999, p. 2).

Suggested reading

There are several excellent accounts of "anxiety and its disorders" and of methods for overcoming these difficulties. These advanced texts include Barlow's (2002) *Anxiety and its disorders*, Brewin's (2003) *Post-traumatic stress disorder – malady or myth?*, D A Clark's (2003) *Cognitive-behaviour therapy for OCD*, D M Clark and Fairburn's (1997) *The science and practice of cognitive behaviour therapy*, Craske's (1999) *Anxiety disorders*, Hawton, Salkovskis, Kirk, and Clark's (1989) *Cognitive behaviour therapy for psychiatric problems*, McLean and Woody's (2001) *Anxiety disorders in adults*, McNally's (1994) *Panic disorder*, Menzies and de Silva's (2003) *Obsessive compulsive disorders*, Resick's (2001) *Stress and trauma* among others. Also, Kafka's *The trial*.

The emphasis of the present book is on anxiety as a psychological phenomenon.

References

Abraham, K. (1927). *Selected papers.* London: Hogarth Press.

Acierno, R., & Cahill, S. (Eds.) (1999). Advances in conceptualization and research into the efficacy and mechanism of EMDR. *Journal of Anxiety Disorders, 13,* 1–236.

Acierno, R. E., Hersen, M., & Van Hasselt, V. B. (1993). Interventions for panic disorder: A critical review of the literature. *Clinical Psychology Review, 13,* 561–578.

Agras, S., Sylvester, D., & Oliveau, D. (1969). The epidemiology of common fears and phobias. *Comprehensive Psychiatry, 10,* 151–156.

Akhtar, S., Wig, N., Verma, N., Pershad, D., & Verma, S. K. (1975). A phenomenological analysis of symptoms in obsessive-compulsive neurosis. *British Journal of Psychiatry, 127,* 342–348.

Arntz, A. (2003). Cognitive therapy versus applied relaxation as treatments of GAD. *Behaviour Research and Therapy, 41,* 633–646.

Arrindell, W. A., Cox, B. J., Van der Ende, J., & Kwee, M. G. T. (1995). Phobic dimensions – II. Cross-national confirmation of the multidimensional structure underlying the Mobility Inventory (MI). *Behaviour Research and Therapy, 33,* 711–724.

Austin, D., & Richards, J. (2001). The catastrophic misinterpretation model of panic disorder. *Behaviour Research and Therapy, 39,* 1277–1292.

Aylward, E. H., Harris, G. J., Hoehn-Saric, R., Barta, P. E., Machlin, S. R., & Pearlson, P. D. (1996). Normal caudate nucleus in obsessive-compulsive disorder assessed by quantitative neuroimaging. *Archives of General Psychiatry, 53,* 577–584.

Baker, T. B., Cannon, D. S., Tiffany, S. T., & Gino, A. (1984). Cardiac response as an index of the effect of aversion therapy. *Behaviour Research and Therapy, 22,* 403–411.

Ballenger J., McDonald, S., Noyes, R., Rickels, K., Sussman, N., & Woods, S. (1988). Alprazolam in panic disorder and agoraphobia: Results from a multicenter trial. Efficacy in short-term treatment. *Archives of General Psychiatry, 45,* 413–422.

Bancroft, J. (1989). *Human sexuality and its problems* (2nd ed.). Edinburgh: Churchill Livingstone.

Bandura, A. (1969). *The principles of behavior modification.* New York: Holt, Rinehart, and Winston.

Bandura, A. (1977). *Social learning theory.* New York: Prentice Hall.

Barlow, D. H. (1988). *Anxiety and its disorders: The nature and treatment of anxiety and panic.* New York: Guilford Press.

Barlow, D. H. (2002). *Anxiety and its disorders* (2nd ed.). New York: Guilford Press.

Barlow, D. H., & Craske, M. (1988). The phenomenology of panic. In S. Rachman & J. Maser (Eds.), *Panic: Psychological perspectives*. Hillsdale, NJ: Lawrence Erlbaum Associates Inc.

Beck, A. T., & Clark, D. A. (1997). An information processing model of anxiety. *Behaviour Research and Therapy, 35*, 49–58.

Beck, A. T., & Emery, G. (with Greenberg, R.) (1985). *Anxiety disorders and phobias: A cognitive perspective*. New York: Basic Books.

Beck, A. T. & Rush, A. J. (1985). A cognitive model of anxiety formation and anxiety resolution. Special issue: Stress and anxiety. *Issues in Mental Health Nursing, 7*, 349–365.

Beech, H. R. (1971). Ritualistic activity in obsessional patients. *Journal of Psychosomatic Research, 17*, 417–422.

Beech, H. R. (Ed.) (1974). *Obsessional states*. London: Methuen.

Booth, R., & Rachman, S. (1992). The reduction of claustrophobia: I. *Behaviour Research and Therapy, 30*, 207–221.

Boring, E. G. (1991). The history of introspection: II. [Trans. A. V. Roshchin and I. V. Tverdovskiy]. *Vestnik Moskovskogo Universiteta – Seriya 14: Psikhologiya, 3*, 54–63.

Borkovec, T. D., & Costello, E. (1993). Efficacy of applied relaxation and cognitive-behavior therapy in the treatment of generalized anxiety disorder. *Journal of Consulting and Clinical Psychology, 61*, 611–619.

Bower, G. H. (1981). Mood and memory. *American Psychologist, 36*, 129–148.

Bradley, B. P., Mogg, K., & Williams, R. (1995). Implicit and explicit memory for emotion-congruent information in clinical depression and anxiety. *Behaviour Research and Therapy, 33*, 755–770.

Bregman, E. (1934). An attempt to modify the emotional attitudes of infants by the conditioned response technique. *Journal of Genetic Psychology, 45*, 169–196.

Brewin, C. R. (1988). *Cognitive foundations of clinical psychology*. London: Lawrence Erlbaum Ltd.

Brewin, C. R. (1996). Theoretical foundations of cognitive-behavior therapy for anxiety and depression. *Annual Review of Psychology, 47*, 33–57.

Brewin, C. (2001). A cognitive neuroscience account of PTSD and its treatment. *Behaviour Research and Therapy, 39*, 373–393.

Brewin, C. (2003). *Post-traumatic stress disorder: Malady or myth?* New Haven, Yale University Press.

Brewin, C., Andrews, B., & Rose, S. (2003). Diagnostic overlap between acute stress disorder and PTSD in victims of violent crime. *American Journal of Psychiatry, 160*, 783–785.

Brewin, C, & Holmes, E. (2003). Psychological theories of PTSD. *Clinical Psychology Review, 23*, 339–376.

Broadbent, D. E. (1958). *Perception and communication*. New York: Pergamon Press.

Broadbent, D. E. (1971). *Decision and stress*. London: Academic Press.

Bryant, R., & Harvey, A. (1997). Acute stress disorder – a critical review of diagnostic issues. *Clinical Psychology Review, 17*, 757–773.

Burish, T. G., & Carey, M. P. (1986). Conditioned aversive responses in cancer chemotherapy patients: Theoretical and developmental analysis. *Journal of Consulting and Clinical Psychology, 54*, 593–600.

Butler, G., Fennell, M., Robson, P., & Gelder, M. (1991). A comparison of behavior therapy and cognitive behavior therapy in the treatment of generalised anxiety disorder. *Journal of Consulting and Clinical Psychology, 59*, 167–175.

Butler, G., & Mathews, A. (1983). Cognitive processes in anxiety.

Advances in Behaviour Research and Therapy, 5, 51–62.

Cairns, E., & Wilson, R. (1984). The impact of political violence on mild psychiatric morbidity in Northern Ireland. *British Journal of Psychiatry, 145,* 631–635.

Carter, M. M., Hollon, S. D., Carson, R., & Shelton, R. C. (1995). Effects of a safe person on induced stress following a biological challenge in panic disorder with agoraphobia. *Journal of Abnormal Psychology, 104,* 156–163.

Cella, D. F., Pratt, A., & Holland, J. C. (1986). Persistent anticipatory nausea, vomiting and anxiety in cured Hodgkin's disease patients after completion of chemotherapy. *American Journal of Psychiatry, 143,* 641–643.

Ceschi, G., van der Linden, M., Dunker, D., Perroud, A., & Bredarts, R. (2003). Further exploration of memory bias in compulsive washers. *Behaviour Research and Therapy, 41,* 737–748.

Chambless, D., & Gillis, M. (1993). Cognitive therapy of anxiety disorders. Special section: Recent developments in cognitive and constructivist psychotherapies. *Journal of Consulting and Clinical Psychology, 61,* 248–260.

Chambless, D., & Hope, D. (1996). Cognitive approaches to the psychopathology and treatment of social phobia. In P. Salkovskis (Ed.), *The frontiers of cognitive therapy.* New York: Guilford Press.

Claparede, M. (1911). Recognition et moiite. *Archives de Psychologie Geneve, 11,* 79–90.

Clark, D. A. (2003). *Cognitive-behaviour therapy for OCD.* New York: Guilford Press.

Clark, D. M. (1986). A cognitive approach to panic. *Behaviour Research and Therapy, 24,* 461–470.

Clark, D. M. (1987). A cognitive approach to panic: Theory and data. *Proceedings of the 140th Annual Meeting of the American Psychiatric Association,* Chicago.

Clark, D. M. (1988). A cognitive model of panic attacks. In S. Rachman & J. Maser (Eds.), *Panic: Psychological perspectives.* Hillsdale, NJ: Lawrence Erlbaum Associates Inc.

Clark, D. M. (1989). Anxiety states: Panic and generalised anxiety. In K. Hawton, P. Salkovskis, J. Kirk et al. (Eds.), *Cognitive behaviour therapy for psychiatric problems: A practical guide.* Oxford: Oxford Medical Publications.

Clark, D. M. (1996). Panic disorder: From theory to therapy. In P. Salkovskis (Ed.), *The frontiers of cognitive therapy.* New York: Guilford Press.

Clark, D. M. (1997). Panic disorder and social phobia. In D. M. Clark & C. Fairburn (Eds.), *Science and practice of cognitive behaviour therapy.* Oxford: Oxford University Press.

Clark, D. M. (1999). Anxiety disorders: why they persist and how to treat them. *Behaviour Research and Therapy, 37,* S5–S27.

Clark, D. M., Ehlers, A., Fennell, M., Hackmann, A., McManus, F., & Waddington, L. (2003). Cognitive therapy versus fluoxetine in generalized social phobia. *Journal of Consulting and Clinical Psychology* (in press).

Clark, D. M., & Fairburn, C. (Eds.) (1997). *Science and practice of cognitive behaviour therapy.* Oxford: Oxford University Press.

Clark, D. M., & McManus, F. (2002). Information processing in social phobia. *Biological Psychiatry, 51,* 92–100.

Clark, D. M., Salkovskis, P., & Anastasiades, P. (1990, November). Cognitive mediation of lactate-induced panic. In R. M. Rapee (Chair), *Experimental investigations of panic disorder.* Symposium conducted at the meeting of the Association for the Advancement of Behavior Therapy, San Francisco.

Clark, D. M., Salkovskis, P., Hackmann,

A., Middleton, H., Anastasiades, P., & Gelder, M. (1994). A comparison of cognitive therapy, applied relaxation, and imipramine in the treatment of panic disorder. *British Journal of Psychiatry, 165,* 557–559.

Clark, D. M., & Wells, A. (1995). A cognitive model of social phobia. In R. G. Heimberg, M. R. Liebowitz, D. A. Hope, & F. R. Schneier (Eds.), *Social phobia: Diagnosis, assessment and treatment.* New York: Guilford Press.

Cloitre, M., Heimberg, R. G., Holt, C. S., & Liebowitz, M. R. (1992). Reaction time to threat stimuli in panic disorder and social phobia. *Behaviour Research and Therapy, 30,* 609–617.

Cloitre, M., & Liebowitz, M. R. (1991). Memory bias in panic disorder: An investigation of the cognitive avoidance hypothesis. *Cognitive Therapy and Research, 15,* 371–386.

Coles, M., & Heimberg, R. (2002). Memory biases in the anxiety disorders. *Clinical Psychology Review, 22,* 587–627.

Constans, J. I., Foa, E. B., Franklin, M. E., & Mathews, A. (1995). Memory for actual and imagined events in OC checkers. *Behaviour Research and Therapy, 33,* 665–671.

Cook, E. W., Melamed, B. G., Cuthbert, B. N., McNeil, D. W., & Lang, P. J. (1988). Emotional imagery and the differential diagnosis of anxiety. *Journal of Consulting and Clinical Psychology, 56,* 734–740.

Cooper, P. J., & Steere, J. (1995). A comparison of two psychological treatments for bulimia nervosa: Implications for models of maintenance. *Behaviour Research and Therapy, 33,* 875–886.

Costello, C. G. (1982). Fears and phobias in women: A community study. *Journal of Abnormal Psychology, 91,* 280–286.

Cote, G., & Barlow, D. (1993). Effective psychological treatment of panic disorder. In T. R. Giles (Ed.), *Handbook of effective psychotherapy.* New York: Plenum Press.

Craske, M. (1999). *Anxiety disorders.* Boulder, CO: Westview Press.

Craske, M. G., Sanderson, W. C., & Barlow, D. H. (1987). The relationships among panic, fear and avoidance. *Journal of Anxiety Disorders, 1,* 153–160.

Curtis, R. C., & Miller, K. (1986). Believing another likes or dislikes you: Behaviors making the beliefs come true. *Journal of Personality and Social Psychology, 51,* 284–290.

Cuthbert, B., & Lang, P. (1989). Imagery, memory and emotion. In G. Turpin (Ed.), *Handbook of clinical psychophysiology.* Chichester: Wiley.

Dalgleish, T. (1994). The relationship between anxiety and memory biases for material that has been selectively processed in a prior task. *Behaviour Research and Therapy, 32,* 227–231.

Davey, G. (1988). Dental phobias and anxieties. *Behaviour Research & Therapy, 27,* 51–58.

Deffenbacher, J. L. (1978). Worry, emotionality and task-generated interference in test anxiety: An empirical test of attentional theory. *Journal of Educational Psychology, 70,* 248–254.

de Silva, P., & Rachman, S. (1984). Does escape behaviour strengthen agoraphobic avoidance? A preliminary study. *Behaviour Research and Therapy, 22,* 87–91.

de Silva, P., & Rachman, S. (1992). *Obsessive compulsive disorders: The facts.* Oxford: Oxford University Press.

de Silva, P., & Rachman, S. (2004). *Obsessive compulsive disorders: The facts* (3rd ed.). Oxford: Oxford University Press.

Devilly, G., & Spence, S. (1999). The relative efficacy and treatment distress of EMDR and a cognitive-behavior treatment protocol in the amelioration of PTSD. *Journal of Anxiety Disorders, 13,* 131–157.

Dickinson, A. (1987). Animal conditioning and learning theory. In H. J. Eysenck & I. Martin (Eds.), *Theoretical foundations of behaviour therapy* (pp. 45–61). New York: Plenum Press.

di Nardo, P. A., Guzy, L. T., & Bak, R. M. (1988). Anxiety response patterns and etiological factors in dog-fearful and nonfearful subjects. *Behaviour Research and Therapy, 21,* 245–252.

Dixon, N. F. (1981). *Preconscious processing.* Chichester: Wiley.

Dugas, M., Gagnon, F., Ladouceur, R., & Freeston, M. (1998). Generalized anxiety disorder – a test of a conceptual model. *Behaviour Research and Therapy, 36,* 215–226.

Durham, R. C., Murphy, T., Allan, T., Richard, K., Treliving, L., & Fenton, G. (1994). Cognitive therapy, analytic psychotherapy and anxiety management training for generalised anxiety disorder. *British Journal of Psychiatry, 165,* 315–323.

Edelmann, R. J. (1992). *Anxiety: Theory, research and intervention in clinical and health psychology.* Chichester: Wiley.

Ehlers, A. (1992). Interoception and panic disorder. *Advances in Behaviour Research and Therapy, 115,* 3–21.

Ehlers, A., & Clark, D. M. (2000). A cognitive model of PTSD. *Behaviour Research and Therapy, 38,* 319–345.

Ehlers, A., Clark, D. M., Hackmann, A., McManus, F., & Fennell, M. (2004). Cognitive therapy for PTSD: Development and evaluation. *Behaviour Research and Therapy* (in press).

Ehlers, A., Margraf, J., & Roth, W. T. (1988). Selective information processing, interoception, and panic attacks. In I. Hand & H.-U. Wittchen (Eds.), *Panic and phobias 2. Treatment and variables affecting course and outcome.* Berlin: Springer-Verlag.

Eich, E., & Macaulay, D. (2000). Fundamental factors in mood dependent memory. In J. Forgas (Ed.), *Feeling and Thinking.* New York: Cambridge University Press.

Eysenck, H. J. (1957). *The dynamics of anxiety and hysteria.* London: Routledge.

Eysenck, H. J. (Ed.) (1960). *Behavior therapy and the neuroses.* Oxford: Pergamon Press.

Eysenck, H. J. (1967). *The biological basis of personality.* Springfield, IL: Thomas.

Eysenck, H. J. (1985). *Decline and fall of the Freudian empire.* London: Penguin Books.

Eysenck, H. J., & Rachman, S. (1965). *The causes and cures of neurosis.* London: Routledge and Kegan Paul.

Eysenck, H. J., Wakefield Jr., J. A., & Friedman, A. F. (1983). Diagnosis and clinical assessment: The DSM-III. *Annual Review of Psychology, 34,* 167–193.

Eysenck, M. W. (1992). *Anxiety: The cognitive perspective.* Hove, UK: Lawrence Erlbaum Ltd.

Fenz, W., & Epstein, S. (1967). Gradients of physiological arousal in parachutists. *Psychosomatic Medicine, 29,* 33–51.

Field, A., Argyris, N., & Knowles, K. (2001). Who's afraid of the big bad wolf: A prospective paradigm to test Rachman's indirect pathways in children. *Behaviour Research and Therapy, 39,* 1259–1276.

Flanagan, J. (Ed.) (1948). The Aviation Psychology Program in the Army Air Forces. *USAAF aviation psychology research report No. 1.* Washington, DC: US Government Printing Office.

Foa, E., Keane, T., & Friedman, M. (Eds.) (2000). *Effective treatments for PTSD.* New York: Guilford Press.

Foa, E. B., & Kozak, M. J. (1986). Emotional processing of fear: Exposure to corrective information. *Psychological Bulletin, 99,* 20–35.

Foa, E. B., Kozak, M. J., Steketee, G. S., & McCarthy, P. R. (1992). Treatment of depressive and obsessive-compulsive symptoms in OCD by imipramine and behaviour therapy. *British Journal of Clinical Psychology, 31,* 279–292.

Foa, E. B., Steketee, G. S., Kozak, M. J., & Dugger, D. (1987). Effects of imipramine on depression and obsessive-compulsive symptoms. *Psychiatry Research, 21,* 123–136.

Follette, W. C. (1996). Introduction to the special section on the development of theoretically coherent alternatives to the DSM system. *Journal of Consulting and Clinical Psychology, 64,* 1117–1119.

Follette, W. C., & Houts, A. C. (1996). Models of scientific progress and the role of theory in taxonomy development: A case study of the DSM. *Journal of Consulting and Clinical Psychology, 64,* 1120–1132.

Frances, A., First, M. B., & Pincus, H. A. (1995). *DSM-IV guidebook.* Washington DC: American Psychiatric Press.

Freeston, M. H., Ladouceur, R., Gagnon, F., Thibodeau, N., Rheaume, J., Letarte, H., & Bujold, A. (1997). Cognitive behavioral treatment of obsessive thoughts. *Journal of Consulting and Clinical Psychology, 65,* 405–413.

Freud, S. (1905). *On psychotherapy.* London: Hogarth Press.

Freud, S. (1910). Reprinted in J. Rickman (Ed.), *General Selection from Works of Freud.* London: Hogarth Press.

Freud, S. (Ed.) (1948). *An autobiographical study.* London: Hogarth Press.

Freud, S. (1949). *Introductory lectures on psycho-analysis.* London: George Allen and Unwin Ltd.

Freud, S. (1950). The analysis of a phobia in a five-year-old boy. *Collected papers of Freud, Vol. 3.* London: Hogarth Press.

Freud, S. (1953). *A general selection from the works of Sigmund Freud.* In J. Rickman (Ed.). London: Hogarth Press.

Frost, R., & Hartl, M. (2003). Compulsive hoarding. In R. Menzies & P. de Silva (Eds.), *Obsessive compulsive disorders.* Chichester: Wiley.

Fyer, A. J. (1987). Simple phobia. *Modern Problems of Pharmacopsychiatry, 22,* 174–192.

Gerull, F., & Rapee, R. (2002). Mother knows best. *Behaviour Research and Therapy, 40,* 279–287.

Giles, T. R. (1993). *Handbook of effective psychotherapy.* New York: Plenum Press.

Gillespie, K., Duffy, M., Hackmann, A., & Clark, D. M. (2002). Community-based cognitive therapy in the treatment of PTSD following the Omagh bomb. *Behaviour Research and Therapy, 40,* 345–358.

Goldstein, A., de Beurs, E., Chambless, D., & Wilson, K. (2000). EMDR for panic disorder and agoraphobia. *Journal of Consulting Clinical Psychology, 68,* 947–956.

Gorman, J. (1987). Panic disorders. In D. Klein (Ed.), *Anxiety.* Basel: Karger.

Gray, J. A. (1971). *The psychology of fear and stress.* London: World University Library.

Gray, J. A. (1982). *The neuropsychology of anxiety: An enquiry into the functions of the septo-hippocampal system.* Oxford: Oxford University Press.

Gray, J. A. (1986). The neuropsychology of anxiety. In C. D. Spielberger & I. G. Sarason (Eds.), *Stress and anxiety.* Washington: Hemisphere Publishing.

Gray, J. A. (1987). *Psychology of fear and stress* (2nd ed.). Cambridge: Cambridge University Press.

Grinker, R., & Spiegel, J. (1945). *Men under stress.* Philadelphia: Blakiston; London: Churchill Livingstone.

Grunbaum, A. (1977). Is psychoanalysis a pseudo-science? In R. Stern, L. Horowitz & J. Lynes (Eds.), *Science and psychotherapy.* New York: Raven Press.

Hackmann, A., Clark, D. M., & McManus, F. (2000). Recurrent images and early memories in social phobia. *Behaviour Research and Therapy, 38,* 601–610.

Hall, G. S. (1897). A study of fears. *The American Journal of Psychology, 8,* 147–249.

Hallam, R. S. (1978). Agoraphobia: A criticial review of the concept. *British Journal of Psychiatry, 133,* 314–319.

Hallam, R. S. (1985). *Anxiety: Psychological perspectives on panic and agoraphobia.* London: Academic Press.

Halligan, S., Michael, T., Clark, D., & Ehlers, A. (2003). PTSD following assault. *Journal of Consulting and Clinical Psychology, 71,* 419–431.

Hammersley, D. (1957). Conditioned reflex therapy. In R. Wallerstein (Ed.), *Hospital Treatment of Alcoholism. Menninger Clinic Monographs,* 11.

Harlow, H. (1954). Motivational forces underlying learning. *Learning Theory, Personality Theory and Clinical Research — Kentucky Symposium.* New York: Wiley.

Harvey, A., & Bryant, R. (2002). Acute stress disorder: A synthesis and critique. *Psychological Bulletin, 128,* 886–902.

Harvey, A., Bryant, R., & Tarrier, N. (2003). Sleep and PTSD. *Clinical Psychology Review, 23,* 377–418.

Harvey, A. G., & Rapee, R. M. (1995). Cognitive-behavior therapy for generalized anxiety disorder. *Psychiatric Clinics of North America, 18,* 859–870.

Hawton, K., Salkovskis, P., Kirk, J., & Clark, D. M. (Eds.) (1989). *Cognitive behaviour therapy for psychiatric problems.* Oxford: Oxford University Press.

Heimberg, R. G. (1996). Social phobia, avoidant personality disorder and the multiaxial conceptualization of interpersonal anxiety. In P. Salkovskis (Ed.), *Trends in cognitive and behavioural therapies.* Chichester: Wiley.

Heimberg, R. G., Liebowitz, M. R., Hope, D. A., & Schneier, F. R. (1995). *Social phobia: Diagnosis, assessment and treatment.* New York: Guilford Press.

Herbert, J., Lilienfeld, S., Lohr, J.,

Montgomery, R., O'Donohue, W., Rosen, G., & Tolin, D. (2000). Science and pseudo-science in the development of EMDR. *Clinical Psychology Review, 20,* 945–971.

Hibbert, G. A. (1984). Ideational components of anxiety: Their origin and content. *British Journal of Psychiatry, 144,* 618–624.

Hirsch, C., Clark, D. M., Mathews, A., & Williams, R., (2003). Self-images play a causal role in social phobia. *Behaviour Research and Therapy, 41,* 909–922.

Hofmann, S., & Barlow, D. (2002). Social phobia. In Barlow, D. (Ed.), *Anxiety and its disorders.* New York: Guilford Press.

Hollander, E., & Liebowitz, M. R. (1990). Treatment of depersonalization with serotonin reuptake blockers. *Journal of Clinical Psychopharmacology, 10,* 200–203.

Hope, D. A., Holt, C. S., & Heimberg, R. (1993). Social phobia. In T. R. Giles (Ed.), *Handbook of effective psychotherapy.* New York: Plenum Press.

Horowitz, M. (1975). Intrusive and repetitive thoughts after experimental stress. *Archives of General Psychiatry, 32,* 1457–1463.

Horwath, E., Lish, J. D., Johnson, J., Hornig, C. D., & Weismann, M. M. (1993). Agoraphobia without panic: Clinical reappraisal of an epidemiologic finding. *American Journal of Psychiatry, 150,* 1496–1501.

Ingram, R. E. (1990). Self-focused attention in clinical disorders: Review and a conceptual model. *Psychological Bulletin, 107,* 156–176.

Insel, T. R. (1988). Obsessive-compulsive disorder: A neuroethological perspective. *Psychopharmacology Bulletin, 24,* 365–369.

Insel, T. R. (1991). Has OCD research gone to the dogs? *Neuropsychopharmacology, 5,* 13–17.

Insel, T. R., & Winslow, J. T. (1992). Neurobiology of obsessive compulsive disorder. *Psychiatric Clinics of North America*, 15, 813–824.

Janis, J. L. (1951). *Air war and emotional stress*. New York: McGraw-Hill.

Jaspers, K. (1963). *General psychopathology* [J. Hoenig and M. W. Hamilton, Trans.]. Manchester, UK: Manchester University Press. (Original work published 1959.)

Jenike, M. A., Baer, L., & Greist, J. H. (1990). Clomipramine versus fluvoxetine in obsessive-compulsive disorder: A retrospective comparison of side-effects and efficacy. *Journal of Clinical Psychopharmacology*, 10, 122–124.

Jenkins, R. (2002). *Churchill: A biography*. London: Penguin Books.

Johnston, M. (1980). Anxiety in surgical patients. *Psychological Medicine*, 10, 145–152.

Jones, E. (1954). *Sigmund Freud: Life and works, Vol. I*. London: Hogarth Press.

Jones, M. C. (1924). A laboratory study of fear. *Pedagogical Seminars*, 31, 308–315.

Juster, H. R., & Heimberg, R. G. (1995). Social phobia. Longitudinal course and long-term outcome of cognitive-behavioral treatment. *Psychiatric Clinics of North America*, 18, 821–842.

Kafka, F. (1977). *The Trial* (original work published 1925), English Edition. London: Pan Books.

Kahneman, D., & Triesman, A. (1983). The cost of visual filtering. *Journal of Experimental Psychology: Human Perception and Performance*, 9, 497–509.

Kahneman, D., Triesman, A., & Burkell, J. (1983). The cost of visual filtering. *Journal of Experimental Psychology: Human Perception and Performance*, 9, 510–522.

Kazdin, A. E. (1978). *History of behaviour modification*. Baltimore: University Park Press.

Kincey, J., Statham, S., & McFarlane, T. (1991). Women undergoing colposcopy: Their satisfaction with communication, health knowledge and level of anxiety. *Health Education Journal*, 50, 70–71.

Kirk, S. A., & Kutchins, H. (1992). *The selling of DSM: The rhetoric of science in psychiatry*. New York: Aldine de Gruyther.

Kirkpatrick, D. R. (1984). Age, gender, and patterns of common intense fears among adults. *Behaviour Research and Therapy*, 22, 141–150.

Klein, D. (1987). Anxiety reconceptualized. In D. Klein (Ed.), *Anxiety*. Basel: Karger.

Klein, D. (1993). False suffocation alarms, spontaneous panics, and related conditions: An integrative hypothesis. *Archives of General Psychiatry*, 50, 306–317.

Klein, D. (1994). "Klein's suffocation theory of panic": Reply. *Archives of General Psychiatry*, 51, 506.

Klein, D. (1996). A reply. [Reply following the article, "Panic attacks: Klein's false suffocation alarm, Taylor and Rachman's data, and Ley's dyspneic fear theory".] *Archives of General Psychiatry*, 52, 83–84.

Klein, D., & Klein, H. (1989). The nosology of anxiety disorders: A critical review of hypothesis testing about spontaneous panic. In P. Tyrer (Ed.), *Psychopharmacology of anxiety*. Oxford: Oxford University Press.

Klein, D. F., Zitrin, C. M., & Woerner, M. G. (1977). Imipramine and phobia [proceedings]. *Psychopharmacology Bulletin*, 13, 24–27.

Klerman, G. L. (1985). Diagnosis of psychiatric disorders in epidemiological field studies. *Archives of General Psychiatry*, 42, 723–724.

Lader, M. (1994). Treatment of anxiety. *British Medical Journal*, 309, 321–324.

Ladouceur, R., Dugas, M., Freeston, M., Leger, E., Gagnon, F., & Thibodeau, N. (2000). Efficacy of cognitive behavioral therapy for GAD. *Journal of Consulting and Clinical Psychology*, 68, 957–964.

Lang, P. (1970). Stimulus control, response

control and desensitization of fear. In D. Levis (Ed.), *Learning approaches to therapeutic behaviour change*. Chicago: Aldine Press.

Lang, P. (1977). Imagery in therapy: An information processing analysis of fear. *Behavior Therapy, 8*, 862–886.

Lang, P. (1985). The cognitive psychophysiology of emotion: Fear and anxiety. In A. Tuma & J. Maser (Eds.), *Anxiety and the anxiety disorders*. Hillsdale, NJ: Lawrence Erlbaum Associates Inc.

Lang, P. J., Levin, D. N., Miller, G. A., & Kozak, M. J. (1983). Fear behavior, fear imagery, and the psychophysiology of emotion: The problem of affective response integration. *Journal of Abnormal Psychology, 92*, 276–306.

Lang, P., Melamed, B., & Hart, J. (1970). A psychophysiological analysis of fear modification using an automated desensitization technique. *Journal of Abnormal Psychology, 76*, 220–234.

Last, C. G. (1987). Simple phobias. In L. Michelson & M. Ascher (Eds.), *Anxiety and stress disorders*. New York: Guilford Press.

Lautch, H. (1971). Dental phobia. *British Journal of Psychiatry, 119*, 151–158.

Lazarus, R. S. (1966). *Psychological stress and the coping process*. New York: McGraw-Hill.

Leon, A. C., Marzuk, P. M., & Portera, L. (1995). More reliable outcome measures can reduce sample size requirements. *Archives of General Psychiatry, 52*, 867–871.

Lewis, A. (1942). Incidence of neurosis in England under war conditions. *Lancet, 2*, 175–183.

Lewis, A. (1980). Problems presented by the ambiguous word "anxiety" as used in psychopathology. In G. D. Burrows & B. Davies (Eds.), *Handbook of studies on anxiety*. Amsterdam: Elsevier/North-Holland.

Ley, R. (1994). The "suffocation alarm" theory of panic attacks: A critical commentary. *Journal of Behavior Therapy and Experimental Psychiatry, 25*, 269–273.

Lohr, J., Tolin, D., & Lilienfeld, S. (1998). Eye movement desensitization and reprocessing. *Journal of Anxiety Disorders, 13*, 185–207.

Mackintosh, N. J. (1983). *Conditioning and associative learning*. New York: Oxford University Press.

MacLeod, C., & Cohen, I. L. (1993). Anxiety and the interpretation of ambiguity: A text comprehension study. *Journal of Abnormal Psychology, 102*, 238–247.

Mannuzza, S., Schneier, F. R., Chapman, T. F., Liebowitz, M. R., Klein, D., & Fyer, A. (1995). Generalized social phobia: Reliability and validity. *Archives of General Psychiatry, 52*, 230–237.

Margraf, J. (1993). Hyperventilation and panic disorder: A psychophysiological connection. *Advances in Behavior Research and Therapy, 15*, 49–74.

Margraf, J., Barlow, D. H., Clark, D. M., & Telch, M. J. (1993). Psychological treatment of panic: Work in progress on outcome, active ingredients, and follow-up. *Behaviour Research and Therapy, 31*, 1–8.

Margraf, J., Ehlers, A., & Roth, W. (1986). Panic attacks: Theoretical models and empirical evidence. In I. Hand & H. Wittchen (Eds.), *Panic and phobia*. Berlin: Springer.

Marks, I. M. (1969). *Fears and phobias*. London: Heinemann.

Marks, I. M. (1987). *Fears, phobias, and rituals*. Oxford: Oxford University Press.

Marks, I. M., Swinson, R. P., Basoglu, M., Kuch, K., Noshirvani, H., & O'Sullivan, G. (1993). Alprazolam and exposure alone and combined in panic disorder with agoraphobia. *British Journal of Psychiatry, 162*, 776–787.

Marks, I., Lovell, K., Noshirvani, H., &

Livanou, M. (1998). Treatment of PTSD by exposure and/or cognitive restructuring. *Archives of General Psychiatry, 55,* 317–325.

Marks, M. (2003). Cognitive treatment for OCD. In R. Menzies, & P. de Silva (Eds.), *Obsessive compulsive disorders.* Chichester: Wiley.

Marks, M. P., Basoglu, M., Alkubaisy, T., Sengun, S., & Marks, I. M. (1991). Are anxiety symptoms and catastrophic cognitions directly related? *Journal of Anxiety Disorders, 5,* 247–254.

Masters, W. H., & Johnson, V. E. (1970). *Human sexual inadequacy.* Boston, MA: Little, Brown.

Mathews, A., Gelder, M. G., & Johnston D. W. (1981). *Agoraphobia: Nature and treatment.* New York: Guilford Press.

Mathews, A., & MacLeod, C. (1994). Cognitive approaches to emotion and emotional disorders. *Annual Review of Psychology, 45,* 25–50.

Mathews, A., MacLeod, C., & Tata, P. R. (1987). An information-processing approach to anxiety. *Journal of Cognitive Psychotherapy, 1,* 105–115.

Mathews, A., Mogg, K., May, J., & Eysenck, M. (1989). Implicit and explicit memory bias in anxiety. *Journal of Abnormal Psychology, 98,* 236–240.

Mavissakalian, M. (1983). Antidepressants in the treatment of agoraphobia and obsessive-compulsive disorder. *Comprehensive Psychiatry, 24,* 278–284.

Mayou, R., Ehlers, A., & Bryant, B. (2002). PTSD after motor vehicle accidents. *Behaviour Research and Therapy, 40,* 665–675.

McEwan, K. L., & Devins, G. M. (1983). Is increased arousal in social anxiety noticed by others? *Journal of Abnormal Psychology, 92,* 417–421.

McGuire, P. K. (1995). The brain in obsessive-compulsive disorder. *Journal of Neurology, Neurosurgery and Psychiatry, 59,* 457–459.

McLean, P., & Woody, S. (2001). *Anxiety disorders in adults.* New York: Oxford University Press.

McMillan, T. M., & Rachman, S. (1988). Fearlessness and courage in paratroopers undergoing training. *Personality and Individual Differences, 9,* 373–378.

McNally, R. J. (1987). Preparedness and phobias: A review. *Psychological Bulletin, 101,* 283–303.

McNally, R. J. (1994). *Panic disorder: A critical analysis.* New York: Guilford Press.

McNally, R. J. (1995). Automaticity and the anxiety disorders. *Behaviour Research and Therapy, 33,* 127–131.

McNally, R. (1999). Research on EMDR as a treatment for PTSD. *PTSD Research Quarterly, 10,* 1–7.

McNally, R. J., Hornig, C. D., & Donnell, C. D. (1995). Clinical versus nonclinical panic: A test of suffocation false alarm theory. *Behaviour Research and Therapy, 33,* 127–132.

McNally, R., Lasko, N., Macklin, M., & Pitman, R. (1995). Autobiographical memory disturbance in combat-related PTSD. *Behaviour Research and Therapy, 33,* 619–630.

Menzies, R., & de Silva, P. (Eds.) (2003). *Obsessive compulsive disorders.* Chichester: Wiley.

Merckelbach, H., de Jong, P., Muris, P., & Van den Hout, M. (1996). The etiology of specific phobias: A review. *Clinical Psychology Review, 16,* 337–361.

Miller, N. E. (1960). Learning resistance to pain and fear. *Journal of Experimental Psychology, 60,* 137–142.

Mineka, S. (1985). Animal models of anxiety-based disorders. In A. Tuma & J. Maser (Eds.), *Anxiety and the anxiety disorders.* Hillsdale, NJ: Lawrence Erlbaum Associates Inc.

Mowrer, O. H. (1939). Stimulus response theory of anxiety. *Psychological Review, 46,* 553–565.

Mowrer, O. H. (1960). *Learning theory and behavior.* New York: Wiley.

Muris, P., Bodden, D., Merckelbach, H., Ollendick, T., & King, N. (2003). Fear of the beast. *Behaviour Research and Therapy, 41,* 195–208.

Newlove, T., & Rachman, S. (1994). *Discounting of praise by social phobics.* Unpublished manuscript.

Nisbett, R., & Ross, L. (1980). *Human inference: Strategies and shortcomings of social judgment.* Englewood Cliffs, NJ: Prentice-Hall.

Nisbett, R., & Wilson, T. (1977). Telling more than we can know: Verbal reports on mental processes. *Psychological Review, 84,* 231–259.

Norton, R., Cox, B., Asmundson, G., & Maser, J. (1995). The growth of research on anxiety disorders during the 1980's. *Journal of Anxiety Disorders, 9,* 75–85.

Ohman, A. (1987). Evolution, learning and phobias. In D. Magnusson & A. Ohman (Eds.), *Psychopathology.* New York: Academic Press.

Ohman, A., Erixon, G., & Lofberg, I. (1975). Phobias and preparedness: Phobic versus neutral pictures as continued stimuli for human autonomic responses. *Journal of Abnormal Psychology, 84,* 41–45.

Ollendick, T., & King, N. (1991). Origins of childrens' fears. *Behaviour Research and Therapy, 29,* 117–123.

Ost, L. G. (1985). Ways of acquiring phobias and outcome of behavioural treatments. *Behaviour Research and Therapy, 23,* 683–689.

Ost, L. G. (1987). Age of onset in different phobias. *Journal of Abnormal Psychology, 96,* 223–229.

Ost, L. G. (1989). One-session treatment for specific phobias. *Behaviour Research and Therapy, 27,* 1–8.

Ost, L. G. (1996). One-session group therapy of spider phobia: Direct vs. indirect treatments. *Behaviour Research and Therapy, 34,* 707–715.

Ost, L. G., & Hugdahl, K. (1983). Acquisition of agoraphobia, mode of onset and anxiety response patterns. *Behaviour Research and Therapy, 21,* 623–631.

Ost, L. G., & Westling, B. (1995). Applied relaxation vs. cognitive behavioural therapy in the treatment of panic disorder. *Behaviour Research and Therapy, 33,* 145–158.

Otto, M. W., Pollack, M. H., Meltzer-Brody, S., & Rosenbaum, J. F. (1992). Cognitive-behavior therapy for benzodiazepine discontinuation in panic disorder patients. *Psychopharmacology Bulletin, 28,* 123–130.

Otto, M. W., Pollack, M. H., & Sabatino, S. A. (1996). Maintenance of remission following cognitive behavior therapy for panic disorder: Possible deleterious effects of concurrent medication treatment. *Behavior Therapy, 27,* 473–482.

Palace, E. E., & Gorzalka, M. M. (1990). The enhancing effects of anxiety on arousal in sexually dysfunctional and functional women. *Journal of Abnormal Psychology, 99,* 403–411.

Parkinson, L., & Rachman, S. (1980). Speed of recovery from an uncontrived stress. In S. Rachman (Ed.), *Unwanted intrusive cognitions.* Oxford: Pergamon Press.

Paul, G. (1966). *Insight versus desensitization in psychotherapy.* Stanford, CA: Stanford University Press.

Pavlov, I. P. (1941). *Conditioned reflexes and psychiatry.* [Trans. W. H. Gantt.] New York: International Publishers.

Peterson, R. A., & Reiss, S. (1987). *Test manual for the Anxiety Sensitivity Index.* Orland Park, IL: International Diagnostic Systems.

Philips, C., & Rachman, S. (1996). *The psychological management of chronic pain.* New York: Springer.

Pigott, T. M., Myers, K. R., & Williams, D. A. (1996). Obsessive-compulsive disorder: A neuropsychiatric perspective. In R. Rapee (Ed.), *Current controversies in anxiety disorders*. New York: Guilford Press.

Pollard, C. A., & Henderson, J. G. (1988). Four types of social phobia in a community sample. *Journal of Nervous and Mental Disease, 176,* 440–445.

Poulton, R., & Menzies, R. (2002). Non-associative fear acquisition. *Behaviour Research and Therapy, 40,* 127–150.

Prigatano, G., & Johnson, H. (1974). Autonomic nervous system changes associated with a spider phobic reaction. *Journal of Abnormal Psychology, 83,* 169–177.

Proust, M. (1981 ed.). *Remembrance of things past. Vol. III.* Translated by C. Moncrieff & T. Kilmartin. London: Penguin Books.

Rachman, S. (1978). *Fear and courage.* San Francisco: W. H. Freeman.

Rachman, S. (1980). Emotional processing. *Behaviour Research and Therapy, 18,* 51–60.

Rachman, S. (1984). Agoraphobia: A safety signal perspective. *Behaviour Research and Therapy, 22,* 59–60.

Rachman, S. (1985). The treatment of anxiety disorders: A critique of the implications for psychopathology. In A. Tuma & J. Maser (Eds.), *Anxiety and the anxiety disorders.* Hillsdale NJ: Lawrence Erlbaum Associates Inc.

Rachman, S. (1990). *Fear and courage* (2nd ed.). New York: Freeman.

Rachman, S. (1991). Neo-conditioning and the classical theory of fear acquisition. *Clinical Psychology Review, 11,* 155–173.

Rachman, S. (1996). The evolution of cognitive behaviour therapy. In D. Clark & C. Fairburn (Eds.), *The science and practice of cognitive behaviour therapy.* Oxford: Oxford University Press.

Rachman, S. (2001). Emotional processing, with special reference to PTSD. *International Review of Psychiatry, 13,* 164–171.

Rachman, S. (2003a). *The treatment of obsessions.* Oxford: Oxford University Press.

Rachman, S. (2003b). Compulsive checking. In R. Menzies & P. de Silva (Eds.), *Obsessive compulsive disorders.* Chichester: Wiley.

Rachman, S., & Bichard, S. (1988). The overprediction of fear. *Clinical Psychology Review, 8,* 303–312.

Rachman, S., Cobb, C., Grey, S., McDonald, B., & Sartory, G. (1979). Behavioural treatments of obsessive-compulsive disorder with and without clomipramine. *Behaviour Research and Therapy, 17,* 467–478.

Rachman, S., Craske, M., Tallman, K., & Solyom, C. (1986). Does escape behavior strengthen agoraphobic avoidance? *Behavior Therapy, 17,* 366–384.

Rachman, S., & Cuk, M. (1992). Fearful distortions. *Behaviour Research and Therapy, 30,* 583–589.

Rachman, S., Gruter-Andrew, C., & Shafran, R. (2000). Post-event processing in social anxiety. *Behaviour Research and Therapy, 38,* 611–617.

Rachman, S., & Hodgson, R. (1980). *Obsessions and compulsions.* Englewood Cliffs, NJ: Prentice Hall.

Rachman, S., Levitt, K., & Lopatka, C. (1987). Panic – 1. The links between cognitions and bodily symptoms. *Behaviour Research and Therapy, 25,* 411–423.

Rachman, S., & Lopatka, C. (1986). Do fears summate? *Behaviour Research and Therapy, 24,* 653–660.

Rachman, S., & Taylor, S. (1993). Analyses of claustrophobia. *Journal of Anxiety Disorders, 7,* 281–291.

Rachman, S., & Whittal, M. L. (1989). Fast, slow and sudden reductions in fear. *Behaviour Research and Therapy, 27,* 613–620.

Rachman, S., & Wilson, G. T. (1980). *The effects of psychological therapy* (2nd ed.). Oxford: Pergamon Press.

Radomsky, A., & Rachman, S. (1999). Memory bias in OCD. *Behaviour Research and Therapy, 37*, 605–618.

Rapee, R. (1995). Psychological factors influencing the affective response to biological challenge procedures in panic disorder. *Journal of Anxiety Disorders, 9*, 291–300.

Rapee, R. (1996). Information processing views of panic disorder. In R. Rapee (Ed.), *Current controversies in anxiety disorders*. New York: Guilford Press.

Rapee, R., McCallum, S., Melville, L., Ravenscroft, M., & Rodney, J. (1994). Memory bias in social phobia. *Behaviour Research and Therapy, 32*, 89–99.

Rapee, R., Sanderson, W. C., McCauley, P. A. & di Nardo, P. A. (1992). Differences in reported symptom profile between panic disorder and other DSM-III-R anxiety disorders. *Behaviour Research and Therapy, 30*, 45–52.

Rapoport, J. (Ed.) (1989). *Obsessive-compulsive disorder in children and adolescents*. Washington: American Psychiatric Press.

Rapoport, J., & Wise, S. P. (1988). Obsessive-compulsive disorder: Evidence for a basal ganglia dysfunction. *Psychopharmacology Bulletin, 24*, 380–384.

Reiss, S. (1987). Theoretical perspectives on the fear of anxiety. *Clinical Psychology Review, 7*, 585–596.

Reiss, S. (1991). Expectancy model of fear, anxiety and panic. *Clinical Psychology Review, 11*, 141–153.

Reiss, S., & McNally, R. J. (1985). Expectancy model of fear. In S. Reiss & R. R. Bootzin (Eds.), *Theoretical issues in behavior therapy*. New York: Academic Press.

Reiss, S., Peterson, R. A., Gursky, D. M., & McNally, R. J. (1986). Anxiety sensitivity, anxiety frequency, and the prediction of fearfulness. *Behaviour Research and Therapy, 24*, 1–8.

Rescorla, R. A. (1980). *Pavlovian second-order conditioning*. Hillsdale, NJ: Lawrence Erlbaum Associates Inc.

Rescorla, R. A. (1988). Pavlovian conditioning: It's not what you think it is. *American Psychologist, 43*, 151–160.

Resick, P. (2001). *Stress and trauma*. Hove, UK: Psychology Press.

Revusky, S. (1979). More about appropriate controls for taste aversion learning: A reply to Riley. *Animal Learning and Behavior, 79*, 562–563.

Saigh, P. A. (1984). Pre- and post-invasion anxiety in Lebanon. *Behavior Therapy, 15*, 185–190.

Saigh, P. A. (1988). Anxiety, depression and assertion across alternating intervals of stress. *Journal of Abnormal Psychology, 97*, 338–341.

Saigh, P., & Bremner, J. (Eds.) (1999). *Post-traumatic stress disorder*. Needham Heights, MA: Allyn and Bacon.

Salkovskis, P. (1985). Obsessional-compulsive problems: A cognitive behavioural analysis. *Behaviour Research and Therapy, 23*, 571–583.

Salkovskis, P. (1996a). The cognitive approach to anxiety. In P. Salkovskis (Ed.), *The frontiers of cognitive therapy*. New York: Guilford Press.

Salkovskis, P. (1996b). Cognitive-behavioral approaches to the understanding of obsessional problems. In R. Rapee (Ed.), *Current controversies in anxiety disorders* (pp.103–133). New York: Guilford Press.

Salkovskis, P. (1996c). Reply to Pigott et al. and to Enright. Understanding of obsessive-compulsive disorder is not improved by redefining it as something else. In R. Rapee (Ed.), *Current controversies in anxiety disorders* (pp. 191–200). New York: Guilford Press.

Salkovskis, P., & Kirk, J. (1997). Obsessive-compulsive disorder. In D. M. Clark & C. Fairburn (Eds.), *Science and practice of cognitive behaviour therapy*. Oxford: Oxford University Press.

Salkovskis, P., & Warwick, H. (1986). Morbid preoccupations, health anxiety and reassurance: A cognitive behavioral approach to hypochondriasis. *Behaviour Research and Therapy, 24*, 597–602.

Sanderson, R., Laverty, S., & Campbell, D. (1963). Traumatically conditioned responses acquired during respiratiry paralysis. *Nature, 196*, 1235–1236.

Sanderson, W., Rapee, R., & Barlow, D. (1989). The influence of an illusion of control on panic attacks. *Archives of General Psychiatry, 46*, 157–162.

Sarason, I. G. (Ed.) (1980). *Test anxiety.* Hillsdale, NJ: Lawrence Erlbaum Associates Inc.

Sarbin, T. R. (1964). Anxiety: Reification of a metaphor. *Archives of General Psychiatry, 10*, 630–638.

Sartory, G. (1989). Obsessional-compulsive disorder. In G. Turpin (Ed.), *Handbook of clinical psychophysiology* (pp. 329–356). Chichester: Wiley.

Sartory, G., Rachman, S., & Grey, S. (1977). An investigation of the relation between reported fear and heart rate. *Behaviour Research and Therapy, 15*, 435–437.

Sbrocco, T., & Barlow, D. (1996). Conceptualizing the cognitive component of sexual arousal. In P. Salkovskis (Ed.), *The frontiers of cognitive therapy.* New York: Guilford Press.

Schacht, T., & Nathan, P. (1977). But is it good for psychologists? Appraisal and status of DSM-III. *American Psychologist, 32*, 1017–1025.

Schmidt, N. B., Telch, M. J., & Jaimez, T. L. (1996). Biological challenge manipulation of PCO levels: A test of Klein's suffocation alarm theory of panic. *Journal of Abnormal Psychology, 105*, 446–454.

Schneier, F. R., & Johnson, J. (1992). Social phobia: Comorbidity and morbidity in an epidemiological sample. *Archives of General Psychiatry, 49*, 282–288.

Seligman, M. (1970). On the generality of the laws of learning. *Psychological Review, 77*, 406–418.

Seligman, M. (1971). Phobias and preparedness. *Behavior Therapy, 2*, 307–320.

Seligman, M. (1988). Competing theories of panic. In S. Rachman & J. Maser (Eds.), *Panic: Psychological perspectives.* Hillsdale, NJ: Lawrence Erlbaum Associates Inc.

Seligman, M., & Hager, J. (Eds.) (1972). *Biological boundaries of learning.* New York: Appleton Century Crofts.

Seligman, M., & Johnston, J. (1973). A cognitive theory of avoidance learning. In J. McGuigan & B. Lumsden (Eds.), *Contemporary approaches to conditioning and learning.* New York: Wiley.

Shafran, R., & Rachman, S. (2004). Thought-action fusion: A review. *Journal of Behaviour Therapy and Experimental Psychiatry.* In press.

Shapiro, F. (1995). *Eye-movement desensitization and reprocessing.* New York: Guilford Press.

Shapiro, L. E., Pollard, C. A., & Carmin, C. N. (1993). Treatment of agoraphobia. In T. R. Giles (Ed.), *Handbook of effective psychotherapy.* New York: Plenum Press.

Sher, K. J., Mann, B., & Frost, R. O. (1984). Cognitive dysfunction in compulsive checkers: Further explorations. *Behaviour Research and Therapy, 22*, 493–502.

Sperling, M. (1971). Spider phobias and spider fantasies. *Journal of the American Psychoanalytic Association, 19*, 472–498.

Spielberger, C. D. (Ed.) (1966). *Anxiety and behavior.* New York: Academic Press.

Spielberger, C. D. (1972). Anxiety as an emotional state. In C. D. Spielberger (Ed.), *Anxiety: Current trends in theory and research* (Vol. 1). New York: Academic Press.

Spielberger, C. D. (1983). *Manual for state-trait anxiety inventory.* California: Consulting Psych-Press.

Spitzer, R. L. (1991). An outsider-insider's

views about revising the DSMs. *Journal of Abnormal Psychology, 100,* 294–296.

Spurr, J., & Stopa, L. (2002). Self-focused attention in social phobia and social anxiety. *Clinical Psychology Review, 22,* 947–976.

Stanley, M. A., & Turner, S. M. (1995). Current status of pharmacological and behavioral treatment of obsessive-compulsive disorder. *Behavior Therapy, 26,* 163–186.

Steketee, G., & Lam, J. (1993). Obsessive-compulsive disorder. In T. R. Giles (Ed.), *Handbook of effective psychotherapy.* New York: Plenum Press.

Sternberger, R. T., Turner, S. M., Beidel, D. C., & Calhoun, K. S. (1995). Social phobia: An analysis of possible developmental factors. *Journal of Abnormal Psychology, 104,* 526–531.

Stouffer, S., Lumsdaine, A., Williams, R., Smith, M., Janis, I., Star, S., & Cottrell, L. (1949). *The American soldier: Combat and its aftermath.* Princeton, NJ: Princeton University Press.

Sutherland, G., Newman, B., & Rachman, S. (1982). Experimental investigations of the relations between mood and intrusive unwanted cognitions. *British Journal of Medical Psychology, 55,* 127–138.

Swinson, R., Antony, M., Rachman, S., & Richter, M. (Eds.) (1998). *Obsessive compulsive disorders: Theory, research and treatment.* New York: Guilford Press.

Tallis, F. (1995). *Obsessive compulsive disorder.* Chichester: Wiley.

Taylor, S. (1995). Anxiety sensitivity: theoretical perspectives and recent findings. *Behaviour Research and Therapy, 33,* 243–258.

Taylor, S., & Rachman, S. (1994). Klein's suffocation theory of panic. *Archives of General Psychiatry, 51,* 505–506.

Taylor, S., Thordarson, D., Maxfield, L., Federoff, I., Lovell, K., & Orgrodniczuk, J. (2003). Comparative efficacy, speed, and adverse effects of three PTSD treatments: Exposure therapy, EMDR, and relaxation training. *Journal of Consulting and Clinical Psychology, 71,* 330–338.

Teasdale, T. (1988). Cognitive models and treatments for panic: A critical evaluation. In S. Rachman & J. Maser (Eds.), *Panic: Psychological perspectives.* Hillsdale, NJ: Lawrence Erlbaum Associates Inc.

Teasdale, J. (1999). Emotional processing, three modes of mind and the prevention of relapse in depression. *Behaviour Research and Therapy, 37,* 553–578.

Teasdale, J., & Barnard, P. (1993). *Affect, cognition and change.* Hove, UK: Lawrence Erlbaum Associates Ltd.

Teasdale, J. D., Segal, Z., & Williams, D. (1995). How does cognitive therapy prevent depressive relapse and why should attentional control (mindfulness) training help? *Behaviour Research and Therapy, 33,* 25–39.

Telch, M. (1988). Combined pharmacological and psychological treatment for panic sufferers. In S. Rachman & J. Maser (Eds.), *Panic: Psychological perspectives.* Hillsdale, NJ: Lawrence Erlbaum Associates Inc.

Thorpe, G., & Burns, L. (1983). *The agoraphobic syndrome.* Chichester: Wiley.

Thyer, B. A., Nesse, R. M., Curtis, G. C., & Cameron, O. G. (1986). Panic disorder: A test of the separation anxiety hypothesis. *Behaviour Research and Therapy, 24,* 209–211.

Treisman, A. M. (1960). Contextual cues in selective listening. *Quarterly Journal of Experimental Psychology, 12,* 242–248.

Tseng, W., Kan-Ming, M., Hsu, J., Li Shuen, Li Wah, Gui-Qian, & Da-Wei (1988). A sociocultural study of koro epidemics in Guandong, China. *American Journal of Psychiatry, 145,* 1538–1543.

Tulving, E. (1983). *Elements of episodic*

memory. Oxford: Oxford University Press.

Turner, S., Beidel, D., & Jacob, R. (1988). Assessment of panic. In S. Rachman & J. Maser (Eds.), *Panic: Psychological perspectives*. Hillsdale, NJ: Lawrence Erlbaum Associates Inc.

Tyrer, P. (1986). Classification of anxiety disorders. *Journal of Affective Disorders*, 11, 99–104.

Valentine, C. W. (1946). *The psychology of early childhood*. (3rd ed.). London: Methuen.

van Balkom, A. J., van Oppen, P., Vermeulen, A., van Dyck, R., Nanta, N., & Vorst, H. (1994). A meta-analysis on the treatment of OCD. *Clinical Psychology Review*, 14, 359–382.

van den Hout, M., & Kindt, M. (2003). Repeated checking causes memory distrust. *Behaviour Research and Therapy*, 41, 301–316.

Wakefield, J. C. (1992). Disorder as harmful dysfunction: A conceptual critique of DSM-III-R's definition of mental disorder. *Psychological Review*, 99, 232–247.

Watson, J., & Rayner, R. (1920). Conditioned emotional reactions. *Journal of Experimental Psychology*, 3, 1–22.

Weiller, E., Bisserbe, J. C., Boyer, P., Lepine, J. P., & Lecrubier, Y. (1996). Social phobia in general health care. An unrecognised undertreated disabling disorder. *British Journal of Psychiatry*, 168, 169–174.

Weller, A., & Hener, T. (1993). Invasiveness of medical procedures and state anxiety in women. *Behavioral Medicine*, 19, 60–65.

Wells, A., & Butler, G. (1997). Generalized anxiety disorder. In D. M. Clark & C. Fairburn (Eds.), *Science and practice of cognitive behaviour therapy*. Oxford: Oxford University Press.

Wells, A., & Mathews, G. (1996). Modelling cognition in emotional disorders. *Behaviour Research and Therapy*, 34, 881–888.

Williams, J., Watts, F., MacLeod, C., & Mathews, A. (1997). *Cognitive psychology and emotional disorders*. Chichester: Wiley.

Wilner, A., Reich, T., Robins, I., Fishman, R., & van Doren, T. (1976). Obsessive-compulsive neurosis. *Comprehensive Psychiatry*, 17, 527–539.

Wine, J. (1971). Test anxiety and direction of attention. *Psychological Bulletin*, 76, 92–104.

Wolpe, J. (1958). *Psychotherapy by reciprocal inhibition*. Stanford, CA: Stanford University Press.

Wolpe, J., & Rachman, S. (1960). Psychoanalytic evidence: A critique based on Freud's case of Little Hans. *Journal of Nervous and Mental Diseases*, 131, 135–145.

Wolpe, J., & Rowan, V. (1988). Panic disorder: A product of classical conditioning. *Behaviour Research and Therapy*, 26, 441–450.

Woody, S., & Rachman, S. (1994). Generalized anxiety disorder (GAD) as an unsuccessful search for safety. *Clinical Psychology Review*, 14, 743–753.

Yule, W. (Ed.) (1999). *Post-traumatic stress disorders*. New York: Wiley.

Zajonc, R. (1980). Feeling and thinking. *American Psychologist*, 35, 151–175.

Zohar, J., Insel, T., & Rasmussen, S. (Eds.) (1991). *The psychobiology of obsessive-compulsive disorder*. New York: Springer.

Author index

Abraham, K. 70
Acierno, R.E. 109, 181
Agras, S. 19
Akhtar, S. 134
Alkubaisy, T. 110
Allan, T. 166
Anastasiades, P. 103, 105, 109, 111, 112, 114, 118, 120
Andrews, B. 179
Antony, M. 144, 145
Argyris, N. 87
Arntz, A. 167
Arrindell, W.A. 20
Asmundson, G. 1
Austin, D. 69, 119
Aylward, E.H. 76

Baer, L. 74
Bak, R.M. 81, 85, 91
Baker, T.B. 82
Ballenger, J. 101
Bancroft, J. 43, 44
Bandura, A. 86
Barlow, D.H. 1, 7, 8, 14, 39, 40, 41, 43, 44, 45, 61, 68, 92, 95, 96, 104, 105, 108, 109, 111, 112, 117, 119, 120, 144, 148, 150, 154, 155, 157, 161, 162, 163, 170, 177, 181, 182
Barnard, P. 54, 58
Basoglu, M. 110, 122

Beck, A.T. 2, 27, 29, 35, 61, 67, 68, 69
Beech, H.R. 137
Beidel, D.C. 104, 148
Bichard, S. 16
Bisserbe, J.C. 148
Bodden, D. 87
Booth, R. 92, 118
Boring, E.G. 72
Borkovec, T.D. 166
Bower, G.H. 51
Boyer, P. 148
Bradley, B.P. 49
Bredarts, S. 48, 49
Bregman, E. 81
Bremner, J. 170
Brewin, C.R. 7, 29, 31, 50, 67, 109, 112, 163, 172, 174, 175, 179
Broadbent, D.E. 58
Bryant, B. 178
Bryant, R. 177, 179
Bujold, A.144
Burish, T.G. 80
Burkell, J. 35
Burns, L. 124, 126
Butler, G. 36, 166, 167

Cahill, S. 181
Cairns, E. 84
Calhoun, K.S. 148
Cameron, O.G. 106
Campbell, D. 83, 106
Cannon, D.S. 82

Carey, M.P. 80
Carmin, C.N. 128
Carson, R. 16, 112, 127
Carter, M.M. 16, 112, 127
Cella, D.F. 80, 18
Ceschi, G. 48, 49
Chambless, D. 48, 115, 157, 166, 181
Chapman, T.F. 148
Claparede, M. 49–50
Clark, D.A. 61, 69, 144
Clark, D.M. 29, 36, 39, 56, 57, 61, 68, 69, 103, 104, 105, 108, 109, 110, 111, 112, 114–120, 128, 144, 150, 151, 152, 153, 154, 156, 157, 166, 175–7, 178, 180
Cloitre, M. 48
Cobb, C. 119, 121, 145
Cohen, I.L. 36
Coles, M. 48
Constans, J.I. 48
Cook, E.W. 82
Cooper, P.J. 118
Costello, C.G. 20
Costello, E. 166
Cote, G. 120
Cottreel, L. 19
Cox, B.J. 1, 20
Craske, M.G. 14, 15, 16, 39, 95, 104, 109, 112, 116, 119
Cuk, M. 43

Curtis, G.C. 106
Curtis, R.C. 153
Cuthbert, B.N. 82

Da-Wei 87
Dalgleish, T. 48
Davey, G. 85, 91
de Beurs, E. 181
de Jong, P. 88
de Silva, P. 15, 132, 133, 142, 144
Deffenbacher, J.L. 40
Devilly, G. 181
Devins, G.M. 152
di Nardo, P.A. 48, 81, 85, 91
Dickinson, A. 89
Dixon, N.F. 58
Donnell, C.D. 107, 108
Duffy, M. 178
Dugas, M. 162, 163, 167
Dugger, D. 74, 121
Dunker, D. 48, 49
Durham, R.C. 166

Edelmann, R.J. 45, 48, 148, 155
Ehlers, A. 36, 39, 95, 104, 105, 110, 119, 157, 175–7, 178, 180
Eich, E. 51
Emery, G. 2, 27, 29, 35, 61
Epstein, S. 10
Erixon, G. 66, 81–2
Eysenck, H.J. 26, 29, 50, 61, 62, 63, 64–5, 72, 73, 77, 79, 83, 124, 172
Eysenck, M. 29, 30, 33, 39, 47, 48, 49, 58, 68, 162, 163, 164

Fairburn, C. 109, 128
Federoff, I. 181
Fennell, M. 157, 166, 178
Fenton, G. 166
Fenz, W. 10
Field, A. 87
First, M.B. 26

Fishman, R. 134
Flanagan, J. 80
Foa, E.B. 48, 54, 74, 121, 174, 177
Follette, W.C. 26
Frances, A. 26
Franklin, M.E. 48
Freeston, M. 144, 162, 163, 167
Freud, S. 69–71, 72, 73, 172, 173
Friedman, A.F. 26
Friedman, M. 177
Frost, R. 143, 48
Fyer, A.J. 92, 148

Gagnon, F. 144, 162, 163, 167
Gelder, M. 15, 105, 109, 112, 114, 118, 119, 120, 126, 166
Gerull, F. 86
Giles, T.R. 92, 115
Gillespie, K. 178
Gillis, M. 115, 166
Gino, A. 82
Goldstein, A. 181
Gorman, J. 104
Gorzalka, M.M. 45
Gray, J.A. 52, 61, 64–7, 73, 77, 126, 165
Greist, J.H. 74
Grey, S. 82, 119, 121, 145
Grinker, R. 51
Grunbaum, A. 52, 62
Gruter-Andrew, C. 153
Gui-Qian 87
Gursky, D.M. 31, 83, 114
Guzy, L.T. 81, 85, 91

Hackmann, A. 105, 109, 112, 114, 118, 120, 154, 157, 178
Hager, J. 66
Hall, G. S. 70
Hallam, R.S. 7, 126
Halligan, S. 180
Hammersley, D. 82

Harlow, H. 14
Harris, G.J. 76
Hart, J. 82
Hartl, M. 143
Harvey, A. 166, 177, 179
Hawton, K. 112, 120, 128, 144
Heimberg, R.G. 48, 149, 155, 157, 159
Henderson, J.G. 148
Hener, T. 31, 38
Herbert, J. 181
Hersen, M. 109
Hibbert, G.A. 109
Hirsch, C. 154
Hodgson, R. 135, 137, 139, 144
Hoehn-Saric, R. 76
Hofmann, S. 157
Holland, J.C. 80, 18
Hollander, E. 74
Hollon, S.D. 16, 112, 127
Holmes, E. 172, 174
Holt, C.S. 48, 159
Hope, D.A. 48, 155, 157, 159
Hornig, C.D. 101, 107, 108
Horowitz, M. 141
Horwath, E. 101
Houts, A.C. 26
Hugdahl, K. 124

Ingram, R.E. 40, 41
Insel, T.R. 74, 75, 76, 145

Jacob, R. 104
Jaimez, T.L. 108
Janis, I. 19
Janis, J.L. 84
Jaspers, K. 132
Jenike, M.A. 74
Jenkins, R. 19
Johnson, H. 82
Johnson, J. 101, 148
Johnson, V.E. 44
Johnston, D.W. 15, 119, 126

Subject index

cognitive analyses of anxiety 67–9
cognitive appraisal in anxiety 31
cognitive aspects of anxiety proneness
  32
cognitive behavioural therapy 92
  fear and 9
  panic and 105, 109, 112, 117–18, 119,
    120
cognitive panic 117
cognitive processing 177
cognitive theory of panic 2, 108–14, 150
  critique 115–19
cognitive theory of PTSD 175, 179
cognitive theory of social anxiety 150–6
  evidence for 154–6
cognitive therapy 92
cognitive vulnerability 32
combat fatigue 80
compulsions 68
compulsive behaviour 75
  characteristics 129–32, 134–5
  hoarding 143
  types 135–6
concentration 36
conditioned anxiety responses 63–4
conditioned nausea reactions 80–1
conditioned stimulus (CS) 89–90
conditioning 61, 69, 89–91
conditioning theory of fear 13–14
  arguments against 84–8, 93
  evidence for 79–83, 93
  nature of 79
congenital hypoventilation syndrome
  106–7
consequences of anxiety 36–7

dark, fear of 20
definition of anxiety 3–8
dental phobia 81, 85
depression 26
  memory in 49
  in obsessive-compulsive disorder 145
  panic and 104
desensitization 51, 92
Diagnostic and Statistical Manual of
  Mental Disorders (DSM) 1, 24, 25–6, 73,
  98, 147, 161
dichotic listening 29

discomfort, fear of 44
distortions of perception 42
distribution of fears 85–6
dogs, fear of 81, 84–5, 90–1
driving phobia 21, 42
drug abuse 2
dual representation theory 172, 174–5
dysfunctional beliefs 151
dysthymia 83

Ehlers–Clark cognitive theory 172, 175–9
emotional processing 53–4, 172
equipotentiality premise 85
escape behaviour 37
expectant dread 70
exposure treatment method 124
extinction 93
eye movement desensitization and
  reprocessing 181–2

facial expressions, fear and 9
failure to acquire fear 84–5
failure, fear of 44
fatigue 36, 54
fear
  components 8–12, 26
  conditioning theory of 13–14
  of failure 44
  nature of 8–12
  subjective 8
  varieties of 19–24
  vs. anxiety 3, 5, 6–7
fear incubation 82
fear of fear 100
fear reduction techniques 46, 56
fear signals 85–6
Fear Survey Schedule 20
fearful distortions 43
fluoxetine 157
food aversions 91
free-floating anxiety 6, 70

generalized anxiety disorder (GAD) 6, 25,
  26, 48, 161–7
  features of 161–2
  lifetime prevalence 162
  safety signals 164–6
  treatment 166–7

habituation 92
health anxiety (hypochondriasis) 68
heights, fear of 19, 20, 26, 88
hoarding 143
humiliation, fear of 44
hypersensitive alarms 106
hyperventilation 114–15
hypervigilance 27, 33–4, 163
hypervigilant monitoring 39
hypochondriasis 68

illness/disease, fear of 19–20, 26, 34, 92
imipramine
  obsessive-compulsive disorder and 74–5
  panic and 102, 103, 104, 120
implicit memory 29, 58
impulsivity 65
in vivo exposures 92
inattentiveness 36
injury, fear of 19–20, 26, 85, 92
innate fear stimuli 65–6
insects, fear of 21, 22
interpretation of information 36
intolerance for uncertainty in generalized
    anxiety disorder 162–3
introversion, vulnerability and 29, 83

koro *86–7*

learned anxiety 50–1, 61–7
learned fears 67
learning theory 61
loss of control, fear of 44

memory 47–53, 59
  confidence in 139–40
  depression and 49
  implicit 29, 58
  in obsessive-compulsive disorder 52
  in post-traumatic stress disorder 50
  repression of 51–2, 71
mental pollution 136
mindfulness training 41, 54
misinterpretation of information 36
model of anxiety 27–37

neurotic anxiety 69
neuroticism, vulnerability and 29

non-associative fears 88
non-cognitive panics 117
non-conscious memorial processes 51
non-reward, behavioural effects of 64

objective anxiety 69
obsessions 68, 140–2
  characteristics 132–3, 134, 135
obsessive-compulsive disorder (OCD) 25,
    26, 34, 40, 48
  affect and 55
  age of onset 133–4
  anxiety and 143
  biological theories of 73–76
  definition 129
  gender and 133
  hoarding and 143
  incidence 133
  memory in 52
  misinterpretation 39
  panic in 95
  persistence 136–40
  reducing hypervigilance 35
  self-focused attention 40
  serotonin theory of 73–6
  treatment 143–5
  see also compulsive behaviour; obsessions
Oedipus complex 71–2
off-duty/on-duty contrast 35
Ondine's curse 106–7
onset of fear 86
ordinary memory system 174, 175
overprediction
  of fear 15, 16–19
  of panic 18

pain, fear of 44
panic 5
  bodily sensations, misinterpretation of
      108–12, 115–16, 119
  definition 95
  cognitive analyses of 68
  cognitive theory of 2, 108–14, 150
  duration 99
  experience of 99–100
  incidence 100–1
  induction 103–4, 111, 113
  nocturnal 115, 116–17